Avoiding Armageddon

Avoiding Armageddon

From the Great War to the Fall of France, 1918–40

Jeremy Black

BLOOMSBURY
LONDON · BERLIN · NEW YORK · SYDNEY

First published in Great Britain 2012

© Jeremy Black, 2012

The moral right of the author has been asserted
No part of this book may be used or reproduced in any manner whatsoever without written
permission from the Publisher except in the case of brief quotations embodied in critical
articles or reviews. Every reasonable effort has been made to trace copyright holders
of material reproduced in this book, but if any have been inadvertently overlooked the
Publishers would be glad to hear from them.

Bloomsbury Publishing Plc
50 Bedford Square
London WC1B 3DP

www.bloomsbury.com

Bloomsbury Publishing, London, Berlin, New York and Sydney

A CIP record for this book is available from the British Library.

ISBN: 978-1-4411-5713-3

10 9 8 7 6 5 4 3 2 1

Typeset by Fakenham Prepress Solutions, Fakenham, Norfolk, NR21 8NN
Printed and bound in India

For
Stephen Cooper

Contents

Abbreviations

Add.	Additional Manuscripts
BL.	Department of Manuscripts, British Library, London
CAB.	Cabinet Office papers
LH	Liddell Hart Archive, King's College, London
MM	Montgomery-Massingberd papers
NA	London, National Archives (formerly Public Record Office)
Rutgers, Fuller	Rutgers University Library, New Brunswick, papers of J. F. C. Fuller
WO	War Office papers

Preface

Variety and unpredictability are the principal lessons from the inter-war period for the present day. Drawing lessons indeed is one of the themes of this book because it is written not only in the conviction that history is of great relevance but also with the view that it is non-linear, so that a period in the past may be more relevant, indeed far more relevant, for the present than more recent periods. And so for the inter-war years.

This point is worth stressing because most of the military history of the twentieth century has been written in terms of total warfare. In this account, the two world wars were linked and were seen as an anticipation of the industrial scale confrontation and destructive capacity of the Cold War. That approach, however, was both unconvincing as an account of the variety of the past and also scant preparation for the nature of conflict across the world since the collapse of the Soviet system in 1989–91.[1]

Instead, it is the inter-war period that is most helpful as an anticipation of the period since 1989, which is one reason why this book is intended not only for scholars and students but also for the general reading public as well as military professionals. Aside from the degree, which is far from coincidental, to which some of the areas fought over in the inter-war period have been centres of more recent conflict, notably Iraq, the North-West Frontier of British India (now the North-West Frontier of Pakistan) and Palestine (now Israel and the Palestinian territories), the types of warfare of recent years can be seen in plenty in the inter-war period. Thus, there was counter-insurgency conflict and resistance to terrorism, alongside more conventional types of warfare. As a result, there has been considerable interest since 2001 and, even more since the outbreak of Iraqi insurrectionary resistance in 2003, in the conflicts of this period, notably the British response to the Iraqi and Palestine risings of 1919 and 1937 respectively, and the British experience of war on the North-West Frontier.

This book captures this variety. It is mindful of the extent to which the Great (First World) War of 1914–18 served to shadow ideas, experience, careers and weapons in the inter-war years, helping affirm or remould the strategic and institutional cultures of particular states and militaries, and the preference for particular weapons and for related operational concepts and doctrinal ideas. Thus, the inter-war years can be presented in terms of the aftermath of the Great War, an aftermath that linked military, political, fiscal, social and cultural considerations.

Moreover, preparations for another major conflict became of increasing importance from the early 1930s, notably in the Soviet Union, Japan and Germany, with Britain becoming more urgently concerned in the late 1930s. Rearmament spread from the authoritarian regimes to the imperial democracies.[2] That is the conventional approach in the established literature and, like most conventional accounts, it contains much of value.

At the same time, there is an effort here to recover a far more complex account than that suggested by the coherent narrative offered in the last two paragraphs, and, therefore, to pose more difficult issues of analysis. The geographical focus of this book also reflects both contemporary and current concerns, notably with the degree of attention devoted to East Asia, but also with due attention to other powers whose importance is currently rising, such as Brazil and India.

Britain, however, is the centre of attention. It had the largest empire by far, and the most important navy in the world. Moreover, the pronounced reluctance of the USA to take on international commitments to match its leading economic strength and wealth and the position of naval parity with Britain agreed by the Washington Naval Treaty of 1922, helped ensure that Britain acted as the strongest power and the would-be guarantor of international order across much of the world. As a result, this book devotes particular attention to British issues and archival sources. These issues and sources very much reflect the issues of prioritization that were more generally at stake, but that were most acute for Britain because its far-flung empire and interests meant that it was concerned about developments across most of the world; although Latin America was more within the American orbit, while the internal affairs of other empires were left to their colonial masters. Nevertheless, the global role of Britain ensured that it was *a*, if not *the*, prime complication, even target, for revisionist powers concerned to change the world system in whole or part.

There was no shortage of these powers. The Great War had left a number of dissatisfied powers, mostly the defeated, especially Germany and Hungary, but also victors, notably Italy, dissatisfied with the outcome. Moreover, from both Left and Right, there were ideological calls for a new order, either a new world order, as advocated by the Communists of the Soviet Union, or a new way of conducting international relations and new regional order, the theme of Italy under its Fascist leader, Benito Mussolini. In the 1930s, Nazi Germany and militarist Japan joined these respective categories.

The cumulative strain of responding to these, and other threats posed a fundamental challenge to Britain's military position, and pushed the political nature of tasking and strategy, specifically questions of prioritization, to the fore. Thus, in 1919–21, British policymakers had to deal with the Communist takeover of Russia, subsequent Soviet expansionism[3], Turkish rejection of the peace settlement, war with Afghanistan, and rebellions in Iraq, Egypt and Ireland, conflict in British Somaliland and on the North-West Frontier of India, as well as worker disaffection in Britain. Questions of military doctrine, force structure and weaponry were secondary to these problems of policy. No other power faced this challenge to the same extent, but the parameters within which other states had to operate were framed accordingly. The parallel with modern America is instructive.

Secondly, current concerns about China encourage a focus on that country in the 1920s and 1930s, which is appropriate as it indeed saw large-scale conflict: conflict that was important both for China and for issues of wider power and influence. Moreover, China experienced a range of types of war, notably conflict between regionally-based warlords, the consolidation of power by a national government, revolutionary and counter-revolutionary warfare arising from the conflict between Communists and the government, limited (but deadly) Japanese intervention, and, lastly, full-scale war in response to Japanese invasion.

Indeed, to describe this period as an inter-war one appears particularly flawed as far as China is concerned. This point invites attention to questions of nomenclature because whatever title is adopted has implications for how the period is viewed. That is also true of more specific episodes such as the Sino-Japanese War and the Arab rising in Palestine.

I have benefitted from the opportunity to develop ideas presented by teaching this period at the University of Exeter and also by being invited to lecture at the Japanese National Institute for Defence Studies, Tokyo; Appalachian State, Athens State, Eastern Tennessee, High Point, Keio, North Carolina Chapel Hill, North Georgia, Southern Mississippi, Waseda and William Paterson universities; Eastbourne and Radley Colleges; and at the 2011 Edinburgh International Book Festival. I also profited from the opportunity to visit Austria, Brunei, China, France, Germany, Hungary, Italy, Japan, Malaysia, Russia, Singapore, Slovakia, Switzerland, Turkey, Ukraine and the USA while working on this book.

History, both the developments of the past and the way in which we understand it, is an accretional process, and I have greatly benefitted from the comments of Ted Cook, Eugenia Keisling, Stewart Lone, Keith Neilson, Liao Ping, Bill Purdue, Roger Reese, Mat Rendle, Bill Roberts, Nicholas Rodger, Kaushik Roy, Frédéric Saffroy, Kahraman Şakul, Anthony Saunders, Barnett Singer, Joe Smith, Larry Sondhaus, David Stone, Richard Toye and Arthur Waldron on an earlier draft or parts of an earlier draft. I have also benefitted from advice from Kate Davison, Leslie McLoughlin and Jon Wise. None are responsible for the opinions expressed here nor for any errors that remain. I would like to thank Robin Baird-Smith for being an exemplary publisher, Jenny Laing for proving an excellent copy-editor, and Kim Storry for acting as Project Manager for Fakenham. It is a great pleasure to dedicate this book to Stephen Cooper, a good friend and fellow-member of the University of Exeter community.

Introduction

Studies of an inter-war period, more particularly the classic inter-war period between the Great and Second World Wars, appear to require an obvious approach: one focuses on the consequences of one war and the causes of another, the former leading clearly towards the latter. That, indeed, is the tendency in the literature on the period 1918–39, and it is one in which military history matches the essential lineaments of other aspects of history of the period, notably political, economic and social. As far as the military history is concerned, there is an attempt to link the discussion of the closing stages of the Great (later First World) War, especially the use of tanks and aircraft by the Allies (Britain, France and the USA) in 1918 to overcome, successfully, the defensive strength of the Germans on the Western Front, with the *blitzkrieg* (lightning war) operations of the Germans in 1939–41, and notably to the rapid conquest of France in 1940.

This pattern provides a clear pattern and a related teleology or apparently inevitable development. These take the form that learning the lessons of the first conflict entailed focusing firepower on mobility and thus making the offensive more effective.

Correspondingly, a failure to understand this pattern apparently consigned some powers, notably France and Britain, to failure in the early stages of the Second World War. Thus, modernity and success are clearly located, part of the teleology that is all-too-common in military history.[1]

This approach is also employed to make sense of conflicts elsewhere in the world. Those of 1919–23 are regarded as consequences of the Great War and are treated in these terms, an approach that brings shape to a complex period of warfare, both international and civil, across Europe and the Middle East, notably the Russian Civil War, the Greek-Turkish conflict, and rebellions against the British in Egypt and Iraq. Secondly, the conflicts of the 1930s, notably the Spanish Civil War of 1936–9, are approached as prefiguring the Second World War, and judged of consequence in so far as they did so.

This approach is not without considerable value, and aspects of it will echo in these pages. There are, indeed, conflicts that have to be discussed and explained, and it is important to do so other than in terms of one war after another. Contemporaries sought and discerned a pattern, in terms of consequences and likely developments, and it is understandable that later commentators have searched for the same.

However, a more complex account will also be offered here, one that seeks to provide a global dimension. In doing so, I challenge the dominant idea that there is, in any given period, an essential style of relevant warfare, and a clear definition of fitness for purpose, with the apparently clear consequences that progress and relative proficiency and strength can be readily assessed. Instead, the focus will be on the variety of warmaking around the world and, in particular, on the validity of types of conflict that relied on irregulars, insurrectionary warfare and counter-insurgency struggles. This approach is important both for the period itself and for twentieth-century warfare as a whole, and also looks toward the present. As an instance of a prescient warning all-too-relevant in recent years, the General Staff of the British War Office pressed the government in March 1920 not to send troops in order to ensure Armenian independence from the Turks. Aside from outlining specific difficulties facing such a mission, the General Staff warned that:

> the resulting operations would partake of the nature of guerrilla warfare, which is a method of fighting above all things to be avoided. The whole spirit of the art of conducting small wars is to strive for the attainment of decisive methods, the very essence of partisan warfare from the point of view of the enemy being to avoid definite engagements. Consequently, it usually happens that many more men are required than were originally estimated, and that warfare of this nature continues for years.[2]

Again, a very contemporary note was struck that June when Sir Henry Wilson, the Chief of the Imperial General Staff, wrote to Winston Churchill, the Secretary of State for War, 'I cannot too strongly press on the Government the danger, the extreme danger, of His Majesty's Army being spread all over the world, strong nowhere, weak everywhere, and with no reserve to save a dangerous situation or to avert a coming danger'. The Air Staff had similar views. Churchill agreed.[3]

Compared to the two world wars, the inter-war period is generally under-rated in accounts of military history, certainly in operational terms; and indeed was by some contemporaries. In large part, this underrating was due to the overshadowing impact of the Great War. The *Evening Public Ledger*, a Philadelphia newspaper, in its issue of 27 July 1922, noted 'since 1918 anything short of cataclysmic fighting is regarded as somewhat inconse-quential'. Moreover, Western commentators tended to underplay conflict in the Far East, notably within China, a pattern already seen in the nineteenth century with the response to the Taiping Revolution.

The focus today, instead, is on the two world wars, with the inter-war period seen as the sequence to the Great War (1914–18) and the preparation for the Second (1939–45). Both of these perceptions are popularly understood primarily in terms of the major Western powers and the ways in which they sought to overcome the impasse of trench warfare. Thus, the evolution of military doctrine and theory is covered in great depth, but this approach is somewhat misleading as an account of inter-war thought, since the prospect of a resumption of symmetrical warfare (warfare using similar techniques and with similar goals) between the major powers seemed limited until the 1930s, and notably until after Japan occupied Manchuria in 1931 and Adolf Hitler gained power in Germany in January 1933.

Earlier, enforced German disarmament after the Great War on land, sea and in the air appeared to have dealt with the major security threat to France and Britain, while the challenges to the new international order were limited and certainly not on the scale of Imperial Germany during the Great War. The most serious challenge, that from the Bolsheviks (Communists), who took over Russia and then sought to spread revolution, was defeated, particularly in Poland in 1920, but also elsewhere, notably when the Communist movement in China was suppressed in the cities in 1927. Soviet forces were withdrawn from Persia (Iran) in 1921 after Reza Khan concluded a treaty with the Soviet Union. Soviet military leaders planned and sought to prepare for a major war, but none was launched.

Other challenges to the international order were limited to the particular countries in which the victorious allies found themselves thwarted, notably Turkey in 1922. Once the Turks had defeated the Greeks in 1921–2 and successfully confronted the British in 1922, there was no attempt to extend Turkish power, for example into the Greek islands in the Aegean or by challenging the British colonial position in Cyprus.

With the exception of Bolshevism, there was no suggestion of a global military threat to the new order. Indeed, American politicians, military planners and commentators felt it possible to argue that European challenges no longer posed a major threat to the USA. Instead, they concentrated on less central issues. Concern about left-wing labour disorder led to planning for military action, notably, with Plan White, immediately after the Great War; and this concern remained an important theme into the late 1930s.[4] Moreover, in broader terms of strategy and policy, there was a marked defensive content and tone in America in the 1920s, particularly with the legislation of 1920 and 1924 limiting immigration. The latter was associated with Bolshevism as part of a more general conservative mindset in this decade of Republican government.

Opposition to American interests in America's 'back-yard' – the Caribbean and Central America – resulted in military commitments, but these local struggles scarcely led to an American effort matching that in the Great War, although the impact on the people of Haiti, Nicaragua and the Dominican Republic was far greater. The Americans also produced colour-coded plans for war with more major states, including, in the 1930s, War Plan Red against Britain, which focused on the conquest of Canada, and envisaged the heavy bombing of Halifax, Montréal and Québec and the use of poison gas.[5] There were also major preparations to defend the Panama Canal against British naval attack. In contrast, the Royal Navy had planned for action against America's coastal cities.

America, and notably its navy, was also aware of Japan as a rising strategic challenge in the western Pacific, but the prospect of war with other major states was scarcely to the fore in the 1920s and the American Army remained small. Moreover, for much of the 1930s, many American politicians believed that neutrality would lessen the need for engaging in large-scale conflict. Looked at differently, although it had a formidable navy, America, in the

1930s, was generally prepared to rely on appeasing Japan as it expanded in China[6], and, in large part, on the safety blanket of the Royal Navy and the French army as far as Germany was concerned. Government policy did not fundamentally change until the Fall of France in 1940.

As so often, the standard approach to military history in the inter-war years also neglects the role of conflict outside the West, both by Western and by non-Western powers, as well, more specifically, as the military-political tasks of the Western and non-Western militaries in the shape of civil wars, counter-insurrectionary struggles, and political policing. For example, in February 1919, in the cosmopolitan city of Pressburg (Bratislava) where the local German and Hungarian population did not welcome inclusion in the new state of Czechoslovakia, a strike called by German and Hungarian socialists was brutally suppressed by Czech forces.

Linked to the importance of considering such tasks is the need not to see the military history of the period, as is so often done, primarily in terms of the policies of the Fascist dictators, Mussolini and Hitler, and the run-up to the Second World War. Instead, it is appropriate to devote due weight both to earlier warfare and to other accounts of the 1930s. While it may be reasonable, in the perspective of hindsight, to focus on moves towards a new Great War, the key problem of the victorious powers in the early 1920s was that of maintaining imperial control and influence. Moreover, the major struggles of the period 1919–36 were civil wars in Russia and China, while that in 1937–9, until the German invasion of Poland, was the attempted Japanese conquest of China.

The central point is that there is no one way to write about military developments in the inter-war period. There is no intention here to suggest that this account is *the* way to write the war. Indeed, whenever I read accounts or reviews that pretend to such definitive status, I know them to be deeply flawed. Instead, there is an attempt both to look at long-term significance and to understand the choices of the period, over force structure, tasking and doctrine, in terms of the uncertainties of these years. For example, there was uncertainty not only about the relationships between surface ships, and submarines and aircraft, and between tanks, and infantry and artillery, but also in the air between long-range bombers, ground-support bombers (especially dive bombers), and fighters.

To use, as is often done, the subsequent conflict, in this case the Second World War, to assess the correctness of particular inter-war policies, for example investment in tanks and aircraft carriers and the development of ground-support doctrine for air forces, is not helpful. This is particularly the case because this approach presupposes that the military tasking that the war was to present had been clear earlier, and, thus underrates the political context that determined tasking.

More specifically, for most of the period, the British armed forces were principally concerned with preparing for war outside Europe, either with resistance to rebellion in British colonies, notably Iraq, India and Palestine, or with protecting them from attack by other powers. This tasking meant planning responses to possible Turkish and Soviet challenges to Britain's position in the Middle East and South Asia in the 1920s, with concern about Turkish claims on northern Iraq where the frontier was only agreed in 1926, and about the possibility of a Soviet advance via Afghanistan against India. The latter offered a new version of anxieties that had been prominent in the late nineteenth century. New technology, such as the supply of Soviet planes to Afghanistan, appeared to make the threat more potent, while there were also fears about the subversive possibilities of Communism. The Soviet and Turkish challenges appeared the most likely cause of war in the mid-1920s. There were also lesser threats, such as that from Ibn Saud, the founder of Saudi Arabia, to British interests and allies, notably in Iraq and Kuwait. This crisis, however, was also settled, notably in November 1925 when the British negotiated boundary settlements between Ibn Saud and both Iraq and Transjordan.

In contrast, a new challenge, Japanese threats to British positions in the Far East, rose greatly in significance in the 1930s. In addition to British colonies, Hong Kong, Malaya, Singapore and north Borneo, there was an important British presence in the trade of China which, in some respects, was a major part of Britain's informal empire.

The tasks outlined in the last two paragraphs required a force structure centred on local garrisons and forces, and a fleet able to move rapidly in order to secure and use naval superiority and cover the movement of reinforcements from units based in Britain. As far as land warfare was concerned, the emphasis was not on tanks, which were not well suited to many tasks in imperial protection and were also cumbersome to move to and within the colonies. The lack of good roads within many colonies, especially in frontier areas, was significant. There were also serious weaknesses in support for mechanized deployment, notably in the provision of petrol. Furthermore, there were major problems in maintaining and repairing vehicles.

Thus, the argument, both at the time and subsequently, that the British should have developed more mechanized forces, including more tanks and ground-support planes (with the tactical doctrine which went with them), in order better to counter the German *blitzkrieg* they unsuccessfully faced in France in 1940, seriously neglects the circumstances that prevailed in the inter-war period. Criticism also underrates British technological achievement.[7]

The learning pattern of the period reflected the range of experience on offer, as well as the extent to which military education had developed as a professional tool. Commanders and commentators alike sought to learn not only from the Great War but also from subsequent wars. The process of learning proved part of the debate about fitness for purpose, not least in contesting claims based on new weapons. This debate was inseparable from issues of cost: all technologies could not be explored because the amount of money available was not sufficient to do so.

Moreover, the impact of new technology alongside politics suggested that there was no fixed point for the learning of lessons but, instead, a need to focus on the most recent conflicts and to consider them in light of the range of events that might occur. For example, far from endorsing the bold claims of air power enthusiasts, in 1936, when he resigned the post of Chief of the [British] Imperial General Staff, Sir Archibald Montgomery-Massingberd, who came from an artillery background, saw the Italian invasion of Abyssinia (Ethiopia) in 1935–6 as demonstrating the inability of a strong air force to ensure an early victory. A memorandum circulated by the Secretary of State for War to his Cabinet colleagues referred to 'the failure of air bombardment to produce a decisive effect on the morale of the Ethiopians'.[8] That this lesson suited Montgomery-Massingberd and his allies in the army did not lessen its weight. Indeed, the same lesson was to be demonstrated over the following years in China as clear Japanese air superiority and damaging bombing with no concern for civilians, did not end Chinese resistance.

However, the Italian air offensive in 1936, in fact played an important role, both in helping the land advance on the Ethiopian capital Addis Ababa and in weakening the cohesion of Ethiopian society, and thus in undermining resistance. Although the scale was very different, the contrast between the situation in Ethiopia and that in China is instructive and underlines the need for caution on the basis of isolated examples.

Lessons were sought because politicians, generals and commentators wished to understand how best to ensure security, and how, if war arose, to succeed without the destructiveness of protracted conflict, the Armageddon that the experience of the Great War and the potential of new weaponry held out as a prospect. A period of flux, an age of uncertainty and variety, the inter-war years provide today a fruitful and fascinating period for consideration, not least as modern strategists have to consider comparable issues of prioritization.[9] The flux of the inter-war years was not just military and technological but also political, specifically what new world order was going to dominate, that of Versailles or the offerings of the Bolsheviks, Fascists and Nazis.

1

The aftermath of the Great War

'The possibilities of manoeuvre have once more reached a pitch of development that has not been seen in Europe since the days of Napoleon. Coming so quickly on the heels of the long stagnation, which was the feature of the war on the Western Front during the Great War [1914–18], the antithesis is all the more striking'. Writing about the wide-ranging and fast-moving Polish-Russian struggle in 1920, a British observer, Major-General Sir Percy Rawcliffe, the Director of Military Operations, drew attention to the manner in which, despite its scale and importance, the Great War on the Western Front had not set the pattern for subsequent conflict in its immediate aftermath[1]; although had his focus been the Eastern Front there would have been more comparison with the Russian Civil War.

Far from being the war to end all wars, as was hoped, the Great War led into a large number of struggles, many of which were large scale. This development was not the intention of the peacemakers, a group led by the 'Big Three', Britain, France and the USA. Instead, the Treaty of Versailles of 1919 with Germany included a clause that fixed the responsibility of the war on Germany, and this war-guilt issue, and the associated reparations (financial retribution for causing the war and for conduct during it), were designed to discourage further aggression by Germany and other powers. Similar clauses were included in the treaties with Austria and Hungary, the defeated successors of Germany's leading ally, Austria-Hungary. American, British,

French and Belgian occupation zones in the Rhineland under the Inter-Allied Rhineland High Commission were a further guarantee of German inactivity.[2]

In addition, as part of a new international order, the League of Nations was established in 1919 in order to maintain peace and deal with any unresolved peace settlement issues. It was the first pan-national organization with a global mission to prevent war. Not all powers joined it, with Congress notably blocking America's accession, but the League represented an important aspiration for a new international order.

Russian civil war

The most striking feature of the Russian situation since the commencement of the struggle against the Bolshevik military forces has been the extraordinary vicissitudes experienced by both sides, first on one front and then on another.

BRITISH WAR OFFICE REPORT, JULY 1919[3]

The new international order failed to determine the largest war of these years, the ongoing Russian Civil War, in which maybe seven million men fought. Russia stood outside the new order as a result of the Bolshevik revolution having been followed by the abandonment of Russia's allies in a peace treaty with Germany. The Russian Civil War (1917–21) began with efforts to overthrow the provisional government that had assumed power after the overthrow of Tsar Nicholas II in March 1917 (February in the Russian calendar). The Bolsheviks were successful in seizing power in November 1917 (October). At first, there was a Bolshevik-dominated coalition government, but the Bolsheviks rapidly seized complete control of the government. Moreover, in the spring of 1918, the Bolsheviks launched a drive for power, initially to remove competing socialist parties once and for all, that led to a civil war.

Already, by late 1917 and early 1918, many elements of the eventual civil war were in place. A volunteer army was emerging in the south, Cossack resistance was growing and the Bolsheviks were involved in fighting these groups as well as separatists in Ukraine. The rival Whites (or conservatives) came to play a major role from the summer of 1918 and large-scale fighting began in

September. In November 1918, Admiral Alexander Kolchak took power in Siberia. Another prominent White, Anton Denikin, a Great War general, had replaced General Lavr Kornilov as commander of the counter-revolutionary forces in the south. Kornilov had been killed on operations in April.

The forces opposed to the Bolsheviks included not only Whites and, at times, Greens (Russia's peasant armies), as well as rival forces on the Left, but also those of non-Russian peoples who had been brought under the sway of the Russian Empire and had separatist agendas of their own, for example Ukrainians and Finns. In addition, there were foreign forces. Although, in combination, this was a formidable array, each of the anti-Bolshevik forces had their own goals, and they sometimes took noncooperation as far as conflict.

The most effectual pressure on the Bolsheviks was exerted by the Don Cossacks to the west of the Volga, and by the Whites, both those under Kolchak to the east of the Soviet zone[4], and those under Denikin from Ukraine to the south. The major industrial centre of Perm fell to Kolchak in December 1918 as Soviet forces in the region facing him were routed. The Soviets lacked both supplies and domestic support as a result of their terrorizing of civilians. By April 1919, Kolchak had overrun the Urals and there were hopes that he would be able to link up with the White forces based in Archangel and Murmansk. In June, Denikin captured the city of Kharkov in northern Ukraine, followed by Kiev, the Ukrainian capital, in August and, on 14 October, with the fall of the city of Orel, he was within 250 miles of Moscow. Moreover, Nikolai Yudenich, another White general, who had advanced from Estonia, was close to Petrograd (St Petersburg).

The fighting quality of these White forces, however, was indifferent. On 1 October 1919, Captain John Kennedy, an artillery liaison officer with the British Military Mission to South Russia attached to Denikin, recorded:

> In the morning the batteries go out, and take up positions, and are followed presently by the infantry. The guns then blaze off at maximum range into the blue, limber up and go on when the signal to advance is given – *followed* by the infantry, who don't like to get in front of the artillery . . . there is but little opposition beyond sniping from machine guns and rifles.

Ten days later, Kennedy attributed the guns firing at the extreme range, which limited accuracy and impact, to their lack of infantry and cavalry protection. He was also unimpressed by the calibre and discipline of the officers.[5]

The Whites, more seriously, proved unable to win and sustain peasant backing. Lacking a broad social base, and largely failing to see the need to create one, their governments were selfish, greedy and incompetent, which helped to alienate support, especially from the peasantry. This lack of support contributed to a shortage of reserves which was serious given the rapid growth in the size of the Red Army. The British General Staff report of 22 July 1919 on the situation in Russia was pessimistic about Denikin's chances: 'Unless he can offer to the wretched inhabitants of the liberated districts . . . conditions of existence better than those which they suffered under the Bolshevik régime, he will in the course of time be faced with revolt and hostility in his rear just at the time when the Bolsheviks will be concentrating large numbers of troops for a counter-offensive'.[6]

The peasantry have emerged in some work as crucial to the course of the conflict. Although this approach simplifies a very complex situation, it has been argued that success in the struggle between Bolsheviks and Whites depended on who was best able to avoid fighting the Greens and, even more, on who was able to win some of their support.[7]

Rallying against the Whites, Green forces helped turn the tide in Ukraine where Denikin's men were driven back. In October 1919, Orel and Voronezh fell to Bolshevik units, which went on to defeat the Whites in November at Kastornoe, a major railway junction. This was a victory in which Bolshevik cavalry under Semen Budënny played a major role.

The Whites were also unsuccessful on other fronts. Yudenich's force included tanks with British crews, but these tanks were unable to overcome defending infantry once their initial panic had been mastered. Moreover, Yudenich was greatly outnumbered and lacked reserves. The defeated Yudenich was driven back into Estonia in late October 1919. His troops were then disarmed and interned. Estonia, indeed, negotiated an armistice agreement with the Bolsheviks, which became a peace on 2 February 1920. Both sides agreed not to allow foreign forces into their territories, nor to permit hostile political organizations to operate. Thus, the Estonians gained a measure of security from subversion but, more significantly, the Bolshevik position in Petrograd (St Petersburg) was now protected, which left a crucial centre of industry and population secure. The fall of Archangel and Murmansk to the Bolsheviks in February-March 1920 further consolidated their position in Petrograd. The Bolsheviks could now focus their attention further south.

There was a serious lack of coordination between the White armies. For example, Kolchak's British-supplied forces retreated in the summer of 1919 just when the Whites in the south were advancing. Kolchak's troops were driven back from the Urals, their overstretched units collapsing in the face of a Red counter-offensive supported by fresh forces. Kolchak's government was weakened by terrible corruption which affected both the army and the economy. Moreover, there was a lack of peasant support for what appeared an old-fashioned Tsarist army and agenda, and high levels of desertion among the brutalized conscripts.

In addition, peasants rose against the Kolchak government, undermining its war against the Reds. Perm fell to the Reds in July 1919, and the outnumbered Whites fell back. Omsk, Kolchak's capital, was abandoned without a fight on 14 November. Seized by the Czech Legion, Kolchak was handed over to the Soviets who shot him on 7 February 1920. Kolchak's regime had been undermined by his brutality and rapaciousness, by its divisions, and by growing Green hostility.

More generally, civilian hostility to conscription and requisitioning undercut the White effort. This was made clear by Kennedy in the months before Denikin's retreat to the Crimea in March 1920. On 11 October 1919, Kennedy recorded 'The Army lives on the fat of the land' and, on 14 February 1920, he added a political note:

we are making a mistake in continuing to support Denikin. Denikin himself is about the only man connected with the movement with any high ideals. When he formed his Volunteer Army, he attracted to it and assimilated very undesirable elements, for instance all the unemployed regular officers of the old regime, who would have to work or starve if there were no fighting, and also all the old rotten aristocracy of Petrograd [St Petersburg] and Moscow and the big landlords . . . His army is one mass of corruption . . . Everybody wants somebody else to do the fighting . . . the disorganisation and confusion and corruption and speculation increases every day. It is a useful experience for us, in that we see how *not* to do everything connected with war.

On 17 March, Kennedy added 'Denikin's robber bands and rabbles . . . They are all in a terrible state of disorganisation'.[8]

The Whites were now under Baron Peter Wrangel, after Denikin's resignation in April following the disastrous end to his campaign. Wrangel, a former cavalry general, advanced from the Crimea into Ukraine on 6 June 1920, seeking to benefit from the Polish offensive. The Whites were able to cross the River Dnieper in October, but were then defeated. In part, this was because an armistice between the Bolsheviks and Poland agreed to in October had freed Soviet troops to launch an offensive on 20 October. Moreover, the land and other policies formulated by Wrangel were outdated and ineffective. After heavy losses, Wrangel's heavily outnumbered force fell back into the Crimea, and was evacuated by the French fleet in November 1920, the effective end of the White threat. In this campaign, the Red Army was helped by the Greens under the anarchist Nestor Makhno, but, once Wrangel was defeated, the Red Army attacked his forces. Widespread fighting across Ukraine led, by August 1921, to Bolshevik success, with mass terror proving particularly effective.

The failure of the anti-Bolshevik forces in Russia owed much to their internal divisions and their political and strategic mismanagement. The White under-estimation of Bolshevik tenacity was also important, as was Bolshevik determination and use of terror. The Bolsheviks' central position was also crucial. They had control of Moscow and Petrograd, the vital populous and industrial areas, as well as of key arms factories around Moscow, notably in Tula, and rail links. As a result, the Bolsheviks fought on interior lines. The industrial centres, where Bolshevik support was greatest, were also the hubs of the transport system. Similarly, in the Mexican Revolution of 1910–17, the Carranza faction came to a commanding position in 1916, in large part thanks to the dominance of the cities and the rail system, although the effective generalship of Alvaro Obregón, president from 1920 to 1924, was also important. In Russia, the Whites, by contrast, lacked manufacturing capacity, although they received supplies from the Allies. In turn, White defeats ensured that some of these supplies came into Bolshevik hands.

The Bolsheviks ruthlessly mobilized all the resources they could for the war effort, although that also harmed their support. For example, in 1918, the Cossack Don Army was able to raise troops against the Red Army because of the harsh nature of Bolshevik grain requisitioning. More generally, conscription was pushed hard, businesses were nationalized, grain seized and a firm dictatorship imposed, with opposition brutally suppressed. The size of the Red Army posed severe problems of supply. It rose to three million men in 1919 and five million by the end of 1920. This was a major achievement given the disintegration of the Tsarist army by late 1917 and the problems that all sides faced from high levels of desertion. Such a large force of the people under arms corresponded with Bolshevik ideas about mass mobilization, and also provided troops for the number of challenges that the Bolsheviks had to confront. However, these numbers posed formidable logistical problems as well as making it difficult to ensure fighting quality and command cohesion. These tasks were handled by Lev Trotsky, People's Commissar for Military Affairs from March 1918 to January 1925, who had earlier served as People's Commissar of Foreign Affairs.

The secret police helped maintain control, but troops were also used to crush opposition within the Soviet-dominated zone. Like the French revolutionaries from 1792, the Bolsheviks overcame their oppositional tendencies and created a new state and military system reliant on force and centralized control in order to direct resources ruthlessly. The Red Army gave force to this internal transformation and also represented it.

Terror, deployed by the All-Russian Extraordinary Commission for Struggle Against Sabotage and Counter-Revolution, or Cheka, established in December 1917, helped greatly in suppressing real or potential opposition to requisitioning and other measures. That December, the Cheka's head, Felix Dzerzhinskii, declared 'we are not in need of justice. It is war now – face to face, a fight to the finish'.[9] Lenin followed up in January 1918 by demanding extra-judicial executions against speculators and bandits causing food shortages. That September, the Cheka was ordered to shoot opponents summarily, launching a 'Red Terror'. Moreover, there were Revolutionary Tribunals from late 1917, including in the army by 1919.

Arbitrary imprisonment, concentration camps, large-scale torture and the mass killings of those suspected, were all integral parts of the October Revolution, and the Cheka was far more brutal and murderous than the Tsarist police had been, albeit in more difficult circumstances. The random as well as large-scale character of the killings reflected the wide and paranoid definition of the counter-revolutionaries supposedly plotting to overthrow the revolution. Despite the propaganda aimed against counter-revolutionaries on the Right, many of those slaughtered were rivals on the Left, notably the Socialist Revolutionaries, because no other interpretation of politics was permitted. Bolshevik violence contributed to a general social and political fragmentation.[10]

At the same time, the Bolsheviks showed, on occasion, an expedient willingness to compromise in order to achieve their goals: far from rejecting hierarchy, the Red Army restored it alongside conscription and the death penalty. Indeed, as a result in large part of Trotsky's concern for discipline and professionalism, at least 30,000 ex-Tsarist officers were employed. Motivated by patriotism, fear or need, they provided a valuable element of experience and continuity. This measure became a cause of contention, with the so-called Military Opposition of Bolsheviks challenging Trotsky's views. Stalin, who distrusted the Tsarist officers, backed this group.

Opposition to the Bolsheviks was encountered not only from the Whites and Greens, but also from the Left. A rising in Moscow in July 1918 by Socialist Revolutionaries who had been in government with the Bolsheviks from December 1917 to March 1918 was suppressed. On 28 February 1921, the sailors and workers on the Kronstadt island naval base to the west of Petrograd, the leading naval base, rose against the government and in favour of Soviet democracy. This was symbolically significant as well as a major threat. Kronstadt had been a bastion of Bolshevik support from February 1917. In the event, covered by heavy artillery, supported by air attack, and organized by Trotsky, 50,000 troops, advancing across the ice on 16–17 March 1921, restored state control after an initial attack on 8 February had failed as the defensive fire from the island fortifications had broken up some of the ice. Those who surrendered were shot without trial or sent to concentration camps. The Finns complained about the number of corpses that washed up on their shore.

The willingness to use force in this fashion was an obvious corollary of its employment against other opponents. Although smaller scale than peasant opposition, these left-wing rebellions were important because they occurred at the centres of power, which were key foci of violence in the inter-war period, unlike during the Great War. Similarly, Shanghai was a central goal and site of conflict in China, whether with the Northern Expedition of the Guomindang, the struggle with the Communists, or warfare with Japan.

In Russia, the fissiparous character of revolutionary movements was clearly demonstrated by these rebellions. Looked at differently, so also was the radical disruption caused by violent changes in authority and the way in which it made renewed uses of violence seem normative.

Peasant opposition to the Bolsheviks reflected the burden of the war, the exactions of the new regime, and opposition to its determination to control rural life. Much of this opposition, especially in the Volga valley, was large scale, and its repression involved a significant deployment of government forces. Famine and exhaustion also helped the Bolsheviks. Over 100,000 troops, supported by planes and using poison gas, and commanded by Mikhail Tukhachevsky, were deployed in June 1921 to overcome the Antonov revolt in Tambov province. There were mass internments, shootings and deportations to concentration camps.[11]

Although less significant than the massive use of violence, the regime also compromised by introducing the New Economic Policy in 1921: allowing the peasants to trade in food and small-scale trade in consumer goods to re-emerge. This measure was essential in order to ensure internal stability after the end of the war and after the disastrous policies of the 'war Communism' period. As such, the political dimension of the conflict was abundantly demonstrated. In contrast, barring Wrangel's too-little, too-late efforts at reform, the Whites offered nothing, even theoretically, to the peasants. Any return to the old regime meant that peasant land gains would be reversed, while the White idea of 'one Russia great and undivided' also alienated the nationalist movements.

The scholarly emphasis can be instructive. A tendency to focus on the New Economic Policy often reflects a failure to discuss the role of large-scale violence in Soviet control of the countryside. In part, this emphasis arises from the degree to which it is easier to comment on the direction of central government legislation, rather than the more obscure processes of rural control.

By retaining control of St Petersburg and Moscow during the Civil War, the Bolsheviks could afford to trade space for time in what was very much a war of movement, and one in which cavalry played a major role. This situation contrasted greatly with the situation in the Great War on many fronts, although there had been important instances of both on the Eastern Front. Trading space for time was also to be a significant component in warfare elsewhere. It was seen for example in the Turkish response to the Greek advance in Anatolia in 1921 and also, repeatedly, during civil warfare in China.

In the case of Russia and Turkey, but less so in China, this willingness was linked to the need to retain control of a centre of power, if not the centre of authority, as this control provided an important level of legitimation. The latter was particularly significant during civil wars. So also was the degree to which control of such centres provided a sense of likely success, which was important in rallying support and discouraging opposition or, at least slackening the latter into neutrality. The alternative emphasis was on controlling, not particular spots, but rather military forces. This emphasis was very much seen in China, both with the warlords and with the Communists, and it was also true, to a degree, of the Guomindang army (see Chapter 3).

Although the Bolsheviks had some skilled commanders, neither side showed much operational or strategic skill. Instead of manoeuvring to obtain the most favourable positions, both sides generally chose to fight where they encountered each other, and success usually came to the one that mounted the offensive; a situation also seen in China in the 1920s. These attacks included frontal assaults on positions, such as Mikhail Frunze's successful storming of the White defences of the Crimea in November 1920. Due to relatively low force-space ratios, this was warfare in which the emphasis was on attacks, raids and the seizure of key governmental positions, rather than on staging large-scale battles from well-prepared positions as if on the Western Front in the Great War. The Red Army tended to rely on prepared offensives, albeit crude ones. The idea was to mass forces in a particular sector for a frontal assault (taran or ram) that was more or less guaranteed to break a thin enemy line and force withdrawal.

The difficulty of sustaining operations, a crucial aspect of logistics, encouraged the emphasis on movement rather than scale, and hence the significance of the railroads. As a result, the situation favoured the offensive over the defensive, as in February 1918 in Russian Central Asia, when the newly established Communist government in Tashkent sent a small force that rapidly seized Khokand, overthrowing the Muslim government that had been established there. Underlining the importance of transport networks, Tashkent was also an important railway town.

Nevertheless, the defensive remained important at the tactical level and, in some respects, more so than in the Great War, because the artillery necessary to suppress defences was in limited supply and was not really useful for fast-moving operations over large areas, in part because the means to move it were limited, which helped explain the importance of armed trains. Their guns provided a form of mobile artillery.

At the same time, the absence of continuous fronts made it easier to outflank defensive positions, as was also amply demonstrated in the fighting of the warlord period in the 1920s in China, and this situation encouraged the stress on advancing. In addition, defensive positions could be stormed. As a result of these factors, and notably of logistical limitations and organizational weaknesses, there were short battles, such as the Red Army's victory over Czech and White Russian forces at Samara on 8 October 1918, and the tank-backed White storming of Tsaritsyn (later Stalingrad) on the second attempt on 19 June 1919 – unlike the long battles, resting on repeated attacks, seen so often in the Great War. Low levels of firepower increased the likelihood of mobile warfare.

Morale played a major role in engagements, again like the situation in China. The Bolsheviks, who had destroyed the coherence of the Tsarist army in 1917 by challenging the disciplinary authority of officers, were greatly helped by the raising of a large conscript army from the summer of 1918. Moreover, from then the emphasis was clearly on regular divisions rather than irregular forces. The Bolsheviks' numerical superiority over the Whites was of considerable importance on a number of occasions early in the struggle and, more generally, in the later stages of the war. Thanks to conscription, the Red Army grew rapidly, especially in early 1919, and heavily outnumbered the

Whites in infantry and artillery; and if not in cavalry, the gap there had been significantly narrowed.

Yet, the issue of numbers has to be handled with care. Although the quality of Bolshevik soldiers varied greatly, numbers could be decisive, but, at the same time, much of the Red Army was dedicated to food requisitioning and otherwise maintaining the rest of the army in the field. Once the impact of desertion is also included, then the effective size of the army was not as large as total numbers might imply, which was also true for the Whites. The threat of the execution of deserters and would-be deserters from the Red Army, a policy pressed by Trotsky, was used to try to control the situation. In practice, manpower was usually too crucial, and deserters were re-enrolled.

Desertion owed much to the need to support family economies and to the terrible conditions of the army. There was a dearth of uniforms and boots, while disease, notably typhus, was a serious problem. It was exacerbated greatly by a lack of medical care. Disease greatly weakened the operational ability of the Red and White armies. There was nothing to match the quality of medical care seen with the British Army on the Western Front, but Britain was richer and the more static nature of the front helped in the build-up of facilities.

The defeat of the Whites helped make foreign intervention redundant. The victorious powers, having, eventually, defeated Germany in a conventional conflict, were to find Russia a more intractable task; although, exhausted, they did not commit a comparable effort to intervention in Russia. Initially motivated largely by a determination to protect supplies of weapons and maintain a presence after the Russo-German peace of March 1918, this intervention rapidly grew in scale and intention. Fourteen states sent troops and weaponry to help the Whites. British forces were dispatched to the Baltic and Black Seas and northern Russia and included an important naval component. The Americans, Canadians, British and Japanese deployed forces in Siberia, and the French in the Baltic and Black Seas and northern Russia. Other participants included Canadians, Italians and Serbs in northern Russia, and Finns, Poles and Romanians to the west of the Soviet zone.

Foreign intervention thus overlapped with the struggle for independence by former subject peoples, which helped explain why foreign forces had their own agendas to pursue including, in some cases, territorial gains and geopolitical interests. As part of their struggle for independence, the Finns sought East Karelia, sending troops to the area in 1918 and 1919, but they lacked international support, notably from the British. The Finns had particularly poor relations with the Whites, who were unwilling to recognize their independence, and, as a consequence, the Finns refused to support Yudenich's advance on St Petersburg. This helped the Bolsheviks concentrate their forces in the region against Yudenich. Their attitude prefigured the later unwillingness to support German attacks on the city in 1941–2.

Geopolitical advantage also played a role in foreign intervention. Looking to the future, the French, for example, wanted a White Russia that would restore the pre-war alliance with France and thus balance German power in Europe: this was a continuous anxiety for French policymakers, one eased but not ended by victory in the Great War. George, Viscount Curzon, the bold British Foreign Secretary, advocated control over parts of the former Russian Empire, a policy seen as a forward-defence for India. There was also concern about the threat of Bolshevik expansion. Sir Halford Mackinder, the British High Commissioner in South Russia, pressed the Cabinet in January 1920 on the danger of 'a new Russian Czardom of the Proletariat' and of 'Bolshevism, sweeping forward like a prairie fire' towards India and 'lower Asia'.[12] There was a general tendency to see anti-imperial rebellions in the British Empire as part of a global Bolshevik conspiracy.

Territorial gains were also sought by Japan, which deployed the largest force of the intervening powers; although, in part, this was because Japan did not have the global commitments of Britain and France. Moreover, Japan had not been exhausted by the Great War, in which its economy had grown greatly, and geographical proximity ensured that the logistical burden of intervention in Russia was less. Japan had negotiated an alliance with Russia in the summer of 1916, but the Revolution overthrew this arrangement and created new fears and opportunities. Seeking gains in the Russian Far East, and determined to strengthen their position in neighbouring Manchuria, the Japanese committed the Siberian Expeditionary Army in 1918. 73,000 men strong, this army was larger than the forces of other Allied powers in Siberia, and led to suspicion by them.[13] The Japanese supported the Whites in Siberia until 1922, and the major centre in the Far East, Vladivostok, the terminus of the Trans-Siberian Railway, did not fall to the Red Army until October of that year.

Foreign forces were important in particular areas of Russia, supplied *matériel* to the Whites and dominated the naval dimension of the struggle, but did not make a decisive impact in the war. There was no coherent White command structure and strategy with which to co-operate. There was, moreover, a lack of agreed aims among the intervening powers and also of resolve. The forces actually committed were small. This had much to do with the general unpopularity at home of intervention. Post-war demobilization and the financial burdens left by the Great War placed obvious limits on interventionism. David Lloyd George, the British Prime Minister, was unenthusiastic about intervention, a course pressed by Winston Churchill, the Secretary for War, and by influential generals. There was also unrest among the conscripts in the British army and navy, which led the government to demobilize more rapidly than it had originally intended. Conscription ended in 1919, and in 1920 the Cabinet turned against its previous emphasis on acting against Bolshevism. There was also unrest and mutiny in the French navy in the Black Sea.

British intervention was, to use a later language, a war of choice. The situation was far less easy for Russia's neighbours, including most obviously peoples seeking independence from Russian rule. In the Caucasus, the British, moving forward from Iraq where they had defeated Turkey in 1918, played a role in protecting the states of Armenia, Azerbaijan and Georgia, which had all become independent from Russia in April–May 1918. The arrival of the Royal Navy in the Black Sea made intervention far easier. In late 1918, the British landed troops in the Black Sea port of Batumi, helping end fighting between Georgians and Armenians. However, under pressure from too many commitments, the British withdrew their forces from late 1919. This withdrawal culminated when Batumi was evacuated in July 1920, the final abandonment of Mackinder's call for the British to hold the rail line from there to Baku.

In turn, the Bolsheviks were able to benefit from the weakness and division of the local republics. The Soviets advanced into Azerbaijan in April 1920, into Armenia in November, and into Georgia in February 1921. As a reminder of the dependence of small states on the politics of the major powers, the fall of these newly independent states owed much to Turkish opposition to Britain, for the British saw these states as a buffer for their interests in Iraq, Persia (Iran)[14] and India, and as a source of raw materials, notably oil from Azerbaijan and access to this oil from Georgia. Seeking to weaken Britain and to win Soviet assistance, including arms, the Turkish nationalists under Atatürk were willing to attack Armenia, while the strong Turkish presence in Azerbaijan, notably in the Azeri army, did not resist the Soviet invasion. Vulnerable to Turkish attack, Armenia followed suit. Surrounded and blockaded, Georgia resisted Soviet invasion, but its forces were heavily outnumbered, and the country fell after a month's struggle. The Soviets had waited until after the situation on their western front, that with Poland, appeared stable. The Turks joined in, in an attempt to gain the port of Batumi.

Further east, Bolshevik forces under Frunze overran Central Asia in 1920, capturing Bukhara and Khiva. As in the Caucasus, this represented a victory both for the centre and for Communism. There had been struggles in the autonomous emirate of Bukhara and the khanate of Khiva, with their autocratic rulers successfully resisting local reform movements, and the Russian Communists intervening. They established a People's Soviet Republic in Khiva in February 1920, and after an expedition had failed that March, a second overthrew the emir of Bukhara in September. On the other side of the Black Sea, the Soviets were able to re-establish control in Transnistria (to the east of the Dniester River), ending any prospect of Romanian expansion beyond Bessarabia (modern Moldova), from which they had already repelled the Soviets. The Franco-Greek force that had landed at Odessa in December 1918 made scant contribution to the White cause in the region and was evacuated the following spring in the face of the Communist advance.

The Soviets proved less successful in the Baltic. In Finland, independence from Russian rule was declared in December 1917, only for a Communist revolt to begin the following year, with Helsinki seized in January 1918. The resulting conflict involved the Red Finns, who were poorly organized; White (conservative) Finns; Germans who allied with the Whites, taking Helsinki in April 1918; and Bolshevik Russians. Anti-Bolshevik forces under Carl Gustav von Mannerheim, a Swedish-speaking Finn of German ancestry who had been a lieutenant-general in the Russian army, became the dominant player; with Mannerheim serving for a while as Regent. Once Mannerheim had overrun the Karelian Isthmus, the axis of advance from Russia, the situation in Finland was under control from the anti-Bolshevik perspective, but a treaty with the Soviets accepting Finnish independence was not signed until October 1920.

The Baltic Republics (Estonia, Latvia, Lithuania) also gained independence from Russian imperial rule. They were helped by the quality and determination of their own troops but also by other forces. Initially, much of the area was occupied by the Germans as a result of their successes in the Great War. However, renouncing their territorial cessions to the Germans under the Treaty of Brest-Litovsk of 1918, the Bolsheviks advanced into the region, capturing Riga, the Latvian centre, on 3 January 1919 and Vilnius/Vilna, the largest city in Lithuania, two days later. In early 1919, the Bolsheviks managed to overrun most of Latvia, much of Lithuania, and part of Estonia, only to be driven back by counter-revolutionary forces supported by German *Freikorps* (veterans), Finnish volunteers and British naval pressure. The importance of the latter was accentuated by the fact that the major cities in Latvia and Estonia were ports.[15]

The *Freikorps* were needed in order to help resist the Bolsheviks on land. The British had preferred to ask for help from the Scandinavian states, which had remained neutral during the Great War, but they refused to get involved. However, the German forces clashed with the local desire for independence as the Germans sought both to dominate the region and, by so doing, to affect the Versailles peace settlement. In the event, the Germans were defeated at Cécis (Wenden) by Estonian and Latvian forces. Subsequently, the attempt of a German force in the White army to seize Riga in October 1919 was stopped by Latvian and Estonian forces, helped by the British navy. In November, the victorious forces took the offensive, driving the Germans from Latvia. Subsequently, the offshore presence of the British navy remained important, as did the Soviet focus on the Poles further south, a focus that ended in Soviet defeat.

Russo-Polish war

Before the Great War, the Russians had ruled much of Poland, only to be driven out by the Germans during the war, Warsaw falling to the Germans in 1915. Once Poland became independent in November 1918, it was unclear where its borders should be, and, particularly its eastern border. The Armistice with the victorious Allies dictated the withdrawal of German forces, but this retreat created a vacuum into which the Bolsheviks advanced. Moreover, local national movements took the initiative, with the West Ukrainian Republic taking control of south-east Poland. Marshal Józef Pilsudski, both Polish Commander in Chief and Head of State, wished to return Poland to her extensive borders prior to the First Partition of Poland in 1772, a plan that, for him, entailed a federation including Belarus, Lithuania and Ukraine. This plan was seen as a way to obtain regional security by ensuring an ability to deter Russian expansion. Rejected by Polish nationalists, who, instead, wanted gains by annexations, this plan was also not welcome to most of the population in these areas, the vast majority of whom were not Polish; but, in November 1918, the Poles occupied Western Ukraine and, in the following spring, the cities of Vilnius/Vilna and Minsk.

By the end of 1919, most of Belarus had also been brought under Polish control. However, the threat from the Red Army led to a willingness to recognize, and ally with, Ukraine against the Soviets. In 1920, Pilsudski negotiated an agreement with Ukrainian separatists by which they ceded Western Ukraine to Poland, in return for Polish help in establishing a Ukrainian government in Kiev. The city fell to the Poles and Ukrainians on 7 May 1920.

As a reminder that conflicts do not take place in isolation, this struggle, however, was impacted in the wider course of the Russian Civil War. Having defeated the Whites, the Bolsheviks were now in a far stronger position, could use nationalistic propaganda to mobilize the population, and also had a battle-hardened army. Using their cavalry effectively, the Bolshevik forces cut the Polish lines of communication and, in June 1920, the Poles were obliged to abandon Kiev and Ukraine. The divided and indifferently led Ukrainians were poorly placed to offer effective resistance, while the Poles, outmanoeuvred and short of supplies, fell back, losing cohesion. The Bolsheviks pressed on to capture Minsk and Vilnius/Vilna in July 1920, and advanced into Poland, intending both to make the country Communist and to use it as the means to spread Communism further into Europe, and, in particular, to Germany. A peace treaty signed with Lithuania in July increased the pressure on Poland.

A pessimistic Sir Maurice Hankey, the British Cabinet Secretary, returning from Warsaw in July, thought Polish collapse likely and warned of the danger that this might lead to an understanding between the Soviet Union and Germany, prompting the French to occupy the Ruhr, the German industrial heartland.[16] On 22 September 1920, Lenin, who had played a larger role in strategy from the summer of 1919, gave a speech to the Communist Party calling for the advance of the Red Army to the German and Czech frontiers.

In response to the advancing Soviets, the Poles sought Anglo-French mediation, offering a provisional eastern boundary that represented a marked reduction of their hopes; but the Communists had no intention of heeding such a mediation. The Communists did not, however, benefit from the expected support of the Polish proletariat. Far from there being a pro-Soviet rising, the all-Polish Government of National Defence established on 24 July won support, notably by backing land reform, the sort of step Kolchak had conspicuously failed to take on behalf of the Whites. Volunteers rallied, taking the army to 900,000 men in an exuberant display of nationalism and opposition to Communism, unexpected by the Bolsheviks, that lent energy to the counter-attack launched by Pilsudski east of Warsaw on 16–18 August. In the most important battle of the 1920s, the Red Army, under Mikhail Tukhachevsky, was defeated near Warsaw between 16 and 25 August 1920 and then driven back, with the Poles subsequently winning fresh battles on the River Niemen and at Szczara.

The Poles benefited from a lack of coordination among the mutually distrustful Bolshevik generals, notably between the forces advancing on Warsaw and those moving on Lvov to the south-east, and from the length of Bolshevik supply lines. Tukhachevsky's failure to concentrate his forces at the key points was also crucial. The Poles also had significant strengths including the availability of French supplies and military advice, and the ability to gain the initiative and then to defeat the Bolshevik forces in detail. The Poles were also superior in intelligence and communications, in part thanks to reading Soviet radio traffic. Ably commanded by Pilsudski, the Poles outmanoeuvred their opponents, who lost over 100,000 men. General Wladyslaw Sikorski, the commander of the Polish Fifth Army, made good use of motorized infantry and armoured cars, providing firepower to supplement the cavalry.

Nevertheless, Polish campaigning had serious weaknesses, and, as is frequent in military history, the conflict was decided by which side was best able to cope with its deficiencies and exploit those of its opponent. That the Soviets were over-extended following a rapid advance, as they were also to be when they approached Warsaw in 1944, was also significant. The British observer, Major-General Sir Percy Rawcliffe, ascribed the contrast between the operational mobility of the Polish campaign and the more static situation on the Western Front in the Great War to the lower density of troops in Poland. This lower density left the Poles weak and, more specifically, without depth and reserves:

> Naturally the attempt to leave no portion of the front uncovered made the Polish forces hopelessly weak everywhere, without cohesion, depth or reserves, and with little more power of resistance than that of a line of seaweed floating on the tide.

There were also more specific problems. A lack of training on both sides, especially in the use of the rifle, undermined the strength of the defensive. Rawcliffe linked fighting quality and mass, arguing that the Bolsheviks were short of both. Claiming that Bolshevik armies were poorly trained, equipped and led, and had low morale, he suggested that, because the Bolsheviks advanced over a very wide front, they lacked depth and nearby reserves. In the battle of Warsaw in August 1920, for the first time in the campaign, the Bolsheviks, having earlier encountered only weak resistance, came up against a continuous line of barbed wire that was moderately well defended. Despite their success, Rawcliffe argued that the Poles lacked training, equipment, organization and good officers, the last particularly significant as, by playing the patriotic card, the Bolsheviks managed to attract a further number of ex-Tsarist generals to join against the Poles. As the terrain was ideal for mobile warfare, but in response to the changing nature of war, Rawcliffe believed that the Polish cavalry should be equipped with machine guns, armoured cars and Ford vans. He also argued that they must have ample reserves echeloned in depth, which would enable them to cope with any breakthrough and also to launch a counter-offensive. Rawcliffe emphasized mobility as the key characteristic of the conflict.[17] Indeed, the campaign was seen by cavalrymen as a vindication of their arm.

This mobility was seen in the aftermath of the victory. Suffering a serious loss of cohesion after their defeat, the Bolsheviks lacked a fall-back position and were also faced with growing disaffection in Belarus and Ukraine. In October 1920, the Poles captured Minsk and advanced to within 90 miles of Kiev, before agreeing an armistice that came into effect on 16 October, in contrast to British hopes of cooperation with the Whites. The eventual Treaty of Riga, of 18 March 1921, left Poland with some territory in Lithuania, Ukraine and Belarus. Poland was left in control of areas that did not have a majority Polish population, and in Western Ukraine this led to resistance into the early 1930s that was repressed by the Polish army.[18] Once Poland had made peace, it was possible for the Red Army to defeat the Ukrainian separatists who had advanced alongside the Poles. Moreover, the Sixth Army which was being moved from the Latvian border to oppose the Poles was now sent south against the Whites based in the Crimea. The sequential character of Soviet offensives helps explain the length of the Russian Civil War, as did its geographical extent; although, unlike the Great War, there was neither a naval nor a trans-oceanic dimension.[19]

Eastern Europe

On a smaller scale, there were also conflicts across much of Eastern Europe in the aftermath of the Great War. The disruptive aftermath of the war combined with the rise of ideological alignments to ensure that political violence became more pronounced in Europe[20], as also (differently) in China. These changes created a more challenging context for regular armies, in terms both of the tasks they faced and of the control they were supposed to exercise. Sectarian and ethnic violence looked towards more recent patterns.

A stress on swift movement in the warfare of the period was encouraged by the need to establish control rapidly in contested areas in order to present peacemakers and other powers with *faits accomplis*. In part, this situation was a response to the failure of peacemakers to accept the complexities of situations. The peacemakers generally had inadequate and partisan information, notably on the local ethnic situation. Frequently, there was also a rejection

of the attempt by outside bodies to dictate developments. Aggressive nation-
alisms gave force to these attempts. The process began in the former Russian
Empire as authority collapsed in the winter of 1917–18, and conflict spread as
the Austro-Hungarian Empire disintegrated in late 1918.

Nationalism worked to justify both independence and expansionism.
Moreover, its ethnic logic was given added force by ideological fears. For
example, in Bessarabia (modern Moldova), which Russia had gained from
the Ottoman (Turkish) Empire in 1812, the Russian Revolution of February/
March 1917, led to pressure for an autonomous Moldavian Republic. As the
Bolsheviks seized power in Russia, so there was a movement to independence,
with the Moldavian Democratic Federated Republic established on 15
December by the National Council. In response to Bolshevik advances, the
Council asked neighbouring Romania to send troops, and a division arrived
in Chişinău, the capital, in January 1918. A declaration of independence
followed, which was widely seen as a prelude to the union with Romania
declared in March.[21]

Before the end of 1918, the collapse of the Austro-Hungarian Empire led
to Germans and Czechs clashing in the Sudetenland (the majority-German
inhabited area of Czechoslovakia), as were the Carinthians and Slovenes in
what became the Austro-Yugoslav border area. Meanwhile, Germans, Poles
and Czechs competed in Upper Silesia. Questions of identity interacted with
often vicious violence, although the latter may have been exaggerated by
contemporaries.[22] Pre-war disputes within empires became post-war clashes,
not least as the Romanians, Serbs, Slovaks and Czechs, who had suffered
within the Habsburg kingdom of Hungary from Hungarian hegemony, united
against Hungary.[23]

There were also clashes across the borders of former empires. Bukovina,
which the Habsburgs had gained from the Ottomans in 1775, was sought
by neighbouring Romania, in large part on the basis that the majority of the
population was Romanian; but the Russians had been interested in northern
Bukovina, where the majority was Slavic. The Russian interest was taken over by
Ukraine and, in late 1918 the commitment of local Romanian leaders to union
with Romania led to the rival dispatch of Ukrainian units which occupied the
capital, Czernowitz. In response, Bukovina's Romanian-dominated National

Council asked for military intervention, and Romanian forces drove out the Ukrainians. On 28 November, Bukovina's national Congress declared for union with Romania.

The Romanian army was also involved at the same time in trying to secure a border with Hungary that matched Romanian territorial claims. The French commander of Allied forces in South-East Europe had drawn a demarcation line in central Transylvania between Hungarian and Romanian forces, but the latter ignored it and pressed on against weak Hungarian resistance. Instructions to stop issued by the Allied Supreme Council were also ignored, and, as a result, the new demarcation line drawn on 25 February 1919 left Hungarian-majority areas under Romanian control. This failure to protect these areas led to the fall of the Hungarian government in March, and its replacement by a Communist-led government which, on 21 March 1919, proclaimed Hungary a Soviet republic. Béla Kun, its head, rejected the February 1919 demarcation line and demanded the November 1918 one, which ended the attempt to reach an agreement between the Allied Supreme Council and Hungary.

As the number of 'players' in conflict rose, the notions of a clear-cut definition of military forces, and of war as the prerogative of the state, were put under severe strain. This obliged newly established regular armies to confront situations in which goals and opponents were often far from clear, while atrocities became more than the small change of war. What would later be termed ethnic cleansing was practiced because of the ethnic basis of the new states.

The Yugoslav re-imposition of rule over Kosovo, seized by Serbia in the First Balkan War of 1912–13 and lost in 1915, was opposed by Albanian irregulars, while Greek and Yugoslav intervention in Albania focused on their attempt to control areas allocated to Albania in 1913. The Yugoslavs justified their intervention in Albania on the grounds that the Italian occupation forces (which were under attack from Albanian irregulars from June 1920) should not be there, but, when Italy withdrew in August 1920, the Yugoslavs sought to strengthen their position. In 1920–1, Aubrey Herbert MP pressed the British government to protest about Yugoslav massacres of ethnic Albanians, in both Albania and Kosovo. On 12 May 1921, he raised the issue in the House of Commons, claiming that on 28 January, two Serbian battalions had occupied four villages 'near Prishtina, driven the male inhabitants above the age of 12 years on to the neighbouring mountain, massacred them with machine guns, proceeded to the villages, set fire to houses and massacred all the women and children, leaving only 14 survivors out of a population of 1,680'.[24] Across Eastern Europe, there was also much murderous anti-Semitic violence, including pogroms which were particularly common in Russia where the Whites killed at least 50,000 Jews.[25] In turn, border regions were deliberately settled in order to justify claims, as with the settlement of Czechs.

The extent to which the regular armies in question were mostly new forces increased the overlap with politics. In 1919, the Czech army took Slovakia from the Hungarians, who were unwilling to accept the separatist drive of the national minorities; and German resistance in the Sudetenland was harshly repressed by the Czechs without a plebiscite, notably with the massacre of Kaaden on 14 March in which 52 Germans were killed.

Moreover, the Romanians, with Czech support, suppressed the Communist regime in Hungary, advancing as far as Budapest. In April 1919, the Romanians responded to Béla Kun by sending their forces further into Hungary, in an attempt to make the Tisza River the frontier. Resistance in eastern Hungary was limited, but it encouraged the Romanians to march on, entering Budapest on 3 August. The Communist government had fallen on 1 August and Béla Kun had fled to Vienna. He was to take refuge in the Soviet Union where he was executed during Stalin's Purges.

A conservative regime led by Miklós Horthy took power in Hungary. Horthy, an admiral under the Habsburgs, had helped suppress the Communists. Under Allied pressure, the Romanians eventually withdrew from Budapest, but the Treaty of Trianon of 1920 left them not only Transylvania but also some Hungarian-majority areas in eastern Hungary. This settlement encouraged Hungarian demands for a revision of the peace settlement.

Instability in Central Europe continued after Trianon. In 1921, the Czechs and Yugoslavs planned to invade Hungary in response to a Habsburg restoration attempt, but they were restrained by Britain and France. In the event, there was no restoration.

Also in 1919, the Poles took the city of Vilnius (Vilna) from Lithuania, while on 12 September an Italian volunteer force under Gabriele D'Annuzio, an exuberant poet intoxicated on nationalism, seized the disputed Adriatic port of Fiume. His was an attempt to force a different outcome to the peace settlement, and one that undermined the authority of the Italian state, although the Liberal governments earlier in the year had already registered their fury with a peace settlement that had failed to accept their territorial pretensions, not least to parts of the Austro-Hungarian Empire, such as Fiume, allocated to Yugoslavia. Indeed, the government, under pressure from the army and navy as well as nationalist opinion, had threatened to hold up the ratification of the German peace treaty.

The Lithuanian seizure of Memel from a French garrison in 1923 represented a different rejection of the peace settlement. Nevertheless, frontier plebiscites helped defuse tension in a number of areas. In Carinthia, where Yugoslav occupying forces were resisted by the *Heimwehr*, a local militia, a plebiscite in October 1920 left most of the territory with Austria. In November 1921, the Great Powers recognized Albanian sovereignty and largely confirmed the 1913 borders, with Delimitation Commissioners instructed to settle issues on the ground.

Alongside nationalism, ideology played a major role in the fighting after the Great War, notably in the suppression of the Hungarian Communists under Béla Kun. Ideological rivalry was also a feature of conflict in post-war Germany, as radical attempts to seize power were violently contested by right-wing paramilitaries, especially in Berlin, as well as in Italy with the rise of the Fascists[26], in Austria and in Hungary. In all these countries, there were paramilitaries on both the Left and the Right.

Ireland

Nationalism and ideology were also at issue in Ireland where, at a very different scale, the Great War closed with another unsettled problem, that of the place of Ireland in the British Empire. A longstanding movement for Home Rule/self-government, supported by much of the (majority) Catholic population, had been opposed by the Protestants, most of whom were concentrated in northern Ireland, the historic province of Ulster. Conflict began in 1916 when a nationalist uprising, centred in Dublin, the Easter Rising, was crushed. The firm, not to say harsh, British response helped radicalize nationalist opinion. The Home Rulers were undermined as political support for independence grew.

In 1919, the Irish Volunteers, soon to rename themselves the Irish Republican Army (IRA), began terrorist activity against the state. They were opposed to conventional politics, which they saw as likely to result in compromise, and their actions helped lead to a situation in which such an outcome was blocked, while the nationalist cause increasingly became both violent and sectarian. Much IRA violence was anti-Protestant. Rival religious groups were defined in what in part became a power struggle between them, as much as a war of national liberation, which was the way in which the IRA presented the struggle.

British refusal to accept independence helped to precipitate a brutal civil war in 1919–21, a war that both illustrated the difficulties of responding to guerrilla warfare and (differently) the effectiveness of terrorism. Although termed a civil war, the emphasis was on terrorism, irregular warfare and martial law measures, rather than battle or even skirmish, which would have exposed the IRA to defeat. Terrorism hit the morale and manpower of the Royal Irish Constabulary and destroyed the ability of the British to convey an impression of maintaining stability, although control over most of the country was sustained. This was an achievement given the shortage of troops arising from widespread pressure on British military resources.[27] This shortage encouraged the controversial use of British auxiliary police, notably the 10,000 strong Black and Tans who were recruited from ex-soldiers. They became associated with reprisals against IRA terrorism, and the use of civilian clothes by the IRA helped encourage a lack of care in the targetting of reprisals.[28]

In tones that were to become familiar from counter-insurgency operations elsewhere, Lieutenant-General Sir Philip Chetwode, Deputy Chief of the Imperial General Staff, claimed, in July 1921, that victory was possible, but only if the army was given more control, including of the police, and the full support of British public opinion:

The full incidence of martial law will demand very severe measures and to begin with many executions. In the present state of ignorance of the population in England, I doubt very much that it would not result in a protest which would not only ruin our efforts, but would be most dangerous to the army. The latter have behaved magnificently throughout, but they feel from top to bottom that they are not supported by their countrymen, and should there be a strong protest against severe action it would be extremely difficult to hold them.[29]

Field Marshal Sir Henry Wilson, the Chief of the Imperial General Staff until February 1922, and an Irish Protestant, was firmly against negotiations. Having ceased to be Chief of Staff and entered Parliament, he was to be shot down on his London doorstep by IRA assassins in June 1922.

It is possible that, with a tough policy, the rebellion could have been put down. Indeed, it has been argued that, far from the British clearly failing, as is often assumed, the IRA did not win in the field, and notably not so in County Cork, a key area of operations. In fact, by the summer of 1921, the IRA was under severe pressure. Over the previous two years, the government and army had developed a series of responses, including internment (detention without trial), the use of wireless telegraphy, air power and the active deployment of fighting patrols. The introduction of these measures meant that the IRA had ceased to provide a significant military threat, and, by 1921, their operations had been reduced to a terrorist challenge, not least using roadside bombs and targeting individuals, rather than a military one. Far from being a rigid force constrained by conventional operations, the ability of the British army to respond flexibly emerges clearly.[30]

As with the (very different) Russian Civil War, however, political and public opinion in Britain lacked enthusiasm for a long, tough struggle. The Liberal Prime Minister, David Lloyd George, who had long had a sympathy for nationalist causes, initially used bellicose rhetoric but later changed his attitude. In the eyes of Conservative backbenchers who pressed for 'No Surrender' in Ireland, as well as 'Make Germany Pay', Lloyd George lacked the necessary firmness. However, even though some of his Conservative coalition ministerial colleagues supported tougher action, the Cabinet did not split.

Under the Government of Ireland Act of December 1920, the British government partitioned Ireland between what were designed to be two Home

Rule states. This legislation was designed as a complement to tough military action as it was intended to take the political initiative from the IRA and lessen its support. The Act established Northern Ireland as a separate territory, dominated by Protestants, and, in June 1921, its first parliamentary session was opened. The following month, in a major shift in policing reflecting the belief of Lloyd George and Churchill that government policy was not working, a truce was agreed between the British and the IRA. This truce was followed by the Anglo-Irish Treaty of December 1921, which accepted both partition and effective independence (rather than Home Rule) for the new Irish Free State (Eire), which became the governing body over most of the island. This treaty superseded the Government of Ireland Act in the South and, instead, the Irish Free State became a self-governing territory, nominally within the British Empire, with a similar status to Australia, Canada and the other dominions.

This treaty, however, did not end instability. In Northern Ireland came the fear of betrayal by the Catholic enemy within as a Catholic minority remained there. Under the Civil Authorities (Special Powers) Act, the Northern Ireland government interned over 900 men and women between 1922 and 1925. Martial law tactics were judged necessary to respond to what was seen as a threatening situation.[31]

The partition, and the failure to secure full independence in the South, was opposed by much of the IRA, the anti-Treaty forces known as the Irregulars. In the face of the nationalist goal of a united Ireland, compromise was unacceptable to them. Mounting a terrorist campaign in Northern Ireland in 1921, the Irregulars also fought the newly independent government in the South in 1922–3. The latter was a more bloody conflict than the War of Independence of 1919–21 against the British. The Irregulars were beaten in Northern Ireland, where they were also to fail to be an effective force able to defend the local Catholics. The Irregulars were also defeated in the Irish Free State where the government launched a vigorous response: the new National Army was given emergency powers, 77 rebels were executed and 12,000 imprisoned. Thereafter, IRA terrorism remained a minor irritant, in both North and South, until the late 1960s.

There was also political stabilization. In the 1923 general election, Sinn Féin, the Nationalist Party under Eamon de Valera, a veteran of the Easter

Rising, who had rejected the Anglo-Irish Treaty of 1921, was defeated, and the Free State government ratified the border with Northern Ireland in 1925. This confirmed partition, and was important to the process by which the new governments in the Irish Free State and Northern Ireland were consolidated. The administrative structures remained those of British Ireland, and the Free State essentially maintained its earlier economic relationship with Britain, selling agricultural goods and importing manufactured products.

Stabilization

By 1925, the political situation across Europe had been stabilized in a fashion that had appeared far less likely in 1919–21 as the high hopes of that period for a new international order had been challenged by continued and new conflicts. In the event, far from the peace settlement sowing the seeds of a major new war, as is frequently claimed, the international system it established worked better in the 1920s, at least from the perspective of Western interests, than was generally appreciated in the 1930s or subsequently.[32] There was domestic instability and international tension in Europe, but this had also been the case prior to 1914, and the Great War and the collapse of the European dynastic empires had left many disputes. However, Britain and France were able to separate key issues of security from others they were prepared to concede. For France, one key issue in 1919 entailed the vetoing of Austrian support for an *Anschluss* (union) with Germany (as demanded by the Austrian National Assembly), as such a step was seen by France as likely to lead to an overly powerful Germany. This issue was a counterpoint to the support for Rhenish separatism, but the latter was not seen as worth pushing hard.

In January 1923, the attempt to enforce the payment of reparations (money to be paid by Germany as part of the peace settlement), led to the dispatch of French and Belgian troops into the Ruhr, the key German economic zone, which had not been part of the occupation zone agreed after the war. This move led not to hostilities, but to large-scale civil disobedience by the local German population. Germany had been restricted to an army of only 100,000 men with no advanced weapons, in the Versailles peace settlement of

1919, and it was in no shape to contest the Franco-Belgian occupation. Civil disobedience in the Ruhr, which was financially supported by the German government, did not lead to guerrilla warfare, nor the people's war pressed by some German commentators, and the crisis was resolved in 1924 before conflict could break out.

Although it was less successful than had been anticipated, passive resistance ensured that the occupiers, despite deploying troops to make the coalminers work, failed to derive the benefits they sought. Furthermore, French relations with Britain and the USA deteriorated. The Americans, whose relations with the Germans had been largely trouble-free, withdrew their forces from their Rhineland occupation zone.[33] The crisis also led to a fall in the value of the franc.

The occupiers withdrew, France having suffered a strategic check, not least as hopes of encouraging Rhenish separatism had been thwarted. This option had been urged by French commentators concerned about continued German strength, especially on the Right. Marshal Ferdinand Foch, the Allied Commander in Chief in 1918, supported the separation of the Rhineland, arguing that the supposedly insufficiently harsh Versailles settlement was only a truce that would last for 20 years. President Raymond Poincaré also wanted a separate Rhineland.[34]

In the event, German reparations were rescheduled in 1924, while the Ruhr crisis demonstrated that France needed the cooperation of both her allies and Germany. Recognition of French reliance on Germany contributed to a *rapprochement* between France and Germany once the Franco-German frontier had been guaranteed by the Treaty of Locarno of 1925.

In 1923, another crisis that threatened war was averted when a Balkan assassination led to armed intervention followed by a diplomatic settlement. On 27 August, General Enrico Tellini, the Italian member of the International Frontier Delimitation Commission tackling the Greek-Albanian frontier, and four of his staff, were murdered on the border. Benito Mussolini, Italy's Fascist leader, blamed the Greeks, demanded an indemnity of 50 million lira, and, when the Greeks refused to pay, occupied the island of Corfu. The crisis provoked the danger of Yugoslav and Bulgarian intervention and threatened to overthrow the principle of settlement via the League of Nations. In the event, the Conference of Ambassadors, the aftermath of the Supreme Council of the Allied Great Powers, found against Greece, which had to pay the indemnity, whereupon the Italians withdrew.

Containing Communism

Another element of post-war stabilization was the containment of Communism. Aside from its hostility to the peace settlements following both the Great War and the Russian Civil War, the very assumptions and core policies of the Soviet Union posed a major and continuing challenge to the international system. If the admission of the Soviet Union to the international system was grudging, Soviet attitudes were also a problem, and there was widespread concern about the Soviet 'aim of world-wide revolution' and about subversion as a result of pro-Soviet activity. Soviet propaganda and the activities, known and suspected, of the Comintern (Communist International), and of Communist parties, went beyond the confines of acceptable diplomacy.[35]

In practice, the hopes of world revolution, with Moscow as the centre and inspiration of the new power of progressive forces around the world, as well as the carrying forward of wartime methods in order to ensure Communist success[36], were, as a result of painful experience, to be subordinated to the more pragmatic interests of the Soviet state. Failure in Poland in 1920 had shown the limits of Bolshevik appeal and power, and helped give rise to a siege mentality.[37] More generally, it proved necessary for the Russian revolutionaries both to accept a new international order[38] and to consolidate their position in a state that was to become the Soviet Union. As a result, in 1921, the People's Commissariat for Foreign Affairs (*Narkomindel*) became more important, and, that year, talented individuals were moved to it from the Comintern.

Diplomatic links were also developed with capitalist states. In March 1921, an Anglo-Soviet trade agreement was used by the Communists to affirm the Soviet Union's legitimate role as a state. An indignant Churchill, who was a fervent anti-Communist, complained that David Lloyd George, the Liberal Prime Minister who had held that post throughout the British intervention in the Russian Civil War, had grasped the 'hairy hand of the baboon' in welcoming the Soviet representative, Leonid Krassin, to No. 10 Downing Street. Lloyd George, in contrast, saw an improvement in relations as a necessary way to counter a threatening situation for which 'the military remedy merely aggravates the disease'.[39]

The hopes of the British government that, as an alternative to force, soft power and engagement in the shape of trade would be a way to dissolve Communism in the Soviet Union proved fruitless, in the face both of the coercive nature of the authoritarian Communist state and of the Soviet leader Lenin's mastery of *realpolitik*. The latter was seen in 1922 when the Treaty of Rapallo with Germany brought two states of very different political type into alliance, as each sought to overcome their diplomatic isolation. In particular, Germany was able to use the Soviet Union for military training that was forbidden under the Versailles peace settlement, thus evading, as the Germans consistently sought to do, the Inter-Allied Military Control Commission established under the peace settlement. The Germans also benefited from a Soviet state that was not aligned with the West.

Rapallo notwithstanding, in 1923, the Soviets planned war with Germany in support of a hoped-for Communist revolution in the country that, due to its industrial development, Karl Marx had seen most favourable for such revolution. Diplomatic efforts were used to support this policy through attempted arrangements with Poland and the Baltic Republics, whose territory separated Germany from the Soviet Union, providing each with the buffer that was to be partitioned out of existence in 1939–40. In the 1923 crisis, there was no division between the realists of the People's Commissariat for Foreign Affairs and the 'bomb-throwers' – revolutionaries – of the Comintern, but rather excessive optimism in both camps at the prospects for revolution.[40]

In the event, there was no revolution in Germany, and the Ruhr crisis did not come together with the potential one in the east; while the Soviet envoy, Viktor Kopp, had also failed to win Polish support for any Soviet intervention. Moreover, an attempted Communist revolution in Estonia in December 1924 was firmly repressed. In 1924, diplomatic relations with Britain were established although alleged Soviet support for subversion in Britain led them to be broken off in 1927.

The pressure in the Soviet Union for a *realpolitik* in international relations that represented the normalization of relations with other states reflected not the abandonment of the Communist cause, but a tactical accommodation. The pursuit of Socialism (i.e. Communism) in one state (the Soviet Union), was justified as gaining time for the strengthening of the cause and intended, in the long term, to be followed by the international expansion of Communism. This emphasis, associated with Stalin, who dominated the state after Lenin's death in 1924, contradicted the more volatile Trotsky's demand for permanent and global revolution. At a meeting of the Politburo in 1926, Trotsky accused his rival Stalin of becoming 'the gravedigger of the revolution'. Trotsky, who had lost his military power-base, was to be forced into exile by Stalin in 1929, and in 1940 was murdered in Mexico in a plot by Soviet Intelligence, the NKVD.

This struggle over policy, control and personalities was also linked to questions of military organization. Trotsky, who was not strong on consistency, both spoke in favour of a workers' militia, which he presented at the Party Congress in 1920 as appropriate for a Communist state and the way to use and retain class consciousness, and also backed technological modernization for the Red Army. The Party Congress led to a militia alongside the regular army. The idea of dependence on a workers' militia was resisted, not least by Mikhail Frunze, with the argument that a standing army was the only way to defeat the regular forces of other states. The workers' militia turned out to be more about mobilizing society and importing successful military ideals into the economy at large, rather than anything to do with the military per se. Committed to professionalism, which was presented as a form of scientific knowledge, Frunze, like Trotsky, was in favour of a career progression for officers rather than their election, and argued for and from centralized, not local, control. Indeed, Trotsky had introduced these elements back into the army from 1918. Trotsky, who, by the mid-1920s, was also in favour of technology rather than revolutionary élan, distanced himself from military affairs from 1923, as part of the pending power struggle, to avoid charges of 'Bonapartism'. With Stalin's support, Frunze's view prevailed, and he succeeded Trotsky as Commissar for Military and Naval Affairs in January 1925. Professionalism was linked to the call for mechanization and for an ability to wage effective offensive warfare, the latter presented as the way to maintain proletarian enthusiasm.

From the mid/late 1920s, Stalin was eager to back the industrialization necessary for large-scale mechanization. He regarded powerful military forces as a way to defend the Revolution against the implacably hostile capitalist states. Moreover, his support for Socialism in one state was not inherently pacific as he used the idea of international crisis to press for an extension of state dominance, notably with the war scare of 1927, which he did not try to defuse.[41]

The new order

The international system adapted not only to the Soviet Union, but also to Turkey's success (see pp. 42–6). The more accommodating Treaty of Lausanne of July 1923 with Turkey replaced that of Sèvres of August 1920. More generally, in the 1920s, there was a strong interest among the European powers in a viable and consensual international order, with new institutions serving as the focus for multilateral diplomacy, adding a newly strong, multi-national dimension to the practice of traditional diplomacy. Attendance at the League of Nations became almost mandatory for its members after 1925.[42]

The Versailles peace settlement was followed by a series of international agreements designed to prevent conflict, notably the Locarno Agreement of 1925 which provided for a mutual security guarantee of Western Europe. Germany was re-assimilated into the international system, perhaps much earlier than many could have expected in 1918. By international agreement, German reparations were rescheduled in 1924 and 1930.[43]

A series of treaties strengthened the peace system, as they were designed to preserve the settlement, and thus to restrain revisionism. The victorious powers also used these treaties to affirm their alliance. For example, in 1926, Romania signed a friendship treaty with France. This treaty both strengthened the French system in Eastern Europe and helped protect Romania against Hungarian and Soviet revisionism. France's system included Yugoslavia and Czechoslovakia.

Given the strengthening of the peace settlement, and the heavy burdens of debt, devastation and dislocation left after the Great War, it was scarcely surprising that investment in the armed forces did not match new military doctrine. Moreover, calls to take advantage of new technology were frequently ignored, though some new weapons were embraced as force-multipliers. For example, rapid economic growth in France in the 1920s was not used to modernize the army, although it eventually benefited the navy.[44] Instead, military-limitation agreements appeared to provide an answer to techno-logical developments, and were instances of the Great Powers trying to legislate against the possibility of a more destructive war. Easy to impose on the defeated, these agreements otherwise proved more difficult, but progress was made, especially at sea (see pp. 102–5).

The military and politics

After the Great War, the military also acted to preserve order and suppress opposition. This was the case for authoritarian states and for democratic counterparts. In Germany, the army overcame a number of Communist uprisings in 1920 and acted against Hitler's unsuccessful Munich putsch in November 1923. Lieutenant-General Hans von Seeckt, the last Chief of the General Staff before it was disbanded in July 1919, had been appointed effective Chief of Staff for the new *Reichswehr* (army) in October 1919 and was in practice its head. Seeckt argued that the German army must remain above party, but there was no doubt of its conservatism under Seeckt, himself a monarchist who was to be dismissed in October 1926 for offering a post to the grandson of the exiled Wilhelm II. Seeckt refused to move against the right-wing Kapp putsch of 1920 although he acted against the Communists that year and opposed Hitler's Munich putsch. Most of the army, indeed, backed the Weimar Republic in its crucial years, largely because it stood for political and social stability and because they hoped to revive Germany's international position. This support was more significant than the hatred for Weimar of the paramilitary *Freikorps*, many of whom were veterans eager to assuage through violence their anger at defeat.

In Britain, in response to labour unrest, 12,000 troops were deployed in Glasgow in 1919, as were tanks. The following March, the General Staff warned that 'In England [meaning Britain], owing to the possibility of industrial unrest, the forces are already dangerously low, and it would only be possible to find a few battalions for service abroad'. In 1921, strikes led the General Staff to think of bringing in troops from foreign postings and to consider calling out reservists.[45] There were also extensive troop movements at the time of the General Strike in 1926, movements designed to intimidate the strikers. In London, troops and police protected volunteers who, in the face of violence by the strikers, drove buses and Underground trains, kept power stations in operation, worked on the docks and distributed food. The rapid end of the strike helped ensure that there was no use of armed force. Troops were deployed to deal with the Winnipeg general strike in 1919 and on a number of other occasions in Canada in the 1920s.

The use of force was far more overt in areas lacking strong processes of order and stability. After the Great War, Albania had seen coups, rebellions and foreign intervention. In 1924, Ahmet Zogu, the young Interior Minister (King Zog, 1928 to 1939), seized power in Albania with the backing of about 2,000 Yugoslav troops, Yugoslav mountain artillery and machine guns, and about 800 Russian mercenaries. He then used force to extend government control into the mountainous interior, and overcame a serious revolt by the Catholic tribesmen of the Dukagjin in 1926, and a Muslim insurrection in 1937. Ten thousand troops and several batteries of guns were used to suppress the tribes of the Dukagjin, although Zogu also had leaders of the revolt assassinated. However, the army played only a small role in building up Zogu's position and, indeed, in the 1920s it caused him considerable difficulty. As a result, he preferred to rely on his own clan retainers and on loyal clans, the leaders of which he made colonels and paid. Zogu's limitation on the right to carry weapons was not extended to tribes on which he depended.[46]

Just as Zogu had seized power through the use of military force, so the same process was seen elsewhere. In Spain, instability and political violence helped prepare the way for the military dictatorship established in 1923. General Miguel Primo de Rivera, the Captain General of Barcelona, seized power supported by military action in Zaragoza and Valencia. He also profited from King Alfonso XIII's refusal to back the civilian government. As with many other coups, this was not a case of a united military seizing power.

Instead, as was the norm, it was action by a determined minority, while the majority did nothing, that was crucial.

Once in office, beside maintaining the war in Morocco (see pp. 46–8), Primo de Rivera's efforts at military reform, in particular to remove some of the large number of superfluous officers in a mostly stagnant economy and country, in which military service provided employment and a role, enraged much of the army. So did his part in military promotion. There was nearly a coup against him in 1926, and, in 1930, the prospect of yet another led Alfonso to force Primo out.[47] In Portugal, the liberal republic was overthrown by an army coup in 1926 that created a conservative order which lasted until 1974.

In May 1926, angry at what he saw as the failure of Polish politicians to provide leadership and unity, Pilsudski led a military revolt demanding a change of government. Advancing on Warsaw, he encountered resistance from pro-government troops led by the Military Governor of Warsaw, Rozwadowski, not the pushover he had hoped for, but, after three days of fighting, the President and Prime Minister resigned and the new regime took power. The coup was popular with many sectors, and the willingness of the railwaymen to strike in support prevented the movement of government reinforcements.[48]

At the close of 1926, there was a coup by army officers in Lithuania, with the army cooperating with the right-wing Nationalist Party and a section of the Christian Democrats. Parliament was occupied and the left-wing government forced to resign. A new government from the Right took power. In Austria a murderous clash between left-wing and right-wing paramilitaries led to a mass demonstration in Vienna in July 1927 in which the Justice Ministry was set alight. The failure of the police to maintain order led Johannes Schober, the Chief of Police, to call in the army, and, by the end of the day, 89 demonstrators were dead. Right-wing paramilitaries helped the government see off the subsequent general strike.

Conclusions

Despite violence and the use of force in many European states it is inappropriate in the 1920s to argue from Versailles to the rise of Hitler. Hitler rejected

Versailles and the international system it sought to create, but he was a failure in the 1920s, his attempted *putsch* in Munich in 1923 rapidly stopped. Instead, the responsible *realpolitik* of the 1920s, one that entailed compromise, and benefited from the idealistic currents of that decade's international relations, focused on another German, Gustav Stresemann, the Foreign Minister from 1923 to 1929. He was far more prominent in the period than Hitler. The rejection of such concepts and agreements by the Soviet Union had been contained, as had Mussolini's bombastic control of Italy from 1922. Thus, a great deal of hostile rhetoric never had much actual impact. Like Stresemann, Austen Chamberlain, the influential British Foreign Secretary from 1924 to 1929, was a believer in the incremental value of negotiations as a way to reduce tension.[49] The Foreign Office view was expressed by Sir Robert Vansittart, Permanent Under Secretary at the Foreign Office from 1930 to 1937, when, in a paper of May 1931 circulated to the Cabinet that December, he wrote of the need to be 'stone-cold', not 'pro-anything, especially in considerable ignorance . . . if we are to avoid the over-secretions of adrenalin so prevalent in Europe'.[50]

Counterfactualism always has its limitations, but it can return us to the unpredictability of the past and the uncertainties of contemporaries. To subtract the failure, protectionism, misery and extremism produced by the Depression from the 1930s, is to suggest that the 1920s' order could have continued, in part because internationalism, liberalism, democracy and free-market capitalism would have retained more appeal, with both electorates and governments. Moreover, in the absence of German rearmament and Soviet expansion, this international order was very much one dominated militarily by France as far as European land strength was concerned. In March 1931, the Chief of the [British] Imperial General Staff, noted that Europe 'contains the greater part of the world's armaments' and observed:

The French army is undoubtedly the most formidable military machine in the world today. The Higher Command is excellent, the moral and fighting qualities exceptionally good, the reserves of material and preparations for industrial mobilisation are probably adequate and the trained reserves total about 5,00,000 men. A most powerful and modern system of fortifications is being constructed along the eastern frontier at a cost of £30,000,000, which will be completed in 1934 or 1935. Not content with this, France has further re-insured by forming a network of military alliances which encircle Germany with a ring of steel. The Little Entente, Belgium and Poland are all the military vassals of France with armies trained on French lines and in some instances by French missions.[51]

The 1920s, therefore, need to be considered separately from what followed, and not seen as its precursor. More particularly, military affairs in the 1920s were quite unlike the Great War and not yet dominated by the technologies that were to be in play during the Second World War. Instead, most of the conflicts of the 1920s were more like wars of the nineteenth century, either the 'small wars' of imperialism or something, as in the case of the Russian Civil War, more akin to the Franco-Prussian War of 1870–1, with its rapid movement and without the emphasis on firepower seen in the Great War.

2

Imperial warfare

Are we to defend Persia or not? If we do not, Persia will be demoralised by
Russian Bolshevism and thereafter devoured by Russian Imperialism.
WINSTON CHURCHILL, 1920[1]

The Great War took Western imperialism to unsurpassed heights, but also
helped foster the dissolution of the Western empires as it weakened them in
both metropoles (home bases) and colonies, and also fostered the spread of
ideas, both nationalism and Communism, that were to be the cause of major
instability. More seriously, the Versailles Peace Settlement exacerbated the
already prominent issue of resistance to imperial control because it added
to the disruption of the Great War by changing imperial control across part
of the world. This was the case both with alterations in the identity of the
imperial ruler, as the German Empire was allocated among the victors, and,
more seriously, with the extension of Western control in the Islamic world,
especially the former Ottoman (Turkish) Empire.

The distribution of the German and Ottoman territories reflected the
determination of the victorious imperial powers to expand their territorial
control of the world. From Germany, Britain gained mandates over German
East Africa (Tanganyika, the continental part of modern Tanzania), and over
parts of Togo and Cameroon, France over most of Togo and Cameroon,
Belgium over what became Burundi and Rwanda, Japan over the Caroline,
Mariana and Marshall Islands in the western Pacific, Australia over German
New Guinea and the neighbouring Bismarck Archipelago, New Zealand over
Western Samoa, and South Africa over South-West Africa, now Namibia.

Powers controlling mandated territories were theoretically answerable to the League of Nations, but, in practice, mandates were colonies.

Similarly, much of the Ottoman Empire was allocated to Britain, which gained mandates over Iraq, Palestine (modern Israel and Palestine), and Transjordan (modern Jordan), or France, which gained Lebanon and Syria. There was resistance to this allocation, but much of it was overcome. Newly established Arab rule in Damascus was brought to an end in July 1920 as a French army advanced on it from Beirut. The extension of imperial control was not only a matter of mandates. In Persia (Iran), which had not been directly involved in the Great War, British influence had increased during the struggle and, in 1919, an Anglo-Persian treaty enabled Britain to supply advisers for both government and army, as well as arms and a loan.

However, it proved far harder than expected to control the situation in the Middle East. Many of the problems were those previously faced by the Ottomans. Thus, in Transjordan, the British confronted internecine tribal conflict and had to adopt the longstanding Ottoman role of defending settler areas against nomadic raiders from the desert fringes. As a result, a force of cavalry and machine-gunners, recruited from Circassians used by the Ottomans to this end, was established by the British in the Transjordan capital of Amman, being designated the 'Reserve Force'. Britain and France also adapted Ottoman techniques of information-gathering and the sedentarization of nomadic tribes.[2]

More seriously, a combination of already-established anti-Western feeling, and the spread of a new impulse of reaction against imperial authority, affected large portions of the colonial world. This situation was particularly intense in the Muslim world, but was also found elsewhere, notably in China and South-East Asia. Opposition had varied causes and consequences. It included hostility to British hegemony in Egypt, Iraq and Persia (Iran); a rising against French rule in Syria; the continuation of resistance in Libya to the rule Italy had sought to impose since 1911; an upsurge from 1921 in action against Spanish attempts to dominate the part of Morocco allocated to it (an opposition that spread into French Morocco); and the Turkish refusal to accept a peace settlement that included Greek rule over the Aegean coast and British troops in Constantinople (renamed Istanbul in 1930).

Turkey

The most serious failure occurred in Turkey, with Greece, one of the wartime Allies, heavily defeated and Britain seriously checked. Misrepresenting in their favour the local ethnic situation at Versailles, the Greeks had pressed for much of western Anatolia in the peace settlement, focusing in particular on the major coastal city of Smyrna/ Izmir, a cosmopolitan centre containing people from many backgrounds but including a large and long-established Greek presence. On 15 May 1919, the landing of a Greek force, designed to force the pace and to give effect to an occupation zone, led to fighting at Smyrna, followed by the looting of the Turkish quarter. The killing of civilians was to be all-too-common in the fighting in Anatolia.

The Greek occupation provided Turkish nationalists with a rallying point and put serious pressure on the armistice with the Allies that had ended the Great War. Mustafa Kemal (later Atatürk), a senior military figure officially entrusted by the defeated Sultan, Mehmet VI, with overseeing the disarmament of Turkish forces in accordance with the armistice, was driven by the Greek landing to coordinate nationalist activity in central Anatolia; at first coordinating so-called defence of rights organizations. When, in 1915, an Anglo-French expeditionary force had threatened to capture Constantinople, preparations had been made by the Turks to wage guerrilla warfare in Anatolia. Arms were dispatched and the necessary organizational infrastructure established. After the armistice in 1918, these bands and local defence organizations rapidly emerged, particularly after the Greek landing at Smyrna. Even before Kemal landed at Samsun on 19 May 1919, these local organizations were in place and very active. He was able to form them into a political movement and an army with a unified command.

When, in response to his role in founding the independence movement, Kemal was called back by the Sultan to Constantinople, he resigned from the military on 8 July 1919. An order was then sent to provincial military officers requiring his arrest. Elections led to victory for Turkish nationalists who took control of the Chamber of Deputies in Constantinople in January 1920, which then demanded full independence for Turkey within the boundaries of the 1918 armistice. These boundaries would have left Turkey in control of all of Anatolia. This demand led to a British takeover in Constantinople on 16 March. As a result, Kemal was able to present himself as the rescuer of the Sultan, who was allegedly held in captivity in Constantinople by the British. Kemal understood the importance of popular support, both at home and abroad. On 23 April, Kemal summoned a national assembly in Angora (Ankara) which elected him provisional head of state.

Unrest in the hinterland of Smyrna became sectarian violence, with claim and counter-claim about atrocities and intentions. In the summer of 1920, the Greeks rapidly advanced from Smyrna, establishing a large buffer zone round the city and also moving forward to the Sea of Marmara. Meanwhile, at Sèvres near Paris on 10 August, a treaty as part of the general Versailles Peace Settlement recognized Turkey's weakness. East Thrace became Greek at once, while Smyrna and its hinterland were to become Greek subject to a plebiscite after five years. Armenia became independent, Kurdistan autonomous, and the French and Italians gained spheres of influence in the south of Anatolia. Kemal's nationalists, however, rejected the treaty, and attempts in early 1921 to negotiate a compromise failed. Kemal was encouraged and helped by the failure of Allied intervention in Russia.

Moreover, Kemal was able to overcome much of the chaos in Anatolia that had followed the close of the Great War. The emergence of warlords had ended the notion of war as the prerogative of the state. Cherkez Ethem (the Circassian), was too powerful to accept subordination to Kemal and he had double-dealings with both him and Greece. In the end, Ethem was driven to take refuge with the Greeks. Demirci Mehmet Efe (the blacksmith) also emerged as a popular bandit in the Aegean region, only for his group to be repressed by Kemal. Many of the brigands were demobilized troops, and they had brought chaos to much of Anatolia. Also in 1920, Kemal defeated the Army of the Caliphate, forces of the Sultan, who had proved willing to accept the Allied terms. In 1920, he also won the help of the Russian Bolsheviks, and was able to develop good relations with Italy (a rival to Greece) which agreed to sell planes to Kemal.

His colleague Kazim Karabekir, the commander of the Eastern Anatolian Army, defeated the new Armenian Republic. Having refused to disband his army in accordance with the 1918 armistice, Karabekir led the only battle-hardened force during the Turkish War of Independence. He ably commanded his troops against the Armenian army which was composed of young and inexperienced militia who made the mistake of fighting in the open field.

The Greek determination to defeat the nationalist challenge reflected a wish to end the political impasse, but also the problems posed by the absence of a readily defensible frontier for their zone of occupation. Instead, the Greeks found their frontier harassed by Turkish irregulars and its communications endangered. This situation led the Greeks in 1921 to decide to advance from the coastal areas onto the Anatolian plateau, even though that move lengthened their supply lines. A Greek advance was defeated in January by Rashid Ismet at the First Battle of Inönü. Backed up by superior firepower, notably artillery but including aircraft, the Greeks in March fought their way up the plateau's escarpment. However, on 31 March, during the Second Battle of Inönü, a Turkish counter-attack under Ismet drove the Greeks back. The improvement in Turkish fighting quality as the nationalists organized their forces was readily apparent.

Nevertheless, a renewed and well-commanded Greek offensive in July 1921, designed to regain the initiative, led to a rapid advance, which was an aspect of the way in which, like the Russian Civil War, this was a conflict of rapid movements with no continuous fronts.[3] The nationalists fell back, giving the Greeks the option of consolidating their hold on their new gains or of advancing further. Moving further into the interior of Anatolia was justified as a way to seize the nationalist capital, Angora (Ankara), but the Greek General Staff lacked a clear strategy or operational plan and, had it occurred, the capture of the city would not have ended the resistance. Moreover, there were no preparations for the grave logistical problems posed by advancing, notably across a large area of salt desert in the summer. Water and food shortages hit the troops, exacerbating disease and exhaustion. Supply shortages were accentuated by the attacks of Turkish irregulars on the Greek supply lines. Kemal, in turn, traded space for time, arguing that 'there is no line of defence but, instead, a surface of defence. That surface is the whole fatherland'. His troops were better able to supply themselves, as a British military observer in the winter of 1919–20 had noted.[4]

The Greeks used British planes for reconnaissance, so that the Turkish army marched at night as it prepared its riposte. Kemal turned to fight near the Sakaria River, digging in on the uplands round Mount Tchal. Launched on 26 August, the Greek attack on this position faced serious difficulties in carrying the defended ridges. Their hungry, exhausted troops ran out of energy, and the Turks, under Kemal, were able to launch a surprise counter-attack which was successful. On 11 September, the Greek forces in the area were ordered to retreat from their surviving gains and to fall back on the Sakaria River. Kemal cautiously pursued them as they retreated.

In August 1922, the Turks rapidly advanced on the remaining Greek positions. Their forces were well trained and benefited from French and Italian arms supplies. The surprised and outmanoeuvred Greeks were swiftly defeated and their army collapsed. On 9 September, Turkish troops entered Smyrna. Massacres soon followed and the burning down of much of the city. All surviving Christian men of military age were deported to the interior where many were killed. Meanwhile, defeat had led to a military coup in Greece that forced the abdication of King Constantine I who had been closely associated with the campaigning.

Moreover, in one of the most forgotten campaigns of the century, Kemal, in part by using guerrilla forces based on brigand bands, had defeated the poorly quipped and supplied French in south-east Turkey in 1921. Although Kemal faced a number of opponents, the issue of too many commitments also worked to his benefit. France had relatively few troops available for service in Turkey because of its commitments in Morocco. The French were persuaded to abandon the struggle in return for the Turks accepting their position in Syria and also allowing France to occupy the region of Alexandretta.[5] This move helped isolate the British.

With its forces in Constantinople since November 1918, and the city formally occupied from 16 March 1920, Britain was left as the major outside force. The advance of Kemal's forces in September 1922 led to a confrontation with British units at Chanak, near the Dardanelles. Both the British government and the empire split over whether to risk war. In Britain, the bulk of the Cabinet, supported by the press, rejected the willingness of Lloyd George and Churchill to do so. Repeating the situation in the Russian

Civil War, public opinion was far from bellicose. Arthur Griffith-Boscawen, Minister of Agriculture, wrote during the crisis, 'I don't believe the country cares anything about Thrace'.

Among the Dominions, only Newfoundland and New Zealand pledged help, a sign of independence suggesting that British assumptions about Dominions' attitudes required revision. At the imperial conferences of 1923 and 1926, the Canadian prime minister, William Mackenzie King, made it clear that his country would not fight in a war simply at Britain's behest, but, instead, that its interests had to be at stake and that the Canadian Parliament would play a crucial role in validating this. The Dominions benefited from the cover provided by British military strength, which enabled them to feel safe with only modest expenditure on defence. Thus, the Canadian navy was greatly run down after the Great War. The limited provision by the Dominions for defence contributed greatly to the more general vulnerability of the British Empire that became apparent in the 1930s.

In 1922, British forces were sent to the region, an aircraft carrier, the *Argus*, being stationed near the Dardanelles, and Lloyd George hoped that Britain would benefit from a revival in the Greek military and from the creation of an anti-Turkish league in the Balkans. However, General Rawlinson, the Commander in Chief India, warned about the danger of conflict spreading across the Islamic world: 'To undertake offensive action against the Turk is merely to consolidate a Pan-Islamic movement', a threat that also concerned the General Staff in London[6], and that was reflected in fictional accounts about the risk of an anti-imperial *jihad*.[7]

It is unclear what would have happened had hostilities occurred. The British were much better placed than during their failure, in the Gallipoli operation, to advance on Constantinople in 1915. Aside from controlling Constantinople, the British benefited from the extent that other post-war challenges, notably in Ireland and the commitment to the Russian Civil War, had already ended. However, politics were to the fore, notably a disinclination to fight.

In the event, the government backed down agreeing, by the Convention of Mudanya, to withdraw its forces. The Turks were able to occupy East Thrace at once. In November, negotiations for a new peace settlement began at Lausanne. The crisis precipitated the fall of the coalition government in Britain. Lloyd

George resigned on 19 October. His Conservative successor, Andrew Bonar Law, had argued that Britain 'cannot alone act as policeman of the world'.[8]

By the Treaty of Lausanne of 24 July 1923, the terms of Sèvres were replaced by ones that acknowledged Turkish success, Turkey receiving Eastern Thrace, Armenia and all of Anatolia. However, the Turkish claim to British-held Mosul was left to future negotiations while the Dardanelles remained demilitarized until 1936. As part of the peace settlement, a large-scale exchange of population between Greece and Turkey was agreed. This idea, brought on the agenda for the first time in 1913, had a major impact on the ethnic composition of Anatolia. Victory led to Kemal becoming first President of the Republic of Turkey on 29 October 1923. After his death in 1937, he was replaced by Ismet, who, from 1923 to 1937, was the first prime minister and who, in 1934, adopted the name Inönü as his surname.

Morocco

A different type of Western defeat was experienced in Morocco, although the eventual outcome was far more favourable for the Western Powers than might have been predicted at one time. Indeed, the ability of Western Powers, if they wished, to sustain a struggle and to return to the attack was an important aspect of their capability.

In the section of Morocco claimed by Spain, the weak state of the colonial administration and military did not dissuade the Spaniards from attempting to expand their control from 1919 when they brought the Tangier peninsula under control. The mineral resources of the Riff Mountains were a goal, while Spain benefited from not having been involved in the Great War. Its neutrality then had permitted a major growth in exports, and thus an improvement in government finances. In 1920, the Spanish offensive broadened, but insufficient effort was made to win local support and, as a result, political advance was not combined with military gains.

In 1921, the Spaniards advanced deeper into the interior, but the opposition, under Muhammed Abd-el-Krim, became better organized, and it moved onto the attack in July. The unprepared and outmanoeuvred Spaniards, poorly led by the feckless and vainglorious Manuel Fernández Silvestre, were unable to hold their ground, a situation exacerbated by the collapse of morale among the Spanish conscripts and by growing dissension among their Moorish auxiliaries, some of whom surrendered. As it fell back, the Spanish force lost cohesion and ran low on ammunition, which the rapid-firing rate of modern firearms made more serious. In contrast, their opponents gained fresh support. In the battle, or rather rout, of Annual on 21 July, 'a gigantic disaster'[9], at least 12,000 Spanish troops were killed. Abd-el-Krim captured large numbers of rifles and pieces of artillery, a crucial addition of strength, although his forces already had effective Mauser rifles and artillery. The Spaniards were then pushed back on their coastal base of Melilla. Success encouraged more tribes to rally to Abd-el-Krim, rather as the Sauds won support in Arabia. Some commentators referred to a holy war.[10] Annual was a disaster that appeared the equivalent to the Ethiopian defeat of invading Italians at Adowa (Adua) in 1896.

Rather than acknowledging failure, as the French, British and Greeks variously did in Turkey, Spain made a major effort to recover its position. New military technology played a role. Tanks, artillery and planes bought from the French were delivered to the Spanish forces in Morocco in 1922. However, the use of light tanks at Ambar in March 1922, their first deployment in Africa, was unsuccessful. Unable to keep up, the infantry could not prevent the tanks from being disabled by Moroccan stone-wielders, while many of the tanks' machine guns jammed due to faulty ammunition.[11]

A renewed Spanish offensive was blocked at Tizi Azza in November 1922, and, in 1923, the Moors resumed the attack as well as proclaiming the Republic of the Riff. A Spanish attempt to secure peace in 1924 by offering autonomy was rejected, and the Spaniards had to evacuate much of what they still held in the interior. The mobile Moors, armed with modern firearms, including machine guns and mountain howitzers, were not dependent on the cumbersome supply routes of their opponents. Spanish positions were supplied by convoys that were easy to harry.[12]

Suffering food shortages in the harsh terrain, however, Abd-el-Krim looked towards the more prosperous French-controlled section of Morocco. He invaded in April 1925, making rapid gains with a number of positions falling after artillery bombardment[13], only to be checked by Marshal Pétain.

By attacking the French, Abd-el-Krim greatly weakened his position, not least because the French and Spaniards agreed to coordinate operations. Moreover, Spanish forces were better armed and trained than hitherto.

In 1925, pressure on the Moors greatly increased. The Spaniards dropped large quantities of mustard gas by air, inflicting heavy casualties on civilians and fighters alike. While the French, deploying about 150,000 troops by late September, attacked in the south, the Spaniards, with French naval support, launched a successful amphibious assault in the Bay of Alhucemas in September, supported by air attack and naval gunnery. The Moors were defeated in pitched battle, and their capital, Ajdir, fell on 2 October.[14] The French used naval and land-based aircraft as well as tanks.

The rebellion was finally crushed in 1926, Abd-el-Krim surrendering to the French on 26 May and being exiled to the Indian Ocean island of Réunion. Suffering from the years of devastating conflict, Moroccan tribes submitted and handed over arms, although, of course, not all arms. Recent developments in Afghanistan have made the Franco-Spanish achievement more impressive; although no two wars are strictly comparable and the scale of the opposition and the operating zone is far greater in Afghanistan.

A number of factors, political, strategic, operational and tactical, contributed to the Moorish defeat. The failure of Spanish liberalism was significant, as the military dictatorship that took power in 1923 was determined to persist with the war and able to focus on it. The lack of any place of refuge in nearby states for the Moors was important (and contrasts with the situation in modern Afghanistan), as was the extent to which, from French entry into the conflict in 1925, their opponents were present in overwhelming force and able to mount simultaneous attacks. Moreover, Moorish fortifications were vulnerable to French and Spanish artillery. Both France and Spain attained their imperial victories not with small, lightly armed, mobile units, but with substantial forces. For Spain, this comprised Moorish auxiliaries, Spanish conscripts and Spanish regulars. The Spanish Foreign Legion, which was established in 1920, was significant among the last. Francisco Franco made his name as commander of the Legion. He was subsequently to seize power in the Spanish Civil War of 1936–9. The fighting in Morocco was harsh with scant quarter given to prisoners. Atrocities were common on both sides.

Dutch and French Empires

As Morocco showed, an impression of general Western failure would be misplaced. The colonial powers still had sufficient military superiority to reimpose control in most cases. The Dutch came under attack in the East Indies from the PKI (Indonesian Communist Party), with uprisings in Java in 1926 and Sumatra in 1927. However, the Dutch benefited from a lack of coordination among the PKI and from the disruption of its leadership by earlier police action, including many arrests. As so often in colonial control, the availability and application of information was important in retaining control.

In 1925, the French faced a Druze rebellion in their new colony of Syria, and it was not a rebellion on the peripheries of French power in Syria. Druze pressure for self-government for the Jebel Druze region near Damascus, the colony's capital, was amplified by demands by Syrian nationalists. In repelling attack, the French utilized the resources of modern weaponry, often to devastating effect. The French used heavy artillery bombardments to thwart Druze progress into Damascus in 1926. Tanks, armoured cars and bombing were all employed, while the city as a whole was encircled by barbed wire and machine-gun posts. Locally raised troops helped the French suppress the rebellion, as did the ability to move units from Morocco once the rising there was settled. The Jebel Druze, into which the French built a railway, was reconquered in April 1926 and the rebellion finally suppressed in early 1927.

The use of local troops was an instance of the extent to which divide, recruit and rule were the crucial object and process of imperialist control. French military control of Syria and Lebanon substantially rested on the *Armée du Levant*, 70,000 strong in 1921, a force largely composed of colonial troops from Africa; as well as on local military and police forces: the *Troupes Spéciales du Levant*, 14,000 strong in 1935, and the *Gendarmerie*. Both had a strong element of local minority groups, such as Christians, that could be relied upon in the event of clashes with the remainder of the population.[15] Similar patterns were followed elsewhere, for example with the Dutch in the East Indies.

The French also encountered problems in Indochina. In response, they turned to new technology but also relied on tried techniques. Thus, air attacks were employed in 1924 and 1929 in an attempt to deal with highland opposition in Vietnam, but the French found that they had to rely on the devastation wrought on the ground by punishment columns.

British imperial defence

The British faced rebellions in the Islamic world, and although the cumulative strain was considerable, achieved several successes. The 1919 rebellion on the mountainous North-West Frontier of India posed serious difficulties, not least because the effective modern rifles used by the tribes led to heavy British casualties in the winter of 1919–20. The regional crisis was exacerbated in 1919 by war with neighbouring Afghanistan, the Third Anglo-Afghan War, a conflict that reflected the determination of the new king, Amanullah, to end British hegemony. The Afghan army was unable to make much of an impact, but Amanullah applied pressure by proclaiming a *jihad* and using tribal forces.[16]

The British, however, responded sensibly by seeking frontier stabilization, rather than intervention in Afghanistan. In reply to Afghan attacks, the RAF bombed Jalabad and the Afghan capital, Kabul, their aeroplanes operating across higher mountains than they had faced in Europe; and the war soon ended. In the event, both sides wished to contain it.

The North-West Frontier quietened down from 1921, with a permanent garrison of 15,000 troops, supported by 10,000 Pathan militia, assigned to Waziristan on the North-West Frontier. However, this large garrison helped provoke a new, and more intractable, revolt in 1936.

There were tactical similarities with the situation in Somaliland, but the context there was different and the outcome was one of British victory. Led by Mullah Sayyid Muhammad, pre-war opposition to the British presence had continued during the Great War, and the British faced opponents who were adaptable in both weaponry and tactics. An intelligence report of 1919 noted the need to respond to new challenges. 'Dervish rushing tactics' had been superseded by a stress on the defence:

> The large increase in the number of rifles in the Mullah's possession and the consequent discard of the spear ... We may expect the Dervishes to

take up defensive positions which they will defend stubbornly behind cover without exposing themselves. We must be ready to carry out attacks against most difficult positions and up narrow and steep-sided valleys, to employ covering fire and frequently to capture the heights or the key to the position before it will be possible to make any headway. It will also be necessary to employ artillery, firing high explosive-shell, if the various Dervish strong-holds are to be captured without very heavy casualties. In short, whereas in the past the training of troops in Somaliland could, in the main, be carried out with a view to meeting one form of savage warfare, namely the Dervish rush in bush country, troops must now be trained to readily adapt themselves to a more varied form of fighting which will in some degree resemble hill warfare in India.[17]

In the event, a combination of the Somaliland Camel Corps and other army forces, with the RAF's Unit Z of twelve DH-9s brought the necessary combination of force and mobility. Naval support, not least in transporting the aircraft, and tribal levies were also important in what was an impressive combination. Launched in early 1920, it saw the Dervishes routed. Their stronghold at Taleh was bombed in January 1920, and Mullah Sayyid fled into the wastes of the lightly-populated Ogaden region, which the British recognized as part of Ethiopia. He was dislodged from there by a British-approved attack by tribal 'friendlies', the Isaqs, and fled, dying in Ethiopia in December 1920 of illness.[18] The opposition to Britain collapsed without his charismatic leadership.

Iraq proved more difficult, in part because it was more populous than Somaliland, although far less so than it was to be in the 2000s. British weakness and Shia activism encouraged the outbreak of an armed revolt in June 1920 and, by late July, much of the mid-Euphrates valley was in rebel hands. The rebellion continued to spread, but the British deployed a substantial force from the Indian Army as well as the RAF[19], while they also benefited from the unwillingness of some tribal sheikhs to support the rebellion. By the end of October, the British had succeeded, having lost about 900 British and Indian soldiers compared to about 6,000 Iraqi dead.

Nevertheless, the rising had revealed serious military and political weaknesses in the British position. As a result, the British devolved their powers to an Iraqi government, a process formalized by an Anglo-Iraqi treaty of 1922 that was supported by a supplementary military agreement in 1924.

Similarly, rebellion in Egypt in 1919 led to Britain unilaterally granting its independence in 1922, although Egypt remained under *de facto* military control. Over 1,000 Egyptians were killed in the rebellion, while there were only 75 British killed or wounded. The rebellion indicated the resources of empire. Warships were sent to Alexandria and the Suez Canal, and a flotilla was dispatched up the Nile, but the British did not want to face a long insurrection. Moreover, abandoning the forward policy of the 1919 Anglo-Persian (Iranian) agreement under which British troops were committed in Persia, British influence collapsed in 1921, as the British accommodated to the rise of Reza Shah. Alongside failure in the Russian Civil War, there was a sense that Britain, like the other European imperial powers, had over-reached itself.

At the same time, throughout the colonial world, there was a deepening of imperial control as areas that had been often only nominally annexed were brought under at least some colonial government. Earlier, the Great War had led to an intensification of European military control in their colonies, as imperial forces manoeuvred in the interior, the British taking over Darfur in western Sudan. In southern Sudan after the war, posts were established by Arab troops under British officers and military patrols were launched. Their effectiveness, however, was limited and the patrols were gradually abandoned.[20] Yet, in the more favourable, drier terrain of northern Sudan, where the forests and swamps of the south were absent, the armoured cars of the machine-gun batteries in the Sudan Defence Force were found effective as a means of maintaining control.[21] Road-building improved the British position on the North-West Frontier of India.[22]

The use of new technology was exemplified by the employment of air power, a process encouraged by Churchill, successively as Secretary for War and then as Secretary of State for the Colonies, and by Hugh Trenchard, in 1918 the first Chief of the Air Staff, whom Churchill recalled to office and made a baronet in 1919. Trenchard used the success in British Somaliland in 1920 in order to support his policy of 'air control', which was applied in Iraq from 1921. Gasoline, incendiary and delayed-action bombs were all employed in the 1920s. Planes were developed or adapted for imperial policing duties, for example the Westland Wapiti, a day-bomber in service from 1928 to 1939 that was used for army coordination, especially on the North-West Frontier.

The RAF spent the 1920s protecting distant interests. In November 1921, a raid of Ikhwan from Arabia on Jordan was caught in the open, suffering heavy casualties. The RAF served against the Nuers in Sudan in 1927–9, was success-fully used against Yemeni incursions into the Aden Protectorate in 1928–9, and in 1928 bombing the Wahabi tribesmen of Arabia who threatened Iraq and Kuwait. 'Aeroplane action' helped stabilize the situation in Kurdistan in 1923 and 1931[23], while its use against the Yemenis served as a background to the 1934 treaty of friendship. The use of the RAF saw an increase of the range of air capability. For example, in 1922, the Vickers Vernon entered service, the first of the RAF's troop carriers. It was based in Iraq. In 1928, Vickers Victorias based there evacuated over 500 civilians from Kabul, which was threatened by insurgents.

The mock bombing attack on an 'enemy village' at the Hendon Air Display of 1921, the second year of RAF pageants, suggested great effectiveness. Drawing on its experience in Iraq, the RAF was convinced that air power could suppress opposition not least by crippling the morale of opponents. The effect of bombing on the economy was also noted, not least the damage to infrastructure and food supplies. However, in June 1920, the General Staff in London claimed 'Whatever the possibilities of replacing troops by aircraft in the future may be, at the present moment the impotence of the Royal Air Force in Mesopotamia to carry out even their present tasks becomes clearer every day'. In part, however, that impotence reflected the limited number of aircraft available. The Civil Commissioner in Baghdad reported the previous month that only eleven were in working order, of which eight were obsolete BE.8s.

In addition, in 1922, a report by the General Staff of the British Forces in Iraq noted 'Aeroplanes by themselves are unable to compel the surrender or defeat of hostile tribes'[24], a point that is pertinent to the modern use of air power. Moreover, the tactical effectiveness of aeroplanes was probably exaggerated once their novelty wore off and tribesmen learned how to evade their attacks.[25] The same was to be the case with the use of American air power in Afghanistan in 2001–2. The debate also reflected the RAF's attempt to avoid being abolished or subsumed into the army. If the RAF could promise that an

independent air force could act effectively (and more cheaply) to police the
empire than could the army, then it had a rationale for its continuing existence
(and budget).

While some opposition could be suppressed by small forces supported by
air power, the overall burden of imperial security remained high. Nevertheless,
real costs were lessened by the use of non-Western forces, both local troops
and those from elsewhere in the empire. As an instance of the increased
proficiency of imperial military forces, regions that had been conquered in
the late nineteenth century or more recently, for example French Morocco,
provided many soldiers for the colonial powers. Both they, and troops from
areas, such as the Punjab in India, that had been ruled for longer, were trained
in Western methods of warfare and organized accordingly. Moreover, hitherto
independent armies of local allies were similarly organized or were integrated
into imperial forces.

The result was a high level of military resource, notably India for the British,
especially the Punjab region where paternalism helped produce a loyalist
ideology.[26] In response to the Arab rising in Iraq in 1920, four divisions were sent
from India. In addition, Iraqi levies were used by the British to drive back Turks
in Kurdistan in 1923, a step taken in order to help end their hostile intrigues
among the Kurdish tribes. In Morocco, the Spaniards used native auxiliaries,
some of whom, notably the *Regulares* of Ceuta, proved reliable, although the
abandonment by others helped cause the disaster at Annual in 1921.

There were serious difficulties in the British Empire. The Amritsar massacre
in April 1919, when General Reginald Dyer ordered troops to fire on a demonstrating crowd, causing nearly 400 fatalities, dented British authority in India
by suggesting that it had an inherently repressive nature.[27] But, that same year,
a Government of India Act established the principle of dyarchy: responsible
self-government in certain areas. However helpful this might be in terms of
the political context, views of the military situation were coloured by racism,
which, indeed, affected debate over Indianization.[28] In 1922, Rawlinson wrote
to a fellow general:

You are wrong to draw a parallel between Ireland and India. The two
problems are entirely different: (1) one is a black country and the other is

a white, (2) no black man, as you well know, would ever have the pluck to do what the Sinn Feiners have done, (3) so long as we have the Army as it is at present, there can be no real danger in the situation.[29]

A racial hierarchy was also understood for the colonies ruled by the Dominions, notably South African-governed South-West Africa. In 1929, protest on the Pacific island of Samoa owing to the suppression of the Fono of Faipule, Samoa's democratic assembly, and organized by the Mau movement, led to an armed police response in which the High Chief was killed, and to the deployment of New Zealand troops.

Libya

Racism also played a role in the violent harshness of Italian conduct in Libya. The Italians had recognized Libyan self-government in 1919, but Benito Mussolini, who gained power in 1922, was not prepared to accept this. Employing great brutality against civilians, of whom over 50,000 were probably killed, the Italians, under Field Marshal Pietro Badoglio, Governor of Libya from 1928 to 1934, who had already served there in 1911–12, subdued the colony in 1928–32. Their tactics included the use of columns of armoured cars and motorized infantry, and the dropping of gas bombs. Auxiliary forces were drawn from the Italian east African colony of Eritrea, rather than from Libya. To destroy the backing for resistance, the population was ruthlessly suppressed. Wells were blocked and flocks slaughtered, both brutally effective means of economic warfare, and the population was disarmed and forcibly resettled in camps in which many died. A largely pastoral society, much of it nomadic, was brought under control.[30]

The Soviet Empire

Islamic opposition was also crushed in the Soviet Union. The Basmachi uprising, a Muslim attempt in the early 1920s to organize a government in Turkestan, was crushed by the local Russians, who had more modern weapons, as well as the benefit of control over the major towns and railways. Subsequently, the Red Army employed the brutal techniques already developed in the Civil War, including mass deportations and execution, in anti-insurgency campaigns in Central Asia and the Caucasus.[31] In addition, overwhelming force, the use of artillery against mountain villages, and the ability to call on some local support, enabled the Soviets to succeed, as when they suppressed an uprising in the Caucasus areas of Daghestan and Chechnya in 1920–1. The Soviets responded similarly to uprisings there in 1924, 1928, 1929, 1936 and 1940.[32]

Soviet policy included not only the social transformation seen elsewhere in the Soviet Union, notably the collectivization of agriculture, but also an attempt at cultural revolution. Muslim courts were suppressed in Central Asia in 1926, followed in 1927 by Muslim schools and colleges as well as an attempt to end the veil. In response, Muslims attacked women who unveiled, and the campaign was called off in 1929.[33] The closure of churches and monasteries led to a revolt in Georgia in 1921–2. Another in 1924 was brutally repressed with about 7,000–10,000 people killed followed by large-scale emigration.

Outside the Soviet Union, in 1921, first White and then Communist forces subjugated Outer Mongolia, hitherto largely autonomous, and a pro-Soviet government was established. This achievement was in part due to technological factors, in particular the gap in firepower between the Mongolians and their invaders, but other factors also played a role, including the low density of the local population.

The Soviets were far less successful in their attempt to become the dominant force in north-east Persia by means of supporting a key local figure, Kuchek Khan. The leader of a revolt in the Caspian province of Gilan from 1917, Khan was forced by the British to stop his expansion in 1918, but in 1920, backed by the Soviets, he announced the foundation of an Iranian Soviet Socialist Republic, and Soviet troops arrived. The Soviets also backed a separatist movement in the Persian part of Azerbaijan. However, in 1921, the Soviets found it expedient to negotiate a treaty with Persia, not least because its new government under Reza Khan was rejecting British influence while Kuchek Khan had turned against the Communists. The Soviets then withdrew their troops. The complex relationships between the Soviet Union, Britain, and the new nationalist regimes of Persia and Turkey, led to concerns about threats to the British Empire notably India.[34] The Soviet-Turkish Treaty of Friendship signed in 1925 sustained these anxieties.

That the Soviet Union acted as an imperial power proved an ironic counterpoint to its hosting, in 1920, of a Congress of Peoples of the East at Baku, an attempt to exploit opposition to imperial rule. In January 1920, the British Admiralty expressed concern that Soviet expansion into the Middle East threatened the oil supplies required by the Royal Navy.[35]

Initial Soviet attempts to destabilize the Western empires, as in the Dutch East Indies, were of limited success. However, the Soviets became influential in China in the mid-1920s when they provided support to the Guomindang. They provided advisers, weapons (from October 1924) and money, but not troops. In 1924, Soviet money funded the establishment of the Whampoa Military Academy near Guangzhou (Canton). It was designed to provide the basis of a Guomindang army modelled on that of the Red Army. Jiang Jieshi was appointed to command the Academy.

American imperialism

The Americans also saw themselves as supporters of liberty, but they enjoyed a quasi-imperial position, supported by extensive and growing trade and investment in the Caribbean and Mexico and an actual imperial position in the Philippines. Although Plan Green, for intervention in Mexico, was not implemented, interventions to protect American interests, in Haiti in 1915 and the Dominican Republic in 1916, led to nationalist resistance.

Popular guerrilla movements in the 1920s proved able to limit the degree of control enjoyed by occupying American forces who found that rebel ambushes restricted their freedom of manoeuvre. American bombing was no substitute, particularly in the face of guerrilla dominance of rural areas at night. However, the Americans were not defeated in pitched battles, and in 1922 the guerrillas in the Dominican Republic conditionally surrendered. American forces left there in 1924.[36] The *Guardia Nacional*, created by the American occupiers as a way to help maintain both order and their interests, became a key force. Moreover, in 1929, Brigadier-General John Russell, the United States High Commissioner, and not President Joseph Bornó, was described as the 'real ruler'.[37]

On the other hand, having withdrawn the Marines from Nicaragua in 1925, the USA sent them back in 1926 in order to end civil war and stop the risk of Soviet-backed Mexican intervention. In 1927, the Americans imposed a settlement, including elections in 1928, which enabled the head of the army, José Maria Moncada, to become president in 1928.

This agreement was resisted by a rebel peasant army under César Augusto Sandino. Sandino took refuge in the mountains and turned to guerrilla warfare. The campaigning revealed the vulnerability of regular troops to ambushes and the problems of fixing opponents:

> The Marines were ambushed . . . as they . . . were going through a narrow pass in single file. When the Marines had reached the middle of the pass the insurgents opened fire from a mountain battery and with automatic rifles and grenades made of glass and scraps of metal attached to sticks of dynamite . . . Finding it useless to fire at the hidden enemy he hurried his men forward through the pass . . . to the outskirts of Quilali where he deployed and engaged the enemy in the open. The insurgents then retired.[38]

The Americans responded with air power, and their planes were held responsible for heavy casualties among Sandino's forces, although the latter also responded with machine-gun fire.[39] The Americans were unable to suppress the rising or capture Sandino, and opposition to the war grew in Congress. In the event, the Americans trained a *Guardia Nacional* and withdrew their troops in 1933. Despite these checks, the Americans dominated the region militarily, not least due to their naval power and to the operational effectiveness of the Marine Corps.[40]

As a parallel, the army was used to tackle race riots in the USA in 1919–20. Black concern with equal rights was seen as a radical and subversive concept. Nevertheless, the army was capable of performing non-partisan duty in ending distrubances.[41]

Pressures on imperialism

It was not only in the Caribbean that informal empire was under pressure. In China, the British abandoned their concessions in Hankou and Jiujiang on the Yangzi, in 1927, after the local British military presence was overawed by massive public protests. A Chinese trade unionist was killed in each city by British troops, but, whereas, in 1925, the British position in Hankou had been underpinned by local warlords, in 1927 there was no such backing.[42] There and elsewhere, the nationalism of the Guomindang challenged Britain's extensive interests.

More generally, within empires, alongside indigenous practices of resistance, many of them central to a peasant culture of non-compliance, there was a growing institutional framework for colony-wide politicization challenging imperial control. The Indian National Congress (1885) and the Egyptian National Congress (1897) were followed by the National Congress of British West Africa in 1920 and the Young Kikuyu Association in Kenya in 1921. Within French Africa, there was the *Étoile Nord-Africaine* in Algeria and the *Destour* in Tunisia. The Algerian Communist Party was established in 1936.

At the same time, the armed resistance to imperial expansion and control seen in the early and mid-1920s largely ended later in the decade. The British had contained opposition in Egypt and Iraq by granting their independence, while there had been no large-scale rebellions in such key colonies as India and Algeria. The disturbances in Punjab in 1919, most prominently remembered for the Amritsar massacre, were not a large-scale rebellion. At one level, the colonial wars of the previous century had not ended, and the ethos of resistance could be triggered by state action or natural catastrophes such as floods.[43] Yet, looked at differently, a *modus vivendi* based on compliance with external control not only pertained but was also strengthened by the resilience of the imperial military.

A The imperial military

Thanks to steamships, troops could be deployed relatively rapidly to colonies. Within colonies, their mobility was improved by better communications and by a degree of mechanization. The experience of the Great War was also valuable.[44] Air power offered an additional form of deployment. Moreover, imperial military forces generally, although not invariably, proved successful in both attack and defence. Prepared units were able to hold off larger attacking forces, as in the OK Pass in British Somaliland in March 1919, where the British lost two men repelling an attack by about 400 supporters of Mullah Sayyid, who allegedly lost 200 men. Success there or, eventually, in Morocco contrasted markedly with the Western intervention in the Russian Civil War, indicating the difficulty of judging overall capability.

Despite the criticism that colonial military forces such as the Indian Army, sometimes received from reformers, not least those keen on mechanization, such as J. F. C. Fuller (see p. 92), these militaries were engaged in their own action-reaction processes, as colonial control warfare was far from static.[45] Indeed, the challenges of counter-insurgency warfare led to the theoretical discussion.[46] The capacity for mobility and tactical advantage offered by air power encouraged particular interest.[47] There was also a role for mechanized capability, as well as interest in the use of gas.[48]

Yet, there was also considerable brutality, not least because, as a special correspondent of *The Times*, in Morocco noted, 'an intense race hatred' was frequently involved. He wrote of 'the hell of warfare which these so-called tribal revolts and their repression entail. There is no mercy asked for or given.'[49]

Conclusions

There was a parallel of sorts between a European situation, in which the Western settlement was well-grounded by the late 1920s (although it had failed earlier in the decade in the Soviet Union), with the position elsewhere. The emphasis outside Europe is on, however, setbacks for Western control: and they were serious. The abandonment of aspirations and positions, notably in Turkey, but also in Iraq, Egypt, Persia and China, marked the start of the ebb of European empire. As with many other important shifts in global power, this abandonment was a recognition of military capability, both absolute and relative, that did not essentially arise from large-scale conflict, but that was as important as any war.

In large part, military limitations reflected a shift in the nature of regional politics as nationalism became far more important, notably in Turkey, China and Egypt, while it was strengthened in Mexico. The politico-military means that had been effective before the Great War were now less so.[50] One commentator observed of the British abandonment under nationalist pressure of its Chinese concession at Hankou in 1927, 'Hankow is perhaps the outstanding example of Europe's humiliation in Asia from the stand-point of the prestige that the White Man built up in the nineteenth century. It marked a surrender dictated by profound changes in bases of conduct in Asia.'[51] Emphasis on the weaknesses of imperial power in the inter-war period serves as a corrective to any focus largely on military developments within Europe and on preparations for the Second World War. This emphasis also looks towards the situation after 1945 when the colonial empires were to collapse within three decades.

As with conflict in inter-war Europe, the nature of imperial warfare was very different to that of the Great War. In an article more generally relevant to the conflicts of the period, both imperial and elsewhere, a correspondent of *The Times* returned from Morocco, and noted in the issue of 20 January 1925:

Four years of warfare in European trenches adjusted the modern mind to the idea of a united front, along which all who fought on the same side could join hands and muster in endless lines without a thought for the safety of their communications and only friends or vanquished behind them.

In order to understand the present situation in Morocco and the events which have led up to it, it is first of all necessary to blot out this picture of an infinite trench and replace it by that of a front – if such a word is permissible in this case – consisting of a series of islets scattered over a country which may have been conquered, but has not yet been pacified. Some of these islets were known as base camps or positions, others were called blockhouses . . . the Moors were at liberty to select both the target and the moment for attacking it.

At the same time, empires were stronger than ever before in world history. Some commitments were abandoned, but there were also successes. The failure of intervention in the Russian Civil War reflected the failures of the White forces, internal and external politics, ambivalence about intervention, and an inadequate military commitment. In contrast, success in British and French-controlled colonies was not only due to the use of local troops and greater political support at home, but also to a clearer sense of purpose. A lack of strength by the rebels compared to the power of the Red Army was also significant, as were technological differences. Not only were the major empires, Britain and France, formidable forces, but lesser ones were also expanding. Thus, the Italians both suppressed opposition in Libya and overran the Sultanate of Obbia in Italian Somaliland. Commitments outside Europe were not simply an add-on to military concerns.

The European empires benefited from the lack of any opposition from their counterparts. There was no counterpart to the pressure put by the Allies on the Soviet Union in 1918–21; and, despite grave concern about hostile Soviet intentions toward the British Empire, no equivalent to the problems that were to be posed for the Western European empires by the Japanese in 1940–2 or, far less seriously, for the Soviets in the Far East by the Japanese in 1938–9. Concerned about the Soviet threat to India via Afghanistan, the British, nevertheless, were not worried about other external threats to this key possession. Thus, for 1927,

> At the present time our policy is to adopt a strict defensive attitude on the north-east frontier [of India, toward Tibet] . . . because we are of the opinion that the Chinese will not for a considerable time be in a position to undertake any important offensive against us, even if they wished to do so.[52]

3

Warfare in the 'Third World' in the 1920s

The term 'Third World' was not yet in currency, but this chapter covers a distinct type of conflict that was separate from imperial warfare. This chapter considers wars involving sovereign countries, or at least countries theoretically sovereign, in which European or American involvement was limited to advisers and technology. As this chapter indicates, such warfare was important.

China

Consideration of conflict within China in the 1920s serves as a corrective to any focus on the contemporary situation within Europe. Much of this conflict appears obscure from the latter perspective, but, from the viewpoint of the early twenty-first century, when China is one of the world's leading powers and potentially the next superpower, the internal military history of China seems of much greater relevance. In addition, in terms of the scale of conflict, these were the largest wars of the 1920s. Moreover, in the inter-war period, the partial defeat of regionalism, in the shape of the power-bases of the warlords, was a key development in Chinese history, as it left the new political-military forces, the Guomindang (Nationalist Party) and the Communists, to battle for control over a country that both wished to keep united. This unity lasted from the end of their direct struggle in 1949 to the present when they remain highly armed opponents from their bases in Beijing and Taibei (the capital of Taiwan).

The 1920s are characterized as the warlord era, but it is necessary, in using the term warlord, to indicate that it was polemical and introduced from the Japanese *gunbatsu*, meaning the militarist interest. Those referred to were generals, mostly members of a fissiparous, but internationally recognized, government in Beijing. Because they lost, where the Guomindang (Nationalist Party), an insurgent movement against that government, won, the generals/warlords are treated as anachronistic and in a pejorative fashion. As Kemal Atatürk and Ibn Saud, however, show, success can provide a very different gloss. The problem with the term warlord is that it suggests that warlord warfare was somehow qualitatively different to the other warfare waged before and after, which is incorrect. Behind the term lies a Marxist/economic theory of warfare that is mistaken.

Long-standing regionalism in China, including historical tensions between north and south, as well as developments prior to the Republican uprising of 1911–12 that overthrew the Qing (Manchu) imperial dynasty, were significant for the nature of military power. These developments, not least the large-scale Taiping civil war of 1850–64, meant that regional military units had gained considerable autonomy, while also needing to control their regions in order to provide for themselves. Defeat by Japan in 1894–5 had led to a second phase in military modernization, which gathered pace, after the failure of the Boxer uprising, in the reform programme adopted by the Qing in the last decade of the empire. A key feature of these new forces was a strong nationalist commitment. Military modernization gathered pace, modern weaponry was adopted, and Western military advisers were employed. The leading figure in this development was Yuan Shikai, commander of the Beiyang (Northern Ocean) army.

The 1911 revolution began with a military uprising and the fate of the Qing was sealed once Yuan, after some hesitation, decided to back it. Alongside the rising influence of the military in local society, specific political developments were responsible for the rise of the warlord era, notably the collapse of the presidency of Yuan (1912–16), who died in 1916, soon after the failure of his attempt to become emperor.[1]

This failure discredited the central government which was based in Beijing, and this government was not strong enough to create a new national order. Many of the first generation of warlords had been officers under Yuan and subsequent rivalries among the now leaderless northern generals, the Northern or Beijing clique, who dominated the Beijing government, were a key element in the breakdown of order. These divisions interacted with the patronage links to the provincial commanders that provided leading generals with greater clout.[2]

One reason for the ascent of the military in Chinese politics after the Republican revolution of 1911 was that there was no other body with the combination of numbers, structure, clarity of outlook, and armed force, to challenge it. However, the Chinese army was riven by personal rivalries. The competing views and both domestic and international links of the leading generals led to clashes between prime minister and successive presidents in 1917 and 1918, with provincial forces called in to help sway the struggle in Beijing. The failure of a reconciliation conference staged in Shanghai in 1919 was followed by a war in 1920 in which the forces of key generals, Wu Peifu and Zhang Zuolin, converged on Beijing, resulting in the overthrow of General Duan Qirui, the head of the Anhui Clique and also prime minister. The latter had lacked enough troops to prevail as well as close links with sufficient other warlords. He took refuge with the Japanese garrison in Tianjin.

Japan had established close links with some of China's regional leaders in the 1890s, but had used the chaos of the 1910s and its position as one of the Allies in the Great War in order to pursue its own ambitions in China and, in particular, in 1915, to establish a powerful presence in the strategically important Shandong region. This presence outraged Chinese nationalist intellectuals who were also offended by the longer-standing territorial presence of Western powers, especially Britain and France, in enclaves within China.[3] These enclaves had resulted from armed attacks on Chinese territory during the nineteenth century.

The overthrow of Duan Qirui saw the power of the warlords brought to fruition. The local commanders were essentially regional figures, but this was not true of the leading generals or warlords. Rather, they used territorial bases to contend for power over all of China. The most powerful was Zhang

Zuolin, the Old Marshal. From a Manchurian peasant background, he had become an enlisted soldier and risen in the newly modernizing army, while also exploiting the breakdown of the empire to become the Manchurian warlord as well as the head of what was called the Fengtian Clique.[4] Zhang benefitted from the economic growth of Manchuria, China's leading industrial region and one of the best served by a major rail network. This meant that he was a key figure also in northern China more generally where none of the local warlords could match his power. However, that influence did not extend further south.

Dominant in central China was Wu Peifu, a crucial figure from 1918, who, thanks to his geographical position, was able to play a role both further north and to the south. In 1921, Wu, the head of the Zhili Clique, conquered the strategically important province of Hunan which had declared self-rule the previous year, while in 1922, in the First Zhili-Fengtian War, Wu defeated Zhang in a struggle for control of Beijing, even though Zhang had numerous troops and weapons. Wu then installed a client central government which was as weak as the others of the period. In response, Zhang declared Manchurian autonomy. Reorganizing and retraining his army, Zhang brought forward younger officers, benefitting from their more recent training, while also trying, in the customary complex politics of the warlord forces, to maintain the backing of his older supporters.

In 1923, Wu's allies invaded Fujian in east China, but, in 1924, a wide-ranging conflict began, the Second Zhili-Fengtian War. Wu's position was challenged in northern and then central China, and, betrayed by a key general (or warlord), Feng Yuxiang, he was driven out of northern China by Zhang. Bar for this betrayal, Wu might have succeeded. However, in 1925 Wu, now helped by Feng and by disloyalty among Zhang's troops, was able to regain his position in central China. In 1926, Wu negotiated a truce with Zhang, and then drove out Feng. Zhang declared himself generalissimo of all Chinese forces.

With politics subsumed by conflict, local society was often left in the hands of gangs. The actions of large bandit gangs complicated the local military and political situation, but, crucially, they lacked the ability of the warlords to use resources and loans in order to obtain weapons from abroad, an ability grounded on their territorial bases. Nevertheless, the bandits challenged the security of the territorial positions from which the warlords raised these resources of men, money and food.

At the same time, there was an overlap between warlords and bandits, with both oppressing the population; this overlap meant that bandit forces could be absorbed into the warlord forces, and particularly undisciplined warlord units could become bandits. In this way, the traditional Chinese hostility to the soldier, seen as a cause of violence and often no more than a bandit, was perpetuated. Large-scale secret societies added to the chaos, especially in areas where the warlords were weak. Warlords concentrated on cities and towns, to control their wealth and benefit from their importance for communications. These societies, notably the Red Spears and the Heavenly Gate Society, resisted both warlords and bandits. They contributed to the centrality of violence in Chinese politics in the 1920s and of the rising tide of violence in Chinese society.

Despite, or perhaps because of, the collapse of traditional stable state structures, the warlords were able to raise and maintain large armies. That of Wu Peifu was 170,000 strong in 1924, while in 1928 Zhang Zuolin and his allies deployed 400,000 men against the Guomindang's 700,000. Although some figures are open to doubt, the size of armies grew during the decades, with the number under arms rising from about half a million in 1916 to about two million in 1928. The length of the individual wars rose with these numbers, as did the burden on the country's economy and society. However, there was an emphasis on rapid victory, which was often obtained when the opponent realized that he had been out-manoeuvred. As with Western military thought in the 1920s, there was no interest in attritional war.

Purchasing modern weapons from Europe in the 1920s, especially from France and Italy, the warlords had plenty of artillery and other arms, including aircraft. Western arms traders were highly active in China's civil wars. Foreign advisers were also important, notably first Soviet and later German for the Guomindang, the nationalist republican movement. Feng Yuxiang had Soviet advisers and arms. Advisers were important if foreign arms were to be used successfully.

An emphasis on foreign arms and advisers makes Chinese warfare seem in part dependent on developments in the West, and therefore apparently helps explain the general focus on the military history of the latter. However, it is likely that the transformative character of both arms and advisers in China has been exaggerated, and notably with the warlord forces. Instead, as an aspect of the way in which the warlords were a mix of the modern and traditional, there was often an 'add-on' quality to this foreign influence, and the influence was fed through existing cultural and institutional preferences and practices. This point is an important one conceptually, as it helps explain the tension between accounts of military history that focus on a paradigm power or system, and the diffusion of its methods, and others that place the emphasis rather on variety and, particularly, a culturally encoded variety. The latter is the focus here.[5] Interwar China merits study on its own right rather than merely as a footnote to Western military history.

'What is true today is almost sure not to be true tomorrow'. The contemporary assessment in the American strategic plan for intervention in China in 1926 was readily comprehensible, as it accurately reflected the inchoate environment of its politics.[6] Much of the warfare of the 1920s there can be seen in terms of the self-interest of the warlords. Their kaleidoscopic alliances appear both as the expression of this self-interest and as the way in which it was structured. Alongside the warlords, the growing power of the Guomindang became a more significant factor. Despite a measure of idealism, the Guomindang came under Jiang Jieshi (Chiang Kai-shek), its effective head from 1926, to act as a form of successful warlordism with more concrete national assumptions and pretensions. Nevertheless, these assumptions and pretensions helped the Guomindang to act and appear (including to the USA and others) as a national force, and this appearance was important to its military rationale and, to a considerable extent, means. Jiang Jieshi, earlier commandant of a military-political academy in South China, lacked the calibre and success of Kemal Atatürk, but he offered China more than Zhang Zuolin.

Alongside elements of continuity, the conflicts of the 1920s also demonstrated the extent of military modernization in China, notably with the use of Great War type equipment, the large-scale production of munitions, especially in Mukden in Manchuria and at Wuhan, and the ability to move troops rapidly by rail. The ready availability of weaponry was noted by commentators. *The Times*' Beijing correspondent reported, in the issue of 3 September

1924, about a confrontation over the lower Yangzi valley, 'Machine-guns and artillery are plentiful on both sides, and each army has a few aeroplanes, while one is credited with gas'.

In the 1920s, a national rail system existed in China. This steel framework was a kind of modern battlefield. Most of the fighting was along, or around, or for, it. The rail system connected mostly relatively new, industrial cities. The rail plus the cities were in effect a separable realm from the countryside and its farmers. As in the American and Russian Civil Wars, the ability to move troops by rail helped shape the conflict, at least in operational terms. Thus, in 1924, Wu Peifu depended on the rail system in order to concentrate his forces against Zhang Zuolin. At the same time, this activity posed a serious logistical strain. The *Times* noted on 26 September 1924:

> Nearly 300 trainloads of troops and supplies have gone forward in 20 days, a considerable performance for a single-line railway. This result has been made possible by withdrawing practically the whole of the rolling stock from all the railways north of the Yangzi river, thereby completely stopping goods traffic and permitting only a precarious minimum mail and passenger traffic.
>
> There is much confusion at the concentration point and the empty trains are not returning. Military officers are seriously interfering with the railway administration and enforcing their demands at the point of the pistol. In one case where a number of officers were disputing for precedence the difficulty was solved by joining five trains together and sending them forward as one train, measuring one and a half miles long. Speed was reduced to a walk, but the "multiple tandem" arrived safely to the satisfaction of the 4,000 soldier passengers. The locomotive crews having objected to long hours are working double shifts, with sentries to see that the men off duty sleep soundly and do not gallivant in the darkness.

The importance of the railways helped ensure that cutting them became a purpose of military moves[7], while advances were described as moving along the railway[8], a process encouraged, as in Russia, by the use of armoured trains. Railway junctions proved key operational goals and garrison points, and notably so if the junctions were also cities as the latter produced revenues and offered legitimacy.

The significance of the railways was enhanced not least by the contrast with the very different communication system used in their absence – coolies, or human porters. Compulsion played a key role. *The Times'* Shanghai correspondent reported in the issue of 6 September 1924:

> There is great indignation owing to the merciless kidnapping by soldiers of thousands of peaceable Chinese for transport and trench-digging in the districts about Shanghai. Male inhabitants of the surrounding district have flocked in a state of terror into the settlement to escape the press gang. Similar reports come from Nanking and Soochow. Both sides are equally blameworthy of this disgraceful oppression.

Men were also seized to dig trenches and build earthworks. The impact of the season, and notably rainfall, on campaigning was another aspect of the traditional practices, although it was also to play a role in modern campaigning.

As with the Russian Civil War, there were not continuous fronts. Their absence contributed to the stress on rapid advances on key positions, for example the Guomindang seizing of the Chinese-governed sector of Shanghai in March 1927. The importance of mobility and the paucity of modern road vehicles helped ensure the continuing role of cavalry[9], which was more important in the drier and flatter lands of northern China than further south. Nevertheless, most troops were infantry, which underlined the significance of railways for transport and logistics.

There was also an emphasis in Chinese politics and conflict on seeking to build up support by winning over warlords. Indeed, the changing allegiances of the warlords resulted in a lack of consistency in the forces engaged. Ideological commitment was very limited and generals, many of whom were former classmates or from a similar military background, changed sides, a process facilitated by payment.[10] Bribed by Japan, Feng Yuxiang of the Zhili faction did so in 1924, undermining Wu's military system and enabling Zhang, the Manchurian warlord, to gain control of Beijing that October.

Moreover, armies lacked cohesion, while troops were motivated by 'the rice-bowl' at a time when soldiering was at least guaranteed employment.[11] Warlord forces were raised largely through personal links between commanders, and local bonds were highly significant. Both factors played a role in the opportunism that encouraged frequent changes of side on the part of individual units. The lack of a unified officer corps in individual warlord armies, and the extent to which these armies were poorly integrated, facilitated this process. In addition, popular mobilization for war, particularly in rural areas, was far less than during the conflict between the Guomindang and the Communists in the 1930s.[12]

At the same time, military leaders had to display considerable adaptability in responding not only to new technology but also to different political circumstances. Whereas the Manchu emperors of 1644–1911 had relied on hereditary military units, the eight Manchu banners, later supplemented by eight Mongol and eight Chinese banners, now, most obviously among the Guomindang, there was a stress on national armies and on new ways of linking society, state and armed forces.[13]

Led by Sun Yat-sen, the Guomindang had failed to establish a nationalist republic in Guangzhou (Canton) in 1918 because some of the southern warlords, who had initially provided support, changed their stance. Nevertheless, in December 1920, Sun Yat-sen established his position anew in Guangdong and when, the following spring, a neighbouring Guangxi warlord army backed by Beijing, advanced on Guangzhou, it was defeated and retreated into Guangxi. However, falling out with the local warlord, Chen Jiongming, Sun fled from Guangzhou in 1922. His forces, which included warlord allies, were soon defeated. In 1923, there was a fresh change as, thanks to a mercenary army he had raised with money from overseas Chinese supporters, Sun was able to take over the city. The mercenaries, however, could only be supported by arbitrary taxation.

Soviet support crucially helped in the development of a more effective Guomindang army. Artillery, rifles and ammunition were provided and in May 1924 a military academy was established on Whampoa Island near Guangzhou. It was placed under Sun's major military aide, Jiang Jieshi, and became the basis of a nationalistic force, many of whom did not look to the Soviets. Jiang had been trained in Japan and had inspected military facilities in the Soviet Union. In 1924, the Guomindang forces defeated the merchants' militia, a conservative group that looked to the British. The following year,

Chen Jiongming was defeated when he advanced on Guangzhou, and, in the Eastern Expedition, his troops were driven back into Fujian.

Sun died in March 1925, leaving no agreed successor. In the subsequent disorder, a rebellion by the mercenaries was crushed. Jiang correctly saw his dominance of the army as a route to power and he soon came to control the Guomindang government. As commander of the Guomindang forces, Jiang commanded the Northern Expedition, a drive north from Guangzhou against independent warlords launched in 1926, which he had first planned in 1917. This operation, which was intended to unify the country and certainly to overawe other forces, benefitted greatly from the Zhili-Fengtian war of 1924 which had weakened the government of northern China.[14] Moreover, the May the Thirtieth (1925) Incident and Movement set the scene for the launch of the Northern Expedition. The incident – the killing of Chinese demonstrators in Shanghai by British-officered police – set in train a series of demonstrations in cities. These helped to give the first phase of the Northern Expedition the character of a popular advance.

Beginning in the summer of 1926, this advance by the National Revolutionary Army benefitted from Soviet military advisers, money and equipment, although the Soviet advisers were disparaging of the Chinese and provided help largely as part of a long-term plan to help the Chinese Communists who were then allied to the Guomindang. Moreover, while claiming to model the army on the Japanese and Soviet forces and with the aim of extirpating the warlords, the Guomindang in fact allied with warlords, notably the Guangxi warlords who commanded an effective force that, in theory, was part of the Guomindang's National Revolutionary Army. More generally, Jiang's attempt to end corruption in the army by centralizing military finance fell foul of his need to propitiate the established military interests. In 1926, Jiang created a coalition of opponents of Wu Peifu and the latter's allies, including Tang Shengzhi, a Hunan warlord who had been driven out by these allies.

In 1926, Jiang advanced, meeting little resistance from the divided Hunan warlords. He entered the Hunan capital of Changsha on 11 July, and gained control of the railway line to the Yangzi. After defeating Wu at Tingsiqiao near Wuchang, Jiang advanced on Wuhan. Wu sought the support of the eastern warlord Sun Chuanfang but, already negotiating with Jiang, the latter preferred to wait on the result of the struggle. Wu was to be forced into retirement. Wuhan fell in October, with Hanyang surrendering after its commander took a bribe.

The Guomindang units had impressed with their dedication and bravery, not least at Tinsiqiao and in besieging Wuchang. There were weaknesses, but fewer than among the warlords' forces. Meanwhile, to the east, Guomindang forces had overrun Fujian and invaded Zhejiang. In each case, success had been obtained by winning over local warlords who had then become commanders in the army. This means of victory without battle reflected a combination of force and politics that was very important to the Chinese warfare of the 1920s and had also been much used in the past, being a Chinese cultural pattern that was extolled in traditional works on war.

The combination ensured success both in the zone of operations and at a distance, as in 1926 when Sichuan's warlords in the north-west agreed to cooperate. Moreover, this combination was important not just to the success of the Guomindang forces but also to relations within them. Jiang had to manage their rivalries with great care, and his allocation of resources and tasks was a central part of this. At the same time, the Guomindang advance also benefitted from a degree of popular support.

After capturing Wuhan, Jiang moved east towards the Yangzi centres of Nanjing and Shanghai, instead of advancing north to Beijing which was the alternative. Rather than pursuing political legitimacy by conquering Beijing, Jiang sought the resources of Shanghai, China's wealthiest centre. At Nanchang, his force was badly checked by Sun Chuanfang's army, but a counter-offensive proved ineffective. In early 1927, the advance resumed with the defeat of the intervening forces of Zhang Zongchang, the warlord based in Shandong. Fighting was linked to the acquisition of backing from local political and military figures through negotiations. Key elements included the large gangster world of Shanghai, with which Jiang had long-standing connections, as well as its business world. The warlord forces offered little resistance as both Shanghai and Nanjing fell in late March.

The Communist allies of the Guomindang were crushed at the same time, beginning a new Chinese civil war (see p. 159). The army played an important role in this violence, in Shanghai, for example seizing the offices of the pro-Communist Labour Federation. The so-called 'white purge' of the Communists underlined the extent to which violence was central to politics, and thus control over its means crucial to political power. The purge helped Jiang win the support of warlords, as most were anti-Communist. Left-wing sections of the Guomindang, an inherently divided movement, who were allied with the Communists, called for the overthrow of Jiang, but the warlords defeated them. Left-wing urban rebellions in the late 1920s failed dismally and forced the emergence of a new, rural-centred, guerrilla movement. As a result of the attack on the Communists, the Soviets pulled out their advisers from the Guomindang.

In response to Jiang's success, Zhang Zuolin, the northern warlord, intervened. He proclaimed himself Grand Marshal on 17 June 1927, organized a military government in Beijing and sent his son, the Young Marshal, successfully south towards Wuhan, while Zhang Zongchang advanced on Nanjing. The latter, however, was pushed back and Jiang's troops then advanced easily north through eastern China. Meanwhile, the Young Marshal was defeated and fell back north of the Yellow River. The Guomindang won the support of important warlords, Feng Yuxiang of Shaanxi, who also had Soviet arms, and Yan Xishan of Shanxi. Both followed Jiang in turning on the Communists.

The British Chiefs of Staff reported in January 1927 that only Japan was in a position to intervene in China on a large-scale.[15] However, Japanese interventions against the Northern Expedition in 1927 and 1928, the two Shandong interventions[16], failed to prevent the consolidation of Guomindang support. The Japanese regarded northern China as part of their sphere of influence and were concerned when, visiting Japan, Jiang informed the prime minister that his goal was to unite China, including reasserting its sovereignty over Manchuria. It seems that a united and strong China was regarded as a threat to Japan's security and especially to its expansion for land and resources.

In April 1928, Jiang advanced on Beijing in alliance with Yan Xishan and Feng Yuxiang. They greatly out-numbered Zhang Zuolin's forces and benefitted from advancing simultaneously from a number of directions. Moreover, the Japanese government made it clear that, while it would not accept the Guomindang taking over Manchuria, it would accept their control of the remainder of China. This stance undermined Zhang. In the face of his converging opponents, Zhang left Beijing on 2 June, only to be assassinated by Japanese officers, dissatisfied with both the Japanese government and Zhang. They detonated a bomb on 4 June as his train passed under a bridge.

Jiang's forces occupied Beijing on 6 July 1928 and agreed terms with the Young Marshal. On 29 December, the Young Marshal pledged allegiance to the National government, now very much under Jiang, and the Young Marshal raised the Guomindang flag, now the national one, over the Manchurian capital, Mukden. The Japanese army, which had mistakenly believed it could control the Young Marshal, was furious. The following month, he had his father's former Chief of Staff, whom he suspected of plotting with the Japanese, shot dead at dinner.[17]

Jiang sought to follow Sun Yat-sen's policy of modernization through centralization, which he also saw as the best way both to protect his own position and to enable China to resist foreign, especially Japanese, pressure.[18] In the process he sought a degree of control over the army that was unacceptable to the warlords who were not interested in being integrated into the system (or bought over) by being given Guomindang posts. Yan Xishan had been made vice-chairman of the Military Council and Feng Yuxiang had been made Minister of War, but they preferred, in 1929, to return to their provincial centres of power, which led Jiang to seek to force them into line or to overthrow them. This crisis resulted in a complex period of political intrigue, in the shape of buying support, and threatening conflict.

The crisis became more serious for Jiang in the summer of 1930 when many of the warlords grouped together against him. They could deploy about 600,000 troops, but were defeated, in the War of the Central Plains, by a combination of Jiang's army, some of which was now German-trained, and the Manchurian army. Divide-and-rule methods also worked, as did a willingness to compromise with those who were defeated, rather than extirpating their local authority. Yan was defeated and exiled, but was allowed back to govern his province from 1931. The Young Marshal's move south, however, was to help leave Manchuria exposed to Japanese expansion.

Jiang's success depended in part on the cooperation of other warlords, notably the Young Marshal, but tension with them continued. From 1935 to

1937, the government was distracted by attempting to suppress the warlords in the south and south-west.

The devastation and cost of the warfare were great and imposed a heavy burden on Chinese society. Although some troops such as those of Feng, the 'Christian Warlord', were generally well behaved, most were not; while war for ideology may be 'scientifically' inhumane, these wars for power were indiscriminate in their violence. The brutalization of the people by troops was commonplace, with killing, rape, looting, extortion, torture and seizing for ransom all frequent.[19] There was also serious damage to the economy, especially food production. Similar devastation had occurred earlier, most recently with the Taiping Rebellion in the mid-nineteenth century and, to a lesser extent, the Boxer Rising at the turn of the centuries, but the geographical extent of the devastation in the 1920s was greater. Moreover, the warlords and other governmental agencies of that period (all weakened by fear and insecurity) were unable to provide an administrative context and structure comparable to that of the late-Qing Empire, however flawed that had been.

On the other hand, the loss of life was not comparable to the carnage of the mid-nineteenth century rebellions. The death toll caused by the Taiping Rebellion has been estimated at 20–30 million. In economic terms, the depredations of the warlord armies undoubtedly caused a great deal of misery to peasants. However, at the same time, exports boomed and there was also considerable growth in industrial production, albeit from a low base. In cultural terms, this was a very lively period. The May Fourth (1919) movement led to an outburst of new writing, striking developments in the graphic arts, and a rejection of Confucianism as the source of Chinese 'backwardness'.

Persia (Iran)

Civil warfare overlapped with state-building in the Islamic world. In Persia (Iran), Reza Khan, a Russian-trained colonel in the Persian Cossack Brigade, suppressed internal rebellions and seized power from the pro-British ruler, Ahmad Shah. Having used the Cossack Brigade to suppress opposition in Azerbaijan in 1920, Reza Khan rose to power in 1921, becoming commander of the army in 1921, prime minister in 1923, and being proclaimed Reza Shah on 15 December 1925. Ahmad Shah had gone abroad in 1923, never to return.

Reza Shah created a new and disciplined national army, 40,000 strong, the loyalty of which he gained by better equipment, regular pay and battlefield success. In part, the army was organized on the British model. It was used to crush opposition. Campaigning from 1921 to 1925 spread governmental power throughout Persia, and the disunited tribes were defeated. Dissidence in Mashhad, Tabriz, Gilan and Kurdistan was crushed, and Khuzistan in the south-west was occupied in 1924. Reza Khan personally led his forces into Khuzistan, breaking the power of Shaikh Khaz'al of Mohammereh whom the British had treated as an independent ruler within their sphere of influence after their 1907 agreement with Russia defining such spheres in Persia for both powers. Reza Khan benefitted from being able to defeat his opponents separately. Thus, in 1921, Gilan was taken over and a rising in Khorasan suppressed, while in 1923 opposition in the south from Bakhtiari and Luri groups was suppressed.

Thereafter, the position of the Persian tribes was further weakened by disarming them and forcibly introducing centralized systems of taxation and conscription, so that conscripted tribesmen could be used against other tribesmen. With these advantages, major tribal rebellions, which owed something to opposition towards conscription[20], were crushed in 1929 and 1932. The tribesmen suffered heavily from the improved mobility of their opponents. Armoured cars and lorries operated on new roads and were supported by the automatic weapons and observation planes of government forces. The combination of technology, expenditure, organization and political skill, shifted the historic balance between the tribes and regular forces, a particular instance of the more general tension between periphery and centre and the way there was a shift of power from the former to the latter in this period.

Afghanistan

New technology played an increasing, but patchy, role in 'Third World' conflict. The effect could be dramatic, especially in the initial stages when there was an important element of novelty. In Ethiopia, a tank was employed to help thwart a coup in 1928. Amanullah, king of Afghanistan, obtained planes from the Soviet Union, and used them against tribal opponents. He also turned to a Turkish military mission in order to try to establish a modern army that was trained as well as loyal to the state (i.e. him), rather than to the tribes. These reforms encountered resistance, both within the army and, from 1924, from particular tribes. In response, Amanullah found his new army of limited effectiveness and, instead, turned to the conventional means of using supportive tribal forces. In this way, the effect of new technology could be short-lived.

Opposition gathered force as Amanullah sought to change conscription from a system controlled by village elders and tribal chiefs to choice by ballot, a measure seen as likely to increase the role of the state. This attack on tribal influence was faced by large-scale resistance in 1928, and the army proved unable to suppress the opposition. Desertion was considerable and tribal loyalties came to the fore, both in the army and in the subsequent conflict between the tribes as Amanullah fell in 1929 to be replaced, first, by Bacha-i-Saqao, a Tajik bandit, and then by Nadir Khan (r. 1929–33) who was able to seize Kabul and become king. The tribes now dominated the country, their forces strengthened by seizing most of the army's weapons.[21] Conflict in Afghanistan was followed closely by the British colonial government of India which feared both the spread of warfare into the North-West Frontier and the possibility that Afghanistan would prove a means for the spread of Soviet power. Neither of these fears was to be proved correct in the 1920s or 1930s.

Arabia

In Arabia, tribal forces again played a major role, but new technology was also valuable. Wireless stations helped Ibn Saud control the situation, notably in directing his campaign in the Azir region in 1926, while trucks equipped with machine-guns were used to provide mobile firepower. However, traditional means of mobility were more significant. In Arabia, after the collapse of Ottoman (Turkish) control and influence, tribal leaders vied for advantage while the major families competed for dominance of the peninsula and for influence further afield. The competition was won by Ibn Saud (1876–1953), who was based in the central region of Nejd round Riyadh. Drawing on the energy and determination of the fundamentalist Islamic Wahhabi movement, which had fought for a previous generation of Al Saud rulers, Ibn Saud gradually extended his position. He defeated the Hashemites, who had been allied to Britain against the Turks in the Great War, in a night attack at Turaba in May 1919. The 8,000 defenders were surprised and slaughtered by the Ikhwan (Brethren) who were committed to the service of Ibn Saud, their Imam, and to the chosen path of Islam. In 1920, Ibn Saud moved north to Hail where he overran and defeated the Al Rashid who surrendered in 1921, destroying the buffer between his territories and Iraq, then under British control. In 1920, the Ikhwan, invaded Kuwait, a British protectorate, but were defeated by the local garrison of the Red Fort at the oasis of Jahra. British reinforcements were then sent to the region, both to protect Kuwait and to thwart Ibn Saud's pressure for a frontier on the Euphrates.

Thereafter, the Hijaz, the region of western Arabia alongside the Red Sea, was the focus of Ibn Saud's operations. This was a conflict of raids and loose sieges. Responding to the fall of the Ottoman Sultan, the Hashemite leader in Arabia, Hussain bin Ali, proclaimed himself Caliph at Jeddah on 5 March 1924, which inflamed the Wahhabis to renew the struggle and to focus on the Hijaz. In doing so, they repeated the Wahhabi attack on the Ottoman/ Egyptian position in the early nineteenth century.

Ibn Saud was greatly helped by serious divisions in the Hashemite family. Branches in Iraq and TransJordan were unwilling to offer help to each other. The Ikhwan sacked the town of Taif on 4 September 1924, slaughtering much of its population. This psychological warfare terrified the population of the Hijaz, leading the inhabitants of Jeddah to press for the abdication of Hussain. The Ikhwan, moreover, captured an undefended Mecca on 16 October 1924. Earlier that month, Hussain was obliged to abdicate the throne of the Hijaz to his eldest son, Ali who was soon besieged in Jeddah. As Ibn Saud preferred to win without relying on frontal assaults, this was a desultory siege. Without hope of relief, Ali, on 20 December 1925, handed over power to a provisional government which surrendered the Hijaz to Ibn Saud on 21 December. Medina had surrendered on 5 December.

Aside from the spiritual importance of the Holy Cities, Mecca and Medina, control over which conferred enormous prestige, the cities were important sources of revenue. Those in the Hijaz also enabled Ibn Saud to present himself as the successor to the Ottoman Sultan who had had garrisons in them before they fell to the Hashemites in the Great War. On 8 January 1926, Ibn Saud was proclaimed King of the Hijaz (being already Sultan of Nejd), and on 23 September 1932 the kingdom of Saudi Arabia was proclaimed.

Ibn Saud had to fight hard to consolidate his position. The Ikhwan revolt from 1928 to 1930 was a major challenge in which British arms supplies were vital to Ibn Saud in helping crush the rebellion. At the battle of Sibilla on 29 March 1929, Ibn Saud won by using trucks with mounted machine guns against the Ikhwan when they were in the open. Later that year, a surprise night attack defeated the Ikhwan at the battle of Hafr Al-Batin. In 1932, a rebellion in the Hijaz armed by the Emir of Transjordan was crushed by Ibn Saud as a result of better intelligence and the use of armoured cars as well as mounted troops. Moreover, the Asir region now became the seat of conflict, with neighbouring Yemen and Ibn Saud supporting rival clients. War between Yemen and Ibn Saud broke out in 1934. Ibn Saud's army was now mostly composed not of Ikhwan, but, instead, of levies. Many moved forward in trucks equipped with machine-guns and radios. This mobile force proved successful in the coastal lowlands, breaking through the Yemenis and capturing the port of Hudaida, but the column that moved through the mountains toward the Yemeni capital, Sana'a, proved vulnerable to ambushes and failed. Its vehicles were not suited to operations in such difficult terrain. As a result, Ibn Saud negotiated a peace in which his claims to Asir were recognized while he withdrew from Yemen.[22]

The trajectories of Saudi Arabia, Iraq, Persia (Iran), and Afghanistan serve as a reminder of the variety of developments within a part of the world that is generally ignored in inter-war military history or, at best, treated as a unit. While the tension between centralizing nationalists viewing their armed forces as sources of integration, and hostile tribes, can be seen as an important theme, one moreover that was more significant than interventions by outside powers, these themes played out through the particular circumstances of the individual states. State-building was more important in Iraq and Saudi Arabia than in Persia, as there was already a state in place in the latter.

Latin America

There was no conflict of the Saudi Arabian type in Latin America, which again underlines the diversity of warfare in this period. State boundaries remained stable, although there were tensions. In 1920, Chile deployed its army to face an apparently imminent attack from Bolivia, eager to regain its Pacific coastline (lost in 1879–83), but the attack never came. In 1929, Chile and Peru settled frontier differences from the same war over control of Tacna and Arica, thanks to American diplomatic assistance. The new frontier was finally agreed in 1932. There was also the risk of conflict between Chile and Argentina over rival territorial claims in the far south. Although the 1902 'Pacts of May' Treaty had broadly given Argentina sovereignty over the land on the Atlantic coastline and the Chileans on the Pacific coast, there were still differences regarding the territorial delineation, notably in the Beagle Channel. However, conflict was avoided.

Rebellions were mostly small-scale, but, in Latin America, the years after the Great War saw a continuation of earlier patterns of conflict. Serious political instability reflected acute economic pressures and social divisions, as well as only limited support for democratic practices. Much conflict was insurrectionary in character. Examples included the failed invasion of Costa Rica in May 1919 by exiles based in Nicaragua; the Liberal revolt in Nicaragua in 1925; and the War of the Cristeros in Mexico in 1927–9.

The last was a major Catholic rising against the revolutionary state with its agrarian reform and its attack on the church. The rising led to guerrilla warfare[23], and the army was used to suppress it. At the outset, unarmed demonstrating masses were machine-gunned. The rising proved intractable, with the army able to control the towns and the railways, but not the countryside. By June 1929, the rising was at its height, but a compromise between church and state that year ended a war which had cost 70,000 lives. American diplomacy again played a role in the settlement.

More generally, the military across Latin America acted against insurrections, and thus enforced the conservative social order. The frequent inability of rebels to confront the army directly, for example in the Chayanta rebellion in Bolivia in 1927[24], encouraged a brutal military policing that frequently relied on acts of terror. The rebellion was harshly put down, as an earlier one in Bolivia at Jesús ale Machaca had been in 1921. There was a socio-ethnic dimension, as the rebels were not only peasants but also from the indigenous Indian population. Similarly, the army was used to put down a miners' strike at Uncía in June 1923, with workers and their families indiscriminately killed in what was to prove the first of a number of mining massacres. The contrast with the far less violent conduct of French troops in the Ruhr that year is readily apparent. Miners' strikes were also broken elsewhere, as in June 1925 when hundreds of nitrate workers were killed in Tarapacá, Chile, once the navy had landed troops. The importance of mineral resources to state finances explained the determination of governments to suppress miners' strikes.

An ethnic dimension also played a role in regional opposition. For example, in 1926–7, the Mexican army, with air support, suppressed the Yaqui Indians in the troublesome province of Sonora. In July 1923, Pancho Villa, who had been a revolutionary leader in Mexico over the previous decade, and an effective guerrilla leader, was assassinated in a plot in which the army was clearly implicated.[25]

In Brazil, the military revolts in 1922 and 1924 were small-scale and suppressed by the loyal majority of the army, being finally defeated in 1927 after an attempt to take refuge in the interior had failed. In Venezuela in 1928, an attempted coup against the dictator, Juan Vicente Gómez, by military reformers backed by the Caracas cadets was suppressed by the garrison. In contrast, in 1925, in Ecuador, young army officers in the *Movimiento Juliano* seized power in a coup.

Military politics and rebellions were also a feature in Mexico. The President from 1920 to 1924 was Álvaro Obregón. He had been a prominent general in the civil wars of the 1910s and had taken power in 1920. In December 1923, Obregón was challenged by an insurrection by former colleagues opposed to his plans for the presidential succession. Obregón won, in part because the rebels were divided, and in part as he received American support, including munitions, aircraft, pilots, and a naval blockade of the strategically more important coast, that on the Gulf of Mexico. After three battles fought over 15 days, notably at Ocotlán, Obregón triumphed and the rebel leaders were shot. Obregón was ready to use exemplary violence to stamp his control on army and state. The execution of former comrades prefigured Stalin's zeal in this respect.[26]

Backed by Obregón, his successor, Plutarco Elias Calles, another nationalist soldier, was able to pre-empt another military rebellion in October 1927, and this proved the occasion for a fresh purge of the military leadership. Obregón was assassinated in July 1928 after being elected to succeed Calles. His successor, Emilio Portes Gil, faced a rebellion by Obregonistas in the army in March 1929, but this was speedily suppressed, the government being helped by the availability of American munitions. American intervention frequently proved critical in Latin America.

Successive purges of generals who were heavily committed to politics were important to the professionalization of the Mexican army by encouraging it to avoid intervention in politics. The purges also helped ensure increased state control, which made the army a reliable tool in the War of the Cristeros. Every country is different, but there were parallels between Mexican, Soviet and Chinese developments, not least revolutions, the disruptive character of civil wars, the issue of foreign intervention, and subsequent concern over control of the army.

In Chile, there was no comparable experience of civil war since 1891, but the military, notably the army which was about 25,000 strong, played a role in politics. In September 1924, President Arturo Alessandri resigned in the face of threatened military action, and a military *junta* took over, only for military action four months later to lead to the installation of another *junta* which let Alessandri back in. He was able to finish his term of office at the close of 1925.

Conclusions

The situation in Latin America was to be very different in the 1930s to that in the 1920s. The same is the case with China. The contrast between the two helps explain why warfare in the 'Third World' is divided between two chapters. At the same time, this contrast serves as a reminder that the developmental character of warfare was not limited to the West nor, elsewhere, a matter of the diffusion of the Western model.

4

Learning lessons

Adapting to the lessons of experience was a normal process for militaries as they sought to retain and enhance effectiveness. However, this process was never free from problems, not least the difficulty of deciding what the lessons were as well as the role in this situation of particular interests within the military. Different constituencies within national armed forces drew different lessons. Far from teaching lessons in an uncomplicated fashion, people derived the lessons they were looking for. The focus on the supposed lessons of the Great War faced the additional problem that there was an hitherto unprecedented range of experience to consider as the war had also seen air and submarine conflict. Commentators had to assess experience, impact and lessons, both on their own and in combination, and did so in terms of their own particular situation. There was an urgent wish to avoid a repetition of the costly stalemate of much of that conflict on the Western Front.[1] 'Never again' referred in military circles to an understanding of the serious consequences of attritional warfare, as well as to the political concern that any further war on that scale would, as in the case of Russia, Germany and elsewhere, undermine political stability, and indeed the entire structure of society.

As a consequence, there was a formal engagement by the military with understanding the recent war. The German army ordered a large number of staff officers to prepare studies of the recent conflict, a methodical instance of the wider process. In Britain, a framework for writing the history of the war was established. It offered a mass of information, though with less clarity about responsibility for failures.[2] The Soviets studied both the Great War and the Civil War. A commitment to the lessons taught by the Great War was particularly apparent in France where victory in the war was presented as demonstrating the value of its military system.[3]

Individual campaigns were considered, as well as warfare as a whole. For example, the German air offensive on London was closely studied by British airmen interested in the strategic potential of air power.[4] In light of the experience of the Great War, the British Treasury emphasized the absolute need to maintain economic strength and stability as a preparation for another struggle, while the Chiefs of Staff considered the implications in that war of weakening Germany by blockade.[5]

Learning lessons was a utilitarian procedure designed to ensure greater success in the next war. In this sense, 'never again' did not mean, 'never again a world war', but, rather, 'never again a world war fought in this manner'. In Britain, Germany, the Soviet Union, the USA, Italy and elsewhere, there was intellectual enquiry about the nature of war-winning, attempts to develop operational doctrine, concern about ensuring manoeuvrability and what would later be termed 'deep battle', and much interest in the potential of tanks, mechanized transport, and air-to-air, air-to-land and air-to-sea warfare, and in the enhanced communication capability offered by radio.[6]

Enhanced firepower also naturally attracted attention. The emergence of three-dimensional warfare in the last 18 months of the Great War was significant. Stagnation and immobility earlier in the conflict were to some degree an illusion as tactically the war was constantly changing; and the revival of successful mobility, both tactically and operationally, in 1918, came from these developments. However, little of this strand of enhanced capability on the Western Front by the closing campaign was evident in the 1920s due to a lack of heavy artillery in the conflicts of the decade.

Meanwhile, the weaponry developments of the Great War, such as the greater use of hand grenades, were absorbed into tactical doctrine. In 1923, General Lord Rawlinson, British Commander in Chief India, called for 'a centre to train all ranks in the scientific use of automatic weapons'.[7] No post-1918 Western army went back to the pre-war ways. Infantry was equipped and trained to fight a flexible battle with a range of weapons. One of the fundamental lessons of the Great War was the importance of training which was regularly updated and reiterated. It was by this means that every British infantryman had become proficient during the war with rifle, bayonet, hand and rifle grenades, and the Lewis gun. The problem for post-war armies was the cost of such training in specialist schools.

A key element in all of this thinking became that of manpower versus machines. Machines cost much money, not only to develop but also to introduce, supply and maintain. This was true both for complex machines, such as planes, and for more simple equipment, such as improved firearms. On the other hand, there were heavy costs entailed in providing for large numbers of troops, notably in training, paying, housing, clothing, and, decisive in wartime, feeding and supplying them. Indeed, much of the army was employed to train the large numbers of conscripts, which was why the French army was opposed to the shortening of military service to one year in 1927–8. To shorten the period, meant spending the money but only enjoying the benefit for a brief period.

Manpower or machines?

The victorious campaigns of 1918 had required both manpower and machines, but the massive expenditure and effort of those years could not be sustained in peacetime. There was a key political dimension, notably in the end or reduction of conscription, and in the limits imposed on the defeated. Britain went back to a system without conscription by choice, while Germany was made to do so. Manpower constraints posed a challenge to tactics and operations requiring the availability of large numbers of troops.

From the late nineteenth century, the organizational centrality of mass armies had been a defining characteristic that was as important as technological change for many powers, but not Britain nor the USA. The situation changed after the Great War. In a context of post-war debt and deflation, there was a political and social imperative to cut expenditure which, for many, increased interest in the idea of machines as a way to deliver increased capability at lower cost. The idea of limiting weaponry as an aspect of disarmament encouraged this process. The preference on the part of many commentators was one for an élite well-equipped force, which also entailed applying something of the navy model to armies. Furthermore, there was Futurism and similar links between modern weapons and certain political ideas.

That option clashed with institutional preferences for continuity and size, and with the careers bound up in traditional military structures. Other factors also played a major role. These included the need for numbers, notably for the maintenance of control in colonies and, if necessary, at home, and also in order to match the armies of other powers. Moreover, in the case of many governments, there was a strong preference for the very idea of a large army which was equated with the impression at least of national strength.

The clash became apparent in Italy. General Antonino Di Giorgio, the War Minister, favoured a small army with modern weapons providing firepower, mobility and offensive capacity; but the military leadership argued that this choice would weaken Italy. The cost was also a major problem.[8] In April 1925, the Fascist leader Benito Mussolini came out against Di Giorgio's proposals as he also wanted a large army. Di Giorgio resigned.

In Japan, the Imperial Way faction in the army pressed for an emphasis on manpower and the military spirit rather than on machines. Their call was for 'flesh before steel' and their belief that Japanese manpower had inherent and unique qualities that made them effective, or what others had called 'human bullets'. In 1928, the army's strategic manual was rewritten accordingly. Whereas, in the context of a serious fiscal situation after the devastating Tokyo earthquake of 1923, General Ugaki Kazushige, the Army Minister, had cut numbers in the mid-1920s in order to focus on equipment, notably planes and armies, General Araki Sadao in the early 1930s, at a time when Japan's economy was reeling from the Great Depression, was a keen supporter of the Imperial Way.[9]

The number of troops in the German army was restricted to 100,000 men under the Versailles Peace Settlement, but, by deliberately appointing a large number of non-commissioned officers, the army prepared for subsequent expansion. Moreover, from 1923 to 1934 the army secretly trained forces and developed weapons in the Soviet Union. The Soviets saw Weimar Germany as less of a threat than Britain and France, and cooperation with Germany as a way of dividing the West.

Soviet planners argued that they could and must have both mass and mechanization;[10] but numbers versus machines was a general issue across nations. It was also complicated by demographics as states with smaller populations than those of potential foes, France as opposed to Germany or Japan as opposed to China, sought ways to compensate for the lack of men. So also did states, such as Britain and the USA, that rejected conscription. Alliances, equipment and morale all appeared necessary solutions to manpower shortages, although, in the early 1930s, Douglas MacArthur, the American Chief of Staff, focused on maintaining manpower rather than on equipment. For France, the decision to build the fortifications of the Maginot Line, on which work began in 1930, was part of the equation in offering protection against German attack. The Maginot Line was both an economy of force measure and a means to create jobs. Collective images were also significant in the numbers versus machines debate. Thus, in Germany, the image of the tank played an important role in accounts explaining the adverse German military experience after 1916: the tank suggested human bravery overcome only by machines.[11]

In practice, ideas about new warfare, notably those of the systematizers of what future war would be like[12], advanced further than technological capability and resource availability, and often much further, as was to be shown in the early campaigns of the Second World War, notably on land and in the air. There were inherent problems with the application in weaponry and battle of many of the technological ideas and innovations, let alone fundamental questions about effectiveness. Moreover, inter-war investment in armed forces, constrained by contemporary economic realities, was too limited to permit an effective implementation of new doctrine, both in equipment and in training. This situation was a problem, for example, for the American army and also for British preparations for amphibious operations[13], although more than resources were involved. For example, thanks to inter-service rivalry, the Americans also found it difficult to develop appropriate combined arms doctrine.[14]

In 1928, Montgomery-Massingberd, then head of Britain's Southern Command, wrote of developments with tanks, 'The whole question is one of money'.[15] The availability of funds was a matter, critics could argue, not only of the choice involved in force structure, but also of the weaknesses of liberal democracy in not permitting effective rearmament until the danger was obvious, when it was generally too late. However, such rearmament would have flown in the face of the new world order decided upon at Versailles with its emphasis on disarmament and collective security through the League of Nations. Montgomery-Massingberd also emphasized the problems of choice, not least in terms of the diversity of developing possibilities in mechanized warfare, and the sense of new potential:

> What we want most at present undoubtedly is light tanks or machine gun carriers, people are not however clear which will be best . . . It looks to me as if the cavalry will want the light tanks and the infantry the machine gun carriers. I don't think there is really very much difference between the two, except that the tanks will have more armour and normally machine guns will fire from them, while it will be the exception to fire from the machine gun carriers, and they will normally be taken out and used on the tripod . . . The latest Carden Lloyd tanks . . a great advance . . . One trial machine did 49 miles an hour, which for a track machine seems almost undreamable.[16]

Such tanks were vulnerable to other tanks and to anti-tank fire, but most of the British tanks of the period focused on speed and manoeuvrability, at the expense of firepower and armour.

British military commitments in the 1920s actually focused on the empire where the experience of the Great War had shaken Britain's authority and there were serious problems in establishing and consolidating new gains. Moreover, both force structure and operational doctrine were affected by the Ten Year Rule, adopted by the British government in August 1919, which argued, with reason, that there would be no major conflict for ten years, and, therefore, that the British did not have to prepare for an imminent war on the Continent. This situation did not preclude interest in capabilities for such a conflict, but ensured that there was a focus on the wider time-scale. In the 1920s, with the Soviet Union checked by the Poles, German armed forces limited by the Versailles settlement, and Balkan tensions containable without war, the most pressing military problems for Britain, France and the USA appeared to be imperial: colonial in the case of the first two, and within the informal American empire for the third.

A lack of funds, moreover, was a major problem for the inter-war American armed forces, and fed through into deficiencies in equipment. Yet, there were also limitations in doctrine. For example, tank warfare was given little role and no independence under the National Defense Act of 1920. Instead, the tank corps was abolished and tanks were allocated to the infantry.[17] The cavalry circumvented the new structure by purchasing tanks and calling them 'combat cars'.[18] However, the American army also made a serious attempt to assess the lessons of the recent war, and devoted much attention to the military education of officers.[19]

Learning lessons was scarcely an easy process for, aside from issues of applying conclusions, there was a lack of clarity as to why the Allies had been successful in 1918. Different arms argued their case. For example, there was resistance to accepting the obsolescence of cavalry. Lieutenant-General Philip Chetwode, the Inspector-General of Cavalry in the British army, complained in 1921 'how much the apparent success of the cavalry in Palestine has mesmerised' the cavalry lobby. He countered that if the Turks in 1918 had had gas, tanks, planes and firepower, the cavalry would have achieved far less.[20]

Very differently, the use of gas in the Great War seemed to offer lessons, as well as require fresh consideration. Charles Foulkes, Director of Gas Services for the British forces in France in 1917–18, toured India in 1919–20 in order to lecture and to consider how best to employ gas against hostile tribesmen on the North-West Frontier, producing a guide, *Gas Warfare on the Indian Frontier*.[21] In 1926, the British Chemical Warfare Research Department proposed the establishment of a small research and experimental organization for India, as it would 'allow a commencement to be made with the investigation of certain offensive aspects of the subject, which can only be done under Indian conditions'.[22]

Neither cavalry nor gas had been crucial in 1918, although much of the artillery had fired gas shells. Instead, the Allies had won thanks to the success of infantry-artillery cooperation. Both sides recognized this as the key from early 1915 onward, and the remainder of the war, at least on the Western Front, can be viewed in terms of the quest for effective infantry manoeuvre under artillery cover. However, this threat was lost after 1918 as air power and mechanization received all the attention. The value of infantry-artillery cooperation was widely overlooked in the 1920s, notably in public discussion, because of greater interest in the potential of mechanized warfare.

Fuller and Liddell Hart

The development of mechanized forces was accompanied by debate about their operational employment, in particular concerning the new tactics of combined arms operations. It was difficult to discern 'correct' doctrine. In the last stages of the war, J. F. C. Fuller, a British colonel responsible for planning tank operations, had, in May 1918, devised 'Plan 1919', a strategy based on a large-scale tank offensive designed to penetrate deep into opposing territory, rather than simply supporting an infantry attack on the front line. Fuller saw this deep penetration as leading to the disintegration of opposition cohesion, and an attendant demoralization that would compromise fighting quality. This offensive strategy, by its impetus, was designed to provide effective protection for the attacking power.[23]

Fuller subsequently served at the Staff College, before becoming an assistant to the Chief of the Imperial General Staff. In 1926, visiting India on behalf of the War Office, Fuller emphasized the need for the Indian Army to mechanize. He presented this as at once an aspect of modernity and a necessary response to a public opinion that, in the aftermath of the Great War, did not want to face heavy casualties. Fuller argued that the navy and air force 'were mechanized forces, materially highly progressive', but he thought the Indian Army reflected 'its surroundings' in being Oriental, a process and term that amounted to condemnation.[24] Promoted to major general, but placed on half-pay in 1930, the independent-minded Fuller was retired for criticizing the quality of generals. He became a military correspondent, notably for the *Daily Mail*.

Following Fuller, Basil Liddell Hart, an ex-army officer turned military correspondent and ardent self-publicist, developed notions of rapid tank warfare, although he also argued that the infantry retained an offensive role. Publicly expressed in his pieces as military correspondent for the *Daily Telegraph* (1925–35) and *The Times* (1935–9), Liddell Hart's ideas also had an influence on British armoured manoeuvres in the 1930s, while he and Fuller were cited by the Inspector of the Royal Tank Corps in his report to the 1926 committee on the reorganization of the cavalry.[25] Both men reflected a characteristic of the period, the drive of a new generation to correct the real and apparent failings of their elders.[26]

Liddell Hart's interest in weaponry and tactics rested on a clear strategic vision. He was particularly keen to advocate advances that did not entail frontal attacks; the 'indirect approach' that emphasized manoeuvre, not the attrition that was held responsible for the casualties and indecisiveness of the Great War. In his *The Decisive Wars of History* (1929), Liddell Hart pressed the case for attacking the enemy where they were not expecting it, and for using mechanized forces to bypass the flanks of enemy armies in order to hit their communications and bases, a theme he returned to in *The British Way of Warfare* (1932). Clausewitz, in contrast, was castigated by Liddell Hart, in the lectures published as *The Ghost of Napoleon* (1933), for an emphasis on mass and direct attack.[27] A stress on the 'indirect approach' also offered the possibility of integrating the amphibious capability brought by naval superiority into British strategy.

Although he was read by those who in the late 1930s pressed for expenditure on the RAF and the navy, rather than the dispatch of an army Field Force to the Continent, Liddell Hart was to exaggerate his influence, and to be accused of 'mis-statement, perversions of fact, half-truths, and quotations taken out of their context'.[28] The complexity of problems was not his forte.[29] It has also been argued that his ideas, along with those of other British exponents of tank operations and reports of British manoeuvres, did not influence German *blitzkrieg* tactics and operational art in the Second World War to the extent that was once claimed, notably by Liddell Hart, but it has also been argued that the Germans were influenced by his early articles.[30]

Mechanized warfare

These tactics and operational art were a development of mechanized warfare and of the offensive tactics and operational art employed by the Germans in 1917–18, and also drew on the emphasis on an effective combined arms doctrine developed under Hans von Seeckt, Commander in Chief of the *Reichswehr* in 1920–6.[31] At the same time, defensive planning remained important in Germany[32], while traditional operational concepts continued to play a central role in the thinking and practice of the German army. This was an aspect of a German conservatism and continuity that can be seen as a source of success in 1939–40. However, German military concepts also reflected a strategic short-sightedness that focused on a battle of annihilation, in the manner of Moltke the Younger in 1914, rather than a consideration of the wider political context, in which the means of converting victory on the battlefield into a successful conclusion to the war played a major role.[33]

The focus in much of the popular literature on new developments in mechanized warfare has to be put in context, especially for Britain in the 1920s. The extent to which large-scale tank attacks were not mounted in the last two months of the war encouraged officers who emphasized the role of more traditional weaponry, particularly artillery[34], and artillery-infantry coordination had indeed played a major role in the Allied victory in 1918. Moreover, Fuller exaggerated what tanks could have achieved in 1919. There were serious operating and tactical deficiencies in their use, while the development of anti-tank doctrine, tactics and weaponry would have affected their tactical effectiveness.[35] Furthermore, the tanks of the 1920s were not sufficiently developed to meet the expectations of Fuller and Liddell Hart. Firepower and armour were crucial to success in battle, but most inter-war tanks were deficient in both. Instead of the more powerfully armed battle tank, the British emphasized the faster, more manoeuvrable so-called infantry tank, which, in the event in the Second World War, proved vulnerable in combat with other tanks. Moreover, the role of the tank was not clearly assessed in inter-war Germany, which did not possess well-armed tanks until the arrival of the up-gunned MkIVs in 1942. The role of tanks changed from infantry support to tank-tank encounters during the Second World War. The ability to aim and shoot on the move was not available until the 1950s and 1960s with the development of stabilized gun systems and fast traversing turrets.

More profoundly, tanks were not yet suited to the operational role given them in plans for a large-scale advance. Logistics, notably the supply of petrol, as well as fuel capacity, range and mechanical reliability, were key issues for breakthrough operations. After the Second World War, multi-fuel engines were a focus of development so that tanks could run on any fuel.[36] Indeed, Soviet planning of the 1920s for breakthrough operations presupposed exploitation largely by cavalry. However, by the late 1920s, the Soviets were building large numbers of tanks to serve that purpose as well. These were small and lightly armoured, and carried machine guns. In 1928, the military's procurement plan was that just under half the tanks it would receive over the next five years would be of this type. The Red Army's massive 1932 tank programme of 10,000 tanks included 5,000 T-27s of this type, and in 1941 there were still 3,000, of various models. These light tanks were intended to take cavalry roles of screening, reconnaissance, raiding and the exploitation of breakthroughs.

As with aircraft, the tanks of 1940 were different to those of 1918 because there were developments in specifications and capabilities. Thus, the Vickers Medium Mark I, of which deliveries began in 1923, was the first British tank in service with a revolving turret. The colonial context also continued to be important. A General Staff minute of September 1919, circulated by Churchill, as Secretary of State for War, to the War Cabinet, focused on the achievements of British armoured cars in France in 1918, adding:

> It is to be noted that these results were obtained in so-called trench warfare, that is when there is no open flank to manoeuvre round. Imagine the possibilities of half-a-dozen such units boldly handled in conjunction with light tanks and a cavalry force where there is an open flank! . . . In all Eastern theatres the value of these cars is constantly being brought to notice, while for internal troubles and industrial "unrest" they are an admirable specific.[37]

Chetwode argued in 1921 that tank specifications and tactics ought to focus on colonial commitments, rather than the possibility of conflict with other regular forces. He pressed accordingly for tanks to be armed with a machine-gun, not a heavier gun, and for training in the use of tanks against opponents equipped with artillery and machine guns, but not tanks.[38] Eight years later, Montgomery-Massingberd commented on the need to develop vehicles able to withstand the rocky terrain of India[39], terrain which was very difficult for armoured cars and much different to the deep clay soils of northern France.

Aside from the question of the terrain for tanks, there was also, as a result of the Great War, a greater commitment to lorries as a part of the supply system, and notably in the absence of rail links. Warning against British intervention in Turkish Armenia in 1920, the British General Staff commented 'before operations could commence, the Trebizond-Erzerum road would require to be remade to take mechanical transport, an immense undertaking considering the distances and the grades'.[40]

While military tasking appeared readily comprehensible, albeit the subject for debate, a sense of flux was very strong in the case of capability and notably the respective advantages of particular arms. Thus, Chetwode suggested in 1921 that 'the tank would not prove to be such a formidable engine of war as people think and that before long it will have lost much of its terror', but he was more convinced of the threat of air attack on ground formations and emphasized that cavalry officers needed to think 'of the war of the future', not least in developing cooperation with tanks and planes.[41] The following year, Rawlinson opposed the proposal of the government of India to abolish a division in order to add two more air squadrons in India.[42] In 1926, Colonel Lindsay, the Inspector of the Royal Tank Corps, was in no doubt that cavalry was too vulnerable to modern small arms:

> All civil evolution is towards the elimination of manpower and animal power, and the substitution of mechanical power. History shows that the military mind has usually lagged behind in its appreciation of civil evolution and its possibilities . . . in the army we must substitute machine and weapon power for man and animal power in every possible way, and that to do this we must carefully watch, and where necessary foster, those trends of civil evolution that will help us to this end.

Lindsay was certain that this capacity was linked to industrial capability: 'We are the nation above all others who can develop the mobile mechanical and weapon-power army, for we have long service soldiers and a vast industrial organisation'.

Other respondents were less happy about the wisdom of dispensing with cavalry and, instead, urged its combination with mechanized forces.[43] It was also unclear which vehicles would be most appropriate. Thus, in 1927, Field-Marshal Sir George Milne, the Chief of the Imperial General Staff, told the officers of the experimental Mechanized Force, that it was necessary to have vehicles that would be immune to poison gas. As an indication of the sense of transience and of the imminent unknowns in military planning, Milne also claimed that 'in a very few years the petrol engine itself will have to give way to something else'.[44]

Greater mobility had a major impact on planning needs and doctrine by accentuating logistical issues and leading to the development of an operational dimension to warfare. The former owed something to the pressures of keeping up with advances and supplying fuel, while the latter responded to the need for a combined arms approach able to make best use of new weapons.

The value of applying present perspectives is exemplified by the subject of this chapter as the recent process and implementation of strategic review in Britain in 2010–11 have been seen to be greatly intertwined with politics, both within the military and beyond. The bitterness of this politics overcame the theory of jointness within the military, and tensions between the branches of the latter were also played out through allies in the press and in public debate. This situation throws light on the debates of the 1920s and 1930s, not least in terms of locating and evaluating the public discussion. Conventionally, this discussion has had the central role in scholarly argument, not least with the attention devoted to Liddell Hart. However, it is apparent from considering the 2010 Strategic Review that the key debates took place within the military and between them and the politicians, and it is on these that attention should profitably focus.

The earlier fixing of naval size by the Washington conference in 1922 ensured that much of the debate in Britain and elsewhere revolved around the army. Moreover, this debate reflected the extent to which, in the eyes of some, the prospect of tank warfare had transformed conflict on land. In the 1920s, the submarine and aircraft did not attract comparable attention at sea as belief in surface ships remained very strong.

For lesser powers, the army tended to be relatively even more important than for their mightier counterparts. If they had a navy or air force, these tended to be weak, and obviously so, while armies were also important for civil control. Lesser powers frequently lacked the industrial capability of producing new mechanized weaponry and also the interests linked to such industrial concerns. However, the active arms trade helped counter this military deficiency. Thus, threatened by Mussolini's expansionism, Yugoslavia in the 1920s was able to obtain arms from France, Belgium and Czechoslovakia. Moreover, the process of alliance deterrence worked to spread the influence of advanced military forces. France's treaty with Yugoslavia in 1927 helped deter Italy. War was inseparable from politics, as was capability from diplomacy.

The social politics of the military

Aside from the role of conventional party politics as well as the significance of patronage within the officer corps, politics in the widest sense was also important to the composition and structure of the military. Class, ethnic and religious distinctions remained highly significant, with inclusion and exclusion both important practices. Traditional concepts about the essential suitability of the landed orders to act as officers and commanders remained strong, as did their converse, the view that peasants and workers inherently lacked the necessary characteristics and value. These assumptions were particularly important for fighting units in armies, and less so for engineering or supply branches.

In functional terms, such ideas represented a limitation on efficiency and excellence, although one that was different in kind to that arising from the exclusion of women from the military process, other than as providers and supporters. In ideological terms, there was an emphasis on professionalism, but, despite the rise of formal military education, this professionalism was constructed in large part in social terms. In particular, there was heavy emphasis on the landed orders, both in entry to military colleges and in subsequent promotion. Ethnicity also played a role. An example is the Indian Army where British racial and religious attitudes played a major role in recruitment with long-standing consequences. In Latin America, officers tended to be of European descent and soldiers of native background.

The social politics of the military interacted with institutional structures and practices, notably in the often harsh treatment of ordinary rankers, whether they were volunteers or conscripts. Such discipline was seen as a necessary means not only for ensuring and maintaining fighting effectiveness, but also to enable the military to be employed for social control.

5

Naval developments

In many senses, the naval situation was similar to that in the contemporary world. After a conflict (the Great War for then, the Cold War for now) that had defined naval superiority, there was no large-scale conflict to chart subsequent shifts in capability nor the impact of technology. The Great War defined naval superiority in terms of Allied, particularly British, predominance, although it left the issue of submarine versus battleship partly unresolved and the role of naval air forces completely undefined. In the inter-war period, shifts in capability and the impact of technology were both important, as was the key role of political concerns in shaping strategic tasking and plans. From the outset, the growth of Japanese naval power proved an unpredictable challenge for Britain and the USA, rather as that of China has been for the USA over the last decade, although China today lacks the aggressive military culture Japan had in the inter-war years. Subsequent to the growth of Japanese naval ambitions, the rise of German and Italian naval power and uncertainties over their naval intentions also became of great significance.

Naval limitations

The Armistice at the close of the Great War was followed by the surrender of the German fleet to the British. At Harwich, 176 U-boats (submarines) surrendered, while the ships of the High Seas Fleet were interned at the British base of Scapa Flow in the Orkneys. The Germans ceased to be a significant naval power. They scuttled their ships at Scapa Flow in 1919, while the Peace of Versailles denied Germany permission to build a replacement fleet, limiting both the number and type of warships it might have. As German air forces were prohibited, there was no fleet air arm. Moreover, as part of the 1919 peace settlement, the merchant ships seized from Germany were allocated to the victors in proportion to their wartime maritime losses.

The Austrian fleet disappeared with the collapse of the Habsburg monarchy and the loss of an Adriatic coastline now divided between Italy and Yugoslavia. Although not so seriously affected, Russia was also hard hit, with its navy and shipbuilding capacity badly affected by the civil war of 1917–22. In 1926, the Russian navy was reduced to a section of the army. It did not regain an independent status until December 1937.

The Great War therefore led to a fundamental transformation in naval power politics. The naval challenge to Britain now came from the increased naval power of two of her wartime allies, the USA and Japan. This competition was to be played out after the war in the diplomacy of naval limitation that led to the Washington Naval Conference of 1921–2 and the Washington Naval Treaty of 1922. However, wartime alliance followed by the success of these negotiations ensured that naval competition ceased to be the key theme that it had been prior to the outbreak of the Great War with the Anglo-German naval race.

Britain's alliance with America during the Great War led to post-war interest in cooperation, as in Halford Mackinder's suggestion, in his *Democratic Ideals and Reality: A Study in the Politics of Reconstruction* (1919), of joint Anglo-American trusteeship over the key naval positions of Singapore, Aden, Suez, Malta, Gibraltar and Panama in order to assure the 'peace of the ocean'. Such notions were fanciful in the context of this period, although they looked toward later cooperation. Moreover, the experience of wartime cooperation played a role in the process by which Britain, in the Washington Naval Treaty, accepted naval parity, a 'one power naval standard', with America, the leading industrial and financial power in the world. Britain did so under pressure from harsh fiscal circumstances and from demands for social welfare, and in the shadow of the build-up of the American navy ordered in 1916 which, had it happened, Britain could not have matched; although Congress did not vote the money for the 'Navy Second to None' until 1940.

This parity was a marked departure from the two power naval standard – a navy equal in size to the next two naval powers – that had been pursued by Britain in the late nineteenth century and the 'one plus sixty per cent' standard pursued pre-war. America's position was also enhanced in 1922 because the Anglo-Japanese Alliance of 1902, which was up for renewal, was replaced, instead, by a Four-Power (Britain, USA, Japan, France) Treaty committing the powers to respect each other's Pacific possessions and to consult in the event of conflict.

In addition, both Britain and the USA acknowledged the fact of Japanese naval power in the Pacific. A 5:5:3 ratio in capital ship tonnage for Britain, the USA and Japan was agreed in the Washington Naval Treaty[1], with 525,000 the total battleship tonnage for each of the first two, while the quotas for France and Italy were 35 per cent of the capital ship tonnage of Britain. The French had unsuccessfully hoped for parity with Japan. Communist Russia was left out of the new agreement. More generally, the treaty comprised an agreement to scrap many battleships, in service or under construction, and to stop new construction for ten years. The latter provision was extended by the London Naval Treaty of 1930, an agreement designed to last until 1936.

By fixing ratios, the Washington Naval Treaty appeared to end the prospect of naval races between the major powers. The treaty also limited warships other than capital ships to 10,000 tons and 8-inch guns (reduced to 6-inch as a result of the 1930 London Conference). In the inter-war period, there was a building of heavy cruisers that met these limits, rather than of the battleships built prior to 1914. Although two battleships (with 16-inch guns) were completed in 1927, Britain, indeed, did not lay down any battleships between January 1923 and December 1936.

The 1922 treaty also included a clause stopping the military development of American colonies in the western Pacific, the British base of Hong Kong, and also of many of Japan's island possessions in the region. This clause greatly affected the American ability to exercise sea power as it meant that naval bases in the western Pacific could not be improved.[2] Despite British efforts in 1922 and 1930, there were no limitations on submarines, although the Peace of Versailles in 1919 had banned Germany from using them. The French were keen to prevent limits on submarine warfare and built the most in the 1920s, in part in response to the limitations on their fleet under the Washington Naval

Treaty and, in part, in response to an emphasis on a defensive fleet: some of the submarines were for coastal defence.[3] The 1930 London Conference's decision that submarines should only sink non-combatant ships after giving fair warning, did not represent a practical limitation on what submarines might do in the future.

The force structure

The combined impact of submarines and air power in the Great War, and their likely future role, suggested to many a fundamental change both in naval capability and in the tactical, operational and strategic aspects of naval power. As a consequence, naval methods and goals had to be rapidly rethought. Thus, submarines had altered the nature of commerce-raiding and made blockade more difficult.

At the same time, submarines had fundamental limitations which were related to their varied specifications and roles. They could not travel submerged for long distances, although the Schnorkel enabled diesel engines to be run while submerged to periscope depth. Only nuclear-powered boats can remain submerged indefinitely. Thus, submarines spent more time on the surface than submerged. There was also a contrast in roles between the emphasis on stealth, which enabled a submarine to mount surprise attacks, and thus to counter the greater firepower advantage of warships, and, on the other hand, the need, if action was to be more effective, to come close to, or to, the surface: in the former case to periscope depth and in the latter to make more speed. However, in doing so, submarines compromised stealth as, even if not on the surface, periscope and torpedo wakes could be tracked. Moreover, close to the surface, submarines were visible to aircraft and vulnerable to air attack. This use of aircraft had developed from the latter stages of the Great War.

Submarine warfare emphasized a major difference between naval and land capability: the former was restricted to a few powers, and thus the options to be considered in terms of strategic goals and doctrine were limited. Admiral Lord Jellicoe, the former British First Sea Lord, argued that submarines destroyed the feasibility of close blockades of opposing harbours so as to prevent hostile warships sailing out, and, instead, led to a reliance for trade protection on convoys protected by cruisers. He was worried that Britain had insufficient cruisers both to do this and to work with the battle fleet in a future war.

British Admiralty concern about the impact of naval limitations on the size and number of ships was also expressed by Admiral Sir Charles Madden, the First Sea Lord, in a meeting of the Cabinet Committee preparing for the 1930 London Naval Conference. He

> . . . explained that it was not possible to build a battleship of less than 25,000 tons with the necessary quantities of armament, speed and protection, which would include an armoured deck of 5" [thick armour] and 6", to keep out bombs and plunging shell, and have sufficient protection under water against mines, torpedoes and bombs . . . The Admiralty required a sufficient number of cruisers to give security to the overseas trade of the Empire against raiding forces of the enemy and a battlefleet to give cover to the trade-protecting cruisers.[4]

The problem with negotiating parity agreements was that every naval power had different force requirements to meet its strategic needs. For example, with less long-range trade to protest, the Americans needed far fewer cruisers than the British, and this difference led to a serious Anglo-American dispute over cruiser numbers at, and after, the Geneva Naval Conference of 1927. The Americans wanted bigger cruisers with longer cruising ranges because they lacked Britain's network of bases at which their ships could re-fuel. Since disarmament agreements worked on the basis of total tonnage, the Americans would have fewer (but bigger) cruisers and the British would have more (but smaller) cruisers. However, for the Royal Navy, if American-style bigger cruisers were built by Japan, then the smaller British cruisers would be out-gunned. Therefore, the British Admiralty wanted qualitative arms limitation rather than quantitative. At the 1930 London Naval Conference, the British government, against Admiralty wishes, agreed to a limit of 50 cruisers.

As had been the case before the Great War, efforts to develop naval strength and weaponry were complicated by acute controversy over the potential of different weapons systems in any future naval war. The respective merits of air power (both from aircraft carriers and shore-based), of surface gunnery (especially from battleships), and of submarines, were all extensively discussed, as well as their likely tactical and strategic combinations. These debates were part of a more long-standing process of naval development seen in the rapid and almost continued adoption of new types of warship, naval armament and naval tactics in the period 1840–1960 in response to fundamental changes in ship power and design. This situation owed much to an industrial culture eager to embrace the positive response to technological innovation.

Although some theorists argued that battleships were now obsolete in the face of air power and submarines, with, for example, a revival in France of the *Jeune École* ideas of obsolescence associated with the battleship, nevertheless, big surface warships had a continued appeal and not simply for the European powers. Indeed, there was opposition to making carriers the key capital ship; in the 1930s, the Americans, British and Japanese put a major emphasis on battle-fleet tactics based on battleships. Given the serious weakness of naval aviation, this emphasis was not simply a sign of conservatism, although that played an important role. However, the British, the most experienced of the major navies, also displayed adaptability in their tactics.[5] The Germans were also fascinated by battleships.

It was argued that battleships could be protected against air attack, while carriers (correctly) appeared vulnerable to gunnery, and the Great War had showed that submarine campaigns could be beaten. Pre-1939 navies, the Japanese providing a particularly good example, conceived of carriers and submarines as a subordinate part of fleets that emphasized battleships, only to find in the Second World War that, while battleships were important, carriers were more useful. Even so many important developments in naval aviation, notably an ability to fly at night and in adverse conditions, did not occur until the 1950s.

The role of battleships was enhanced by the absence of a major change in battleship design comparable to those in the late nineteenth century and the 1900s. Indeed, with the arrival of the dreadnoughts, battleship archi-tecture had reached a new period of relative stability and existing battleships remained effective. For example, the USS *New York* (BB-34) of 1914, *Texas* (BB-35) of 1914, and *Nevada* (BB-36) of 1916, participated in the D-Day bombardment in 1944. The *Texas*'s ten 14-inch guns could fire 1½ rounds per minute; each armour-piercing shell weighing 1,500 lb. There was still great interest in such weaponry, both for ship destruction, of comparable and different ships, and for shore bombardment including the destruction of harbours and the covering of amphibious attacks.

Moreover, there were considerable efforts to strengthen battleships, as well as other ships, in order to increase their resistance to air attack. Armour was enhanced to resist bombs, outer hulls added to protect against torpedo attack from planes, submarines or surface ships, and anti-aircraft guns and tactics developed, not least with improved fire-control.[6] Furthermore, more accurate fire with the main battleship guns was achieved through the addition of computers to integrate course and speed calculations into fire-control systems. Air spotting for naval gunfire also developed in the 1920s and 1930s. This improvement in battleship capability is a reminder of the danger of assuming that a weapons system is necessarily static, which is a conclusion too often drawn when discussing battleships.

In the Second World War, surface ships were crucial for conflict with other surface ships. Moreover, although there were spectacular losses, many battleships took considerable punishment before being sunk by air attack. Battleships were not supposed to operate by themselves but in tandem with auxiliary ships that could serve to enhance anti-aircraft capabilities. Air attack was less effective against armoured ships than the Royal Navy had expected, and most losses were to submarines or other armoured surface ships. The real surprise was to be the vulnerability of smaller ships to air attack. For the British, an anti-warship and anti-submarine air capability was not pushed to the fore pre-war while the Royal Air Force (RAF) controlled the delivery of maritime air power and focused on its preferred option of a strategic bombing force, although it is important to remember the extent to which standard histories of naval aviation involve myths, in this case Royal Navy accounts designed to attack the RAF.

In a reminder of the need not to focus simply on one element, other factors also encouraged an emphasis on capital ships. Until reliable all-weather day and night reconnaissance and strike aircraft were available (which was really in the 1950s), surface ships provided the means of fighting at night. In addition, battleships were still necessary while other powers maintained them because they provided the required offensive armament and defensive armour with which to confront other battleships.

Naval air power

There was no experience before the Second World War, of conflict between aircraft carriers, but there was considerable confidence in their potential. In 1919, Jellicoe, who was very concerned about the strategic relationship with Australia and New Zealand, pressed for a British Far East Fleet, to include four carriers as well as eight battleships, in order to deter Japan[7], while, in 1920, Rear-Admiral Sir Reginald Hall MP argued in *The Times* that, thanks to aircraft and submarines, the days of the battleship were over. The British Admiralty remained convinced of the value of battleships but was not opposed to carriers. Inter-war planning called for a carrier to every two or three capital ships, and every two or three cruisers on the trade routes. The key to British attitudes was that aircraft had to be integral to the fleet, whereas in the American and Japanese navies carriers operated separately and were variously regarded as auxiliaries and rivals to battleships.

A determination to employ the new capability offered by naval aviation was rapidly apparent. Carriers were used when Britain intervened against the Communists in the Russian Civil War, while the varied attacking capability of the Royal Navy was also shown in the successful motor torpedo boat attack on the Soviet naval base of Kronstadt in August 1919. In addition, the carrier HMS *Argus* was stationed near the Dardanelles during the Chanak crisis between Britain and Turkey in 1922. There was also a carrier on the China Station in the late 1920s, first *Hermes* and then *Argus*. *Argus* landed six planes at Shanghai in 1927[8], strengthening the European position in the face of the conflict between Chinese forces. Another carrier, *Furious*, took place in the major naval exercises in the late 1920s.[9] The *Eagle*, commissioned in 1923, was the first British flush-deck carrier, while the Fleet Air Arm of the RAF was formed the following year. The number of planes in the Fleet Air Arm rose, but only to 144 by the end of the 1920s.

The *Eagle* was a converted dreadnought, while *Argus* was built on a hull intended for a passenger liner and *Furious*, *Glorious* and *Courageous* were converted from the battle cruisers of those names. Prior to the *Illustrious* class, only *Hermes* (commissioned 1924) of Britain's original six carriers was built keel up as a carrier. *Furious*, when first converted, had separate fore and aft decks separated by the ship's original centreline battle cruiser superstructure, and therefore did not become a flush-deck carrier until a subsequent more radical reconstruction.

At sea, air power was greatly restricted in the 1910s and 1920s by the difficulty of operating aeroplanes in bad weather and the dark, by their limited load capacity and range, and by mechanical unreliability, but improvements continued, especially in the 1930s. New arrester gears were fitted which helped slow planes down while landing on carriers. Because the equipment could be reset automatically it could handle sequential landings. Hydraulically reset traverse arrester gear was in use by the Royal Navy by 1933.

Carrier doctrine and tactics also advanced. The need to attack first was taken for granted as hitting the enemy carrier first would hinder its ability to respond. Reliable defence against air attack was difficult. Defending fighters and their control system lacked this capability, while anti-aircraft guns were of only limited value, not least in protecting such a big target.

The Americans and Japanese made major advances with naval aviation and aircraft carriers, in part because they would be key powers in any struggle for control of the Pacific.[10] The *Langley*, a converted collier, was, in 1922, the first American carrier to be commissioned, followed, in 1927, by two converted battle cruisers, the *Lexington* and the *Saratoga*. This basis helped ensure that American carriers were very fast: 33 knots against a 21-knot battle fleet, which forced the carriers to operate separately and made it difficult for the American navy to develop an integrated naval system. The *Lexington* and *Saratoga* were each designed to carry 63 planes. The Japanese commissioned six carriers between 1922 and 1939: some converted but others purpose-built as carriers. The *Akagi*, a converted battle cruiser, commissioned in 1927 was designed to carry 91 planes, the *Kaga*, with 90 planes, following in 1928.

Britain was part of the same process as it had a carrier fleet intended to compete with that of Japan. In contrast, Germany, Italy and the Soviet Union did not build aircraft carriers in the inter-war period, and France only had one, the *Béarn*, a converted dreadnought which was insufficiently fast to be considered an important asset. Moreover, concern about its vulnerability to shore-based Italian planes, restricted its value in the Mediterranean. The

Soviet emphasis, not on carriers but on shore-based planes, reflected the Soviet assumption that their naval operations would take place in the Gulf of Finland or otherwise close to Soviet-controlled coastlines.

Britain's carrier construction gave an important added dimension to her naval superiority over other European powers. In addition to the carriers in commission in the 1920s, four 23,000-ton carriers, the *Illustrious* class, each able to make over 30 knots and having a 3-inch armoured flight deck, were laid down in 1937, following the 22,000-ton *Ark Royal,* laid down in 1935 and completed in November 1938. British and American carrier and aircraft design diverged because of differing conceptions of future naval war. In the Second World War, the British armoured-deck carriers proved less susceptible to bombs and Japanese *kamikaze* aircraft than the American wooden-deckers as they tended not to penetrate the former. The 23,450 *Implacable* was laid down in February 1939, although it was not commissioned until August 1944.

The organization of air power in the inter-war period remains significant to debates about the role and capability of air power today. In the inter-war period, this organization was linked to fundamental issues of strategic, operational and tactical capability and conduct. Despite pressure from the Royal Navy, naval air power in Britain lacked a separate institutional framework, because naval air power was placed under the RAF between 1918 and May 1939, when it was returned to the navy by the Inskip Award of 1937. Moreover, the RAF was primarily concerned with land-based aeroplanes, and had little time for their naval counterparts.[11]

In France, the Air Ministry, established in 1928, gained nearly all naval air assets, and this helped ensure that plans for more carriers were not pursued there until 1938 when a second, the *Joffre,* was laid down. In 1936, the French navy had regained control of naval aviation. Nevertheless, more effective land-based aircraft in the 1930s threatened carrier operations in European waters, notably in the Mediterranean, and this lessened French interest in such warships. In Germany, the *Luftwaffe* took control over all military aviation, angering the navy which had earlier developed an air capability forbidden under the peace settlement. In the USA, there was a very different situation thanks to the Bureau of Aeronautics of the American navy created in 1921, which stimulated the development of effective air-sea doctrine, operational policies and tactics.

In addition to developments in aircraft carriers, there were also marked improvements in aircraft, notably as air frames became larger and more powerful in the 1930s. The Americans and British developed dive bombing tactics in the 1920s and, subsequently, dive bombers. However, they did not replace torpedo-bombers (aircraft launching torpedoes). Torpedo-bombers were vulnerable to defensive firepower but best able to sink armoured ships.[12] American air-to-sea doctrine also developed, notably with an emphasis on attacking capital ships. The number of planes in the American Naval Air Arm rose from 1,081 in 1925 to 2,050 in 1938; a larger figure than in the Army Air Corps.

Tasks and roles

The likely geostrategic character of any future major conflict ensured that there would be different naval requirements to those on the eve of the Great War. In particular, the focus was less on the confined waters off north-west Europe, the centre of attention in that war because of the centrality of conflict between Britain and Germany, the two leading naval powers of the period. Instead, much of the focus was now on the vast expanses of the Pacific.

Even before the close of the Great War, there had been an awareness that new technology was likely to lead to a very different naval situation in any future conflict. Arthur Balfour, British Foreign Secretary and former First Lord of the Admiralty, argued in May 1918 that a peace settlement that left the Germans with overseas colonies would pose a great problem:

> a piratical power, prepared to use the submarine as Germany had used it in this war, and possessed of well placed bases in every ocean, could hold up the sea-borne commerce of neutral and belligerent alike, no matter what were the naval forces arrayed against it.[13]

Similarly, Italian diplomats cited the threat from submarines as a reason for their concern about the future of Albania.[14]

Planning for the Pacific

In 1919, an Admiralty memorandum warned that the British navy was likely to be weaker than that of Japan in the Far East. It suggested that using Hong Kong as a base would expose the British fleet to overwhelming attack from Japan, and recommended that Singapore should be developed instead, as it was sufficiently far from Japan to permit reinforcement without peril.[15] The Treasury, however, proved reluctant to share the Admiralty's concerns.[16]

Japan certainly represented a different threat. Hitherto, the challenge to Britain's position in Asia had been the land threat from Russian expansion, particularly across Central Asia toward Iran, Afghanistan and India, but also toward Manchuria in northern China. The British response to Russia had been military and diplomatic policies focused on the land mass, with the Royal Navy playing only a supporting role. Now there was the prospect of a naval challenge to Britain in Far Eastern or even Indian waters that could not be countered by British strength in home waters. In the Great War, Japan, as an ally with Britain since the treaty between the two powers in 1902, had deployed her navy to distant waters, attacking German bases in the Pacific, escorting British convoys from Australia, hunting German raiders, and in 1917 sending warships to assist the Allies in the Mediterranean.

The end of the alliance in 1922 made this Japanese capability threatening. In his *Rulers of the Indian Ocean* (1927), G. A. Ballard, a British admiral, argued that the rise in Japanese and American naval power meant that it was no longer sufficient for Britain to prevail over European rivals in order to win global naval dominance. He presented the British Empire as particularly vulnerable in the Indian Ocean:

> As regards its present form or fabric, the Empire may be roughly divided into an occidental half – including the British Isles – and an oriental; which are held together commercially and strategically by the Imperial lines of communication across the Indian Ocean . . . If those connections are cut, the two halves of the Empire will fall apart as surely as night follows day.

The Americans also were increasingly concerned about Japanese intentions and naval strength. Furthermore, there were specific American interests in the western Pacific, including the territories of the Philippines, Guam and Samoa, trade, and a strong commitment to the independence of China and to an 'open door' allowing other powers, notably the USA, to share in Chinese trade. This concern led to American planning for war with Japan, hypothetical exercises that were a bridge from the naval thought of the pre-1914 Mahanian period to the strategy pursued in the Second World War. Plan Orange of 1924 called for the 'through ticket': a rapid advance directly from the American base in Hawai'i to Manila, the capital of the Philippines, a decisive battle, and then starving Japan by blockade.

This plan was superseded by greater interest in a slower process of seizing the Japanese islands in the Pacific – the Marshalls, Carolines and Marianas, which they had gained from Germany as mandates in the Versailles Peace settlement. The capture of these islands would provide the Americans with forward bases en route to the Philippines and deny them to the Japanese. Without control of this area, it was argued, a naval advance to the Philippines would be unsuccessful. There was concern about fighting Japan near its bases and resources.[17]

War games prepared options. In 1927, Lieutenant-Commander Tagaki Sokichi planned an attack by two aircraft carriers on the Hawaiian American base of Pearl Harbor as part of his graduation exercises at the Japanese Naval War College, but was held in the war game to have suffered heavy losses. Aside from the Navy Fleet problems (manoeuvres) aimed against Japan, the Americans played war games with model ships on the floor of a lecture theatre. In one 1933 exercise, Captain Ernest King chose a northern attack route on Japan via Hawai'i-Midway-Wake and the Mariannas, while the President of the Naval War College, Rear-Admiral Laning, preferred a southern route, beginning with Micronesia, and criticized King's plans as the worst possible.[18] A decade later, King put his plan into action while MacArthur put Laning's plan into action, but they each took far longer than expected. Moreover, virtually all the American inter-war plans, at least until 1937, ignored practicalities such as fuel. Less plausibly, the Americans had also prepared plans for war with both Britain and Japan.

The likely character of a major future war in the Pacific led to a new geography of commitment and concern that was reflected in the development of naval bases, for example those of Britain at Singapore, which in 1932 the British Cabinet decided to complete, and of the USA at Pearl Harbor on the Hawai'ian island of Oahu. The switchover from coal to oil as the power source of the Royal Navy helped ensure that the previous system of coaling bases was obsolete. Moreover, the major expansion in the size of battleships from the deployment of the dreadnoughts in the mid-1900s had made the existing imperial harbours at Hong Kong, Singapore and Trincomalee (in Sri Lanka) inadequate. The Chiefs of Staff urged that Singapore should be not only a modern naval base but also the location of an army force able to act as a strategic reserve forward of India.[19] The strategic value of Pearl Harbor for controlling the eastern Pacific and advancing across the western Pacific was clear to the American Joint Army and Navy Planning Committee in 1919.[20]

A far greater role for aircraft carriers in the Pacific than in the North Sea and the Mediterranean was envisaged. As tensions mounted in the Far East in the 1920s and, even more, 1930s, with Japanese expansionism at the expense of China from 1931 and full-scale war from 1937, and an increase in the size of the Japanese navy, so it was necessary to plan for conflict across very large bodies of water.

In response, there was an emphasis on a greater range for ships and planes. For example, the range, size and speed of submarines improved. The American S class of 1918–21, with a range of 5,000–8,000 miles at a surface speed of 10 knots, was replaced by the B class (12,000 miles at 11 knots), and then by the P-boats of 1933–6, which were the first American submarines with a totally diesel-electric propulsion. These were followed by the Gato class introduced in 1940: double-hulled, all-welded-hull submarines with a range of 11,800 miles and a surface speed of 20–25 knots. By the time of the Japanese attack on Pearl Harbor in December 1941, the American navy had 111 submarines in commission, while the Japanese had 63 ocean-going submarines. Their Type 1-400 submarines had a range of 37,500 nautical miles, a surface speed of 18.7 knots, and carried supplies for 60 days.

In the event of war with the USA, the Japanese planned to use their subma-rines to sink American warships steaming from Hawai'i into the western Pacific. They therefore intended to employ their long range as a major prelim-inary component in fleet action. In the event, Japanese submarines failed to fulfil expectations, which was unsurprising as pre-war exercises had indicated significant deficiencies.

The need to plan for conflict with Japan accentuated the problems for Britain and the USA, powers with commitments in both Atlantic and Pacific, for they had to think about how best to distribute naval forces, and how vulnerabilities would affect policy.[21] There was a *de facto* division of spheres of activity, with the USA dominant in the Pacific, but having no naval role in the Indian Ocean which was very much a British sphere. The British were more prominent than the Americans in the South Atlantic and in East Asian waters, although the Americans had a small Asiatic Fleet to defend the Philippines and their interests in China. As Admiral Montgomery Taylor, the Asiatic Fleet commander from 1929 to 1933, pointed out, this force was too small to thwart Japanese moves.[22]

The British failed to agree among themselves or with the Americans on how best to contain the Japanese threat. In response to Treasury opposition in 1934 to sending a fleet to the Far East and, instead, concern about Germany and support for a focus on air power, it was argued by both the Admiralty and the Dominions Office that this was unacceptable because of the impact on Australia and New Zealand of leaving them without support.[23] The Admiralty was ready to consider a forward policy based on protecting Hong Kong, to provide support against Japan, but that required an American willingness to move naval units to East Asian waters which, the Americans feared, would leave Hawai'i vulnerable. The American Naval Department, which anyway included anglophobes, was unwilling to support such a scheme and relations between the two were poor.[24]

The outcome was not a forward policy, but a British plan to send much of the fleet to Singapore in the event of war with Japan. Indeed, in 1941, Churchill decided to send a modern battleship to Singapore in order to deter the Japanese and impress the Americans.[25] However, the availability of warships for Singapore depended on commitments against Germany and Italy in Home, Atlantic and Mediterranean waters, and on the fate of the British fleet in any conflict that might arise.

In 1935–6, in the Second London Naval Conference, Japan demanded equality of tonnage with Britain and the USA, which would have meant Japanese naval superiority in the Pacific and Far East. British attempts at compromise failed and the Japanese left the talks in January 1936. This withdrawal led to the unilateral Japanese disavowal of existing limits under the Washington Naval Treaty, and the launching of the Marusan Programme of shipbuilding designed to prepare for victory over British and American fleets.[26] The build-up of their navy included the largest capital ships in the world, the 'super-battleships' *Yamato* and *Musashi*, ordered in 1937, each displacing 72,000 tons and carrying nine 18.1 inch guns. Their size was designed to compensate for being heavily outnumbered, but they were to be sunk by the Americans in 1944 and 1945.

The militaristic nature of Japanese naval policy and culture calls into question claims that navies have generally been associated with liberal, commercial values.[27] The Japanese focused on the force structure of a large navy based on battleships and on the goal of victory stemming from a decisive battle comparable to Admiral Togo's triumph at Tsushima over the Russians in 1905, a success that had helped lead to a desired outcome to the Russo-Japanese War of 1904–5.

Seeking international power through naval strength and naval strength through international power, many naval commanders and planners opposed the naval limitation treaties because they believed that the Japanese navy should be closer in size to the American navy, an idea first expressed in 1907 when a ratio of 70 per cent or more had been advanced. As a consequence, the 1922 ratio of 60 per cent was seen as unreasonable, a humiliation, and a threat both to national defence and to the ability of the navy to act as a deterrent force.[28] In November 1930, Prime Minister Osachi Hamaguchi was assassinated after he signed the London Naval Treaty. Throughout the inter-war period, the Americans were seen as the likely enemy by Japanese naval planners, and those who opposed this stance lost their position in the navy as the Fleet Faction consolidated its dominance. A purge in 1934 led to the promotion of aggressive officers. As a result, naval preparation centred on preparing for war with the USA.

Deterrence was more generally a point in inter-war military planning. There was an emphasis on the availability of force to provide a deterrent capability that would offer both security and an ability to pursue limited goals in safety. Such an approach, however, appeared threatening to others which encouraged them to respond and thus end the element of security. This course of development might appear as obvious, but a belief in inherent competition was strong in this period. The Japanese focus was very much on opposing the USA, as Britain did not appear a comparable threat. Aside from adding armour and upgrading engines, the Japanese increased the gun elevation of their warships in an attempt to outclass the Americans at extreme range, and thus be able to damage them prior to conflict at closer range, only for the Americans to do the same in an effort to have the ability to secure an initial advantage.

Both the Japanese and the American naval leadership focused on a decisive battle centred on battleships, with air and submarine attacks being preliminary blows. The Japanese also put an emphasis on preliminary damage from night-time cruiser and destroyer torpedo strikes, and produced an effective surface-launched torpedo, the oxygen-fuelled Type 93 or 'Long Lance'. Moreover, as an instance of the relationship between tactics and equipment, the Japanese increased their capability for night-time attack by developing effective light-gathering optical devices as well as high-explosive propellants that were nearly flashless.[29] The Americans lacked a comparable torpedo (and comparable propellants), and the contrast in tactics affected conflict in the Solomon Sea in 1942.[30]

Despite Japanese efforts, their fleet, by 1940, was only 7:10 in strength relative to the American. Franklin Delano Roosevelt, who became President in March 1933, was a keen supporter of the navy. He had been Assistant Secretary of the Navy under Woodrow Wilson. The Vinson-Trammel Act of March 1934, followed by the 'Second Vinson Act' of May 1938, had set out to rearm the American navy and remedy an earlier situation in which there had been a failure in the 1920s and early 1930s, to construct what was allowed by the Naval Conferences, a failure that hindered the American ability to respond confidently to Japanese pressure on China.[31] In 1939, the authorized strength of the American navy was upped to 145,000 men. In July 1940, when Britain appeared defeated by Germany, Congress passed the Two Ocean Naval Expansion Act, which was designed to produce a fleet larger than that of the second and third ranking naval powers combined. This fleet would enable the Americans to wage naval war against both Germany and Japan, a necessity that seemed increasingly apparent.

European challenges

The development of the German and Italian navies indicated that both powers would contest European waters. Already, under the Weimar Republic, the Germans had enhanced their naval strength through responding to the Versailles (1919) constraints on the maximum tonnage of German battleships by designing the *Deutschland* class. The *Deutschland* was classified by Germans as a *panzerschiff* or armoured ship, and, by others as a pocket battleship. Exploiting the discrepancy between the Versailles treaty which bound them, and the Washington treaty which bound everyone else (11-inch guns against 8-inch) the firepower of this class was superior to the cruisers of other navies. Moreover; their new diesel propulsion gave them a speed of 28 knots, which was faster than most other battleships, offering a mobility designed to allow the *Deutschland* class the opportunity to engage with a target of opportunity, but to escape if the situation proved hazardous. Laid down in 1928, the *Deutschland* was commissioned two months after Hitler came to power. Over the following years, the specifications of the class improved and their official displacement was raised to 18,000 tons, instead of the 10,000 tons laid down by Versailles. In practice, the ships did not equal their promise as they were badly overloaded and their engines extremely unreliable.

This development was an instance of German strategic culture. In the first half of the century, the stress was on using technology to permit a major change in the international system. Surface warships and submarines provided key instances, whereas in Britain technological developments, such as changes in battleships, were pursued according to a more defensive strategic culture.[32]

Under the Anglo-German Naval Treaty of 18 June 1935, a British attempt to provide an acceptable response to German demands for rearmament, the Germans were to have a quota equivalent to that of France or Italy under the 1922 Washington treaty, with a surface fleet up to 35 per cent the size of that of Britain, and the submarine fleet of 45 per cent, later 100 per cent. Hitler, however, ignored these restrictions in his naval build-up. Like Stalin, Hitler was fascinated by battleships, ordering the *Bismarck* and *Tirpitz*, each of which displaced 45,000 tons, and he then planned another six battleships. In March 1939, Hitler arrived in the *Deutschland* at Memel (modern Klapeida) to take control of his new acquisition from Lithuania, thus displaying power as well as avoiding the need to cross Poland. When he attacked Poland in September, the latter's navy was heavily outnumbered.

This focus on battleships was to the detriment of smaller, frequently more effective, warships.[33] Indeed, Germany only had 57 submarines, of which 23 were seagoing, all of obsolete design, at the outset of the Second World War.[34] The navy's commander, Admiral Erich Raeder, was also committed to battleships, arguing that anti-submarine warfare by Germany's rivals would counter the German submarines. The build-up of the navy was designed for conflict with Britain and the Soviet Union, but did not assume war until the mid-1940s, by which time a far larger German navy was planned.

The German emphasis on battleships did not mean that submarines were ignored. Banned under the Versailles treaty, they were built in the 1930s. Karl Dönitz, who was appointed Chief of the Submarine Force in 1935, developed wolf-pack tactics in which a group of submarines, coordinated by radio, was to attack convoys on the surface at night-time, overwhelming the escorts. Aimed at the British, this tactic was to be used with considerable success in the Second World War. Dönitz sought to create a capability that was more effective than that seen in the Great War.

Meanwhile, Benito Mussolini, the Italian dictator from 1922, greatly expanded the Italian navy in rivalry with France and in order to challenge the British position in the Mediterranean, the crucial axis of the British Empire, and one that was dependent on naval power and related bases at Gibraltar, Malta and Alexandria (in Egypt). However, Mussolini was less interested in naval affairs than the situation on land, and he lacked both relevant knowledge and an understanding of the strategic situation. It was possible to talk of unlocking the gates of the Mediterranean at Gibraltar and Suez, but, as the ambitious Italian Naval Staff noted, there was really only hope of Italy controlling the central Mediterranean. A lack of carrier air cover, and a battle fleet that could not match those of Britain and France, rendered other schemes futile. The Italian navy also had tactical and weaponry deficiencies, notably weaknesses in gunnery training and shell manufacture, and the building of outdated submarines.[35]

Britain and Italy came close to conflict as a result of the Italian invasion of Ethiopia in 1935–6, a step condemned by the League of Nations. In October

1933, the Chiefs of Staff Sub-Committee of the Committee of Imperial Defence had warned that 'our defensive arrangements in the Mediterranean are in many respects obsolete and have not been adjusted to the development of the French and Italian navies, and the increasing range and strength of French and Italian military aircraft'.[36] However, in 1935–6, despite weaknesses, including a lack of sailors, reserves and anti-aircraft ammunition, and concerns about Italian submarines based at Leros in the Dodecanese Islands (an Italian colony), the Royal Navy, with its bases at Gibraltar, Malta and Alexandria, was confident of success. As a might-have-been war, this confrontation was significant in the establishment of relative capability and in the development of plans. The British planned a carrier attack on the Italian fleet in harbour at Taranto. One, indeed, was to be successfully launched in November 1940.

In the event, in 1935–6, the British government considered oil sanctions as well as closing the Suez Canal, but did not wish to provoke war with Italy, not least as it hoped to keep Mussolini and Hitler apart, and did not intend to antagonize the Americans by stopping their tankers. The British failure to intimidate Italy was more a consequence of an absence of political will, than of a lack of naval capability.[37] A failure to secure a promise of French naval cooperation was also significant.

Having competed with Italy in the 1920s and responded, in particular, to the Italian-Spanish alignment under Mussolini and Primo de Rivera, the French were challenged in 1928 when Germany lay down the first of three new *panzerschiff*-class ships. This led the French to lay down new battleships in the early 1930s, the *Dunkerque* and the *Strasbourg*, the name of the latter an affirmation of France's commitment to the territory regained from Germany in 1918–19. Designed to pursue the *panzerschiff*, these battleships were fast. In turn, these ships were followed by the 35,000-ton *Richelieu*-class battleships. In response to the German naval build-up, the French navy re-focused its attention from the Italians and the Mediterranean, and established a battleship-based *Force de Raid* at Brest, France's major Atlantic base. This force was designed to protect French trade routes. As a result, the French fleet had effective ships that were to be important to the power politics of 1940–2, notably in the Mediterranean.

The Soviet navy

The development of the Soviet navy reflected not so much alterations in weapons capability as changes in strategy and doctrine that primarily arose from political considerations. The naval example is more generally instructive of the widespread relationship between these factors. There was significant continuity into the Soviet era from the Tsarist period, not least in terms of doctrine and leadership. The emphasis, under what was later called the 'Old School', was for a defensive posture in both the Gulf of Finland (to the west of St Petersburg/Petrograd/Leningrad) and the Black Sea. Submarines and torpedo boats were to weaken attacking fleets, most probably the Royal Navy, prior to a battle in which the Soviet navy would use its full power in a decisive engagement. This strategy accorded with the state and size of the Soviet navy, which did not benefit from new construction.

The drive for something more than a defensive strategy, combined with ideological, political and generational contrasts, to lead the 'Young School' (based on the French *Jeune École* of the 1880s) to challenge these ideas from the late 1920s. The Young School were Communists and they also sought a strategy that conformed more to the attacking plans of the Red Army. Arguing from the role of submarines and aircraft, the Young School questioned the idea of command-of-the-sea as well as belief in a superior navy with the attendant stress on powerful surface ships. In contrast to the Old School and the more general international adherence to Mahanian ideas, the Young School argued that a decisive battle was a mistaken goal and, instead, that the submarines, torpedo boats and planes of the Soviet navy could nullify the impact of the opposing fleet, so as to enable the Soviet navy to assist the army. This approach pleased Stalin who, in 1930, purged the navy and promoted the Young School.

As a result, in the early and mid-1930s, the new group's ideas shaped doctrine, training and procurement. The second Five-Year Plan (1933–7) called for 310 submarines. The annual manoeuvres of the Baltic Fleet which, in the late 1920s, had emphasized a defensive response to an attacking fleet, the latter modelled on the Royal Navy, and had focused on the combined arms tactics required, instead now focused on amphibious attacks in support of the army.

In 1937–8, there was a reversal in doctrine. Stalin had come to focus on big ships, in part in response to the commitment to such ships by Germany, Japan and Britain. He planned a 59,000-ton battleship, the *Sovetskii Soiuz*, but was thwarted in his plans to order the world's largest battleship from an American yard.[38] By 1939, there were three battleships of this class under construction in the Soviet Union as well as two 35,000-ton battle cruisers, which were designed to be faster. None was ever completed. Instead, the Soviet navy's three battleships were all Tsarist-era (pre-1917), and their inadequate armour made them vulnerable.

The purge in the navy that accompanied the purge in the army in 1937 reinforced Stalin's commitment to big ships, by destroying the Young School. As part of the process of transformation, as in the army, the system of 'dual command' was reintroduced with political commissars given the task of jointly signing orders with commanding officers. That these commissars were called military commissars did not lessen their political rationale.

However, there was no time to create a fleet of big ships, while disruption continued because the initial purge of 1937 was followed by fresh killings. The purges helped ensure a serious shortage of experienced officers, and of non-commissioned officers as the latter were promoted to fill gaps. Training regimes were seriously affected, the frequency of accidents rose, and there was less emphasis on annual manoeuvres. As a result, the effectiveness of the navy at combined arms operations, notably coordination with aircraft, declined. The purges also affected the shipyards and greatly exacerbated the problems created by Stalin's unrealistic assumptions. The consequence was a serious decline in quality, with much of the armour of Soviet warships inadequate. Complex gun mountings posed a particular problem. Much of the investment of resources was wasted.

Significant deficiencies in Soviet naval forces at the close of the 1930s included the absence of dive bombers, advanced torpedoes or sonar equipment, and the fact that only one ship was equipped with radar. Although there was a large submarine force, it was poorly trained and, in the event, its wartime effectiveness proved limited. In part, this was because submarine aiming and firing techniques were poor, while Soviet doctrine emphasized remaining in fixed positions and waiting for enemy vessels to appear. Soviet motor torpedo boats also proved of limited effectiveness. Thus, as with the air force, the major build-up attempted under Stalin proved to be of restricted value only. In part, this result reflected the severity of the discontinuity during the Russian Civil War, but there is also a more general conclusion about the difficulty of developing capability and the requirement for more than resources.

Soviet naval doctrine in the late 1930s focused on the battleships that Stalin wanted. The Combat Manual of the Soviet Naval Forces issued in March 1937 emphasized the need for battle without the support of minefields and coastal artillery. At the same time, there was a continuing call for a capability for amphibious operations in support of the army.[39]

Stalin's focus, anyway, remained focused on the Red Army. As a result, from the naval perspective, there was a clear logic to the Nazi-Soviet Pact of 1939, as it freed the Soviets from the need to defend the Gulf of Finland from the larger German navy. At the same time, the conflicts with Japan over Manchuria in 1938 and, even more, 1939 were limited in space and time. As a result, the vulnerable Soviet Far East was not exposed to attack by the greatly superior Japanese navy. The main Soviet naval base in the Far East, at Vladivostok, was also very vulnerable to land attack from Japanese forces in neighbouring Manchuria.

Latin America

Some lesser powers also developed their navies. Siam (Thailand) added large Italian-built torpedo boats to a British-built Great War vintage destroyer. In Latin America, tensions between Peru, Chile and Argentina over border disputes led to naval races. The USA built four submarines for Peru which were commissioned in 1926–8. The Chileans regarded their existing destroyers as inadequate in countering these boats, which would make the battle group built round the British-built dreadnought *Almirante Latorre*, a surface action group, vulnerable to attack. The Peruvians, in turn, had no surface vessels to challenge the *Almirante Latorre*. Strengthened by new British-built destroyers from 1929, its battle group was then seen as able to counter the Peruvian submarines.

The perceived naval threat to Chile from Argentina increased from the mid-1920s when the government of the latter authorized an expenditure of 75 million gold pesos on a ten-year naval building programme. This ambitious programme was to remain mostly intact. The Argentineans bought two heavy cruisers, a light cruiser, twelve destroyers and three submarines. The building work was mainly divided between Britain and Italy.

The Chileans sought to achieve parity by modernizing their fleet with the new destroyers, as well as three submarines and an extensive refit of *Almirante Latorre*. The submarines, together with a large submarine depot ship, were all constructed at Barrow-in-Furness in England by Vickers-Armstrong. The Chilean navy intended to use the submarines to counter threats from both Peru and Argentina, with the depot ship in support to add to the operational range. Moreover, the Chilean naval air arm grew in size and significance in the 1920s. Significantly, it constructed bases in the south, in Puerto Montt and Punta Arenas, and a joint exercise with the fleet was held in 1926 in the southern channel, which suggests that naval air power would have played a part in any conflict with Argentina. By the mid-1930s, the navy had formulated a plan for a decisive naval battle with Argentina. The Chileans divulged this plan to the British in an unsuccessful effort to order two 8-inch-gun heavy cruisers from British yards.[40]

The British Empire

In part, this drive to develop naval forces also reflected the sense on the part of coastal states that naval power was important as a sign of sovereignty. Thus, visiting Australia in 1919, Jellicoe was made aware of opposition to subsuming the Australian navy into an imperial force. However, within the British Empire, there was a failure to match naval forces to resources. Australia was reluctant to spend while the Canadian navy was greatly run down after the Great War: it had only 366 men in 1922. As a result, the empire was not in a position to provide Britain with much naval support. In 1938, Australia, which had partly modernized its navy in response to the Japanese challenge, had six cruisers and five destroyers, Canada only six destroyers and five minesweepers, New Zealand two light cruisers, and India only eight small coastal ships. Cooperation with Britain, nevertheless, was eased by the extensive use of British or British-derived equipment and tactics.

Although equality of size had been conceded to the Americans at the Washington conference in 1922, the British navy remained the world-leader in prestige and reputation, while also having an unrivalled chain of fleet bases, which, in effect, were battleship bases.[41] As a sign of their standing, British warships occupied pride of position on the *Bund* at Shanghai[42], the prime anchoring position in China. As a consequence, in part, of the economic difficulties, social policy and disarmament priorities of the Labour government of 1929–31, British naval expenditure had been cut seriously in 1929–34, leading, by 1936, to a degree of obsolescence. Cuts in fuel and ammunition in 1931 hit training.[43] However, the threatening international situation then led to naval rearmament.[44] The February 1934 report of the Defence Requirements Sub-Committee of the Committee of Imperial Defence noted of the navy: 'The greatest potential threat lies in the acquisition of submarines and aircraft by Germany'.[45]

The Royal Navy was therefore prepared for a far more varied conflict than what might result from a German battle-fleet offensive alone. Due to the time taken to build ships, the British would also know some years ahead whether or not Germany would have a battle fleet. British naval planning anticipated that war with Germany would result in a determined air-sea offensive against the British maritime system. Thus, the British understanding of German naval strategy was more sophisticated than is commonly assumed.[46] Moreover, it was located within an understanding that a lengthy struggle of industrial attrition would have a central naval dimension.

From 1936, helped by an increase in the navy estimates, the Admiralty was free to pursue ambitious policies. Many carriers, battleships, cruisers and destroyers were laid down: the battleships those of the 35,000-ton King George V class. Moreover, the Fleet Air Arm was greatly expanded. Radar sets were installed in British (and German) warships from 1938. There were weaknesses in 1939, not least a lack of mines and torpedoes, but the Royal Navy was in a much better state than it had been in 1931.

Amphibious operations

More generally, amphibious operations were not to the fore in inter-war naval thinking, which, in part, was a consequence of the lack of joint (i.e. joint service) structures and planning. British amphibious warfare capability was weak, but an invasion of France in a future war, as was to occur in 1944, was not anticipated. France, Germany and the Soviet Union lacked specialized amphibious craft. Nevertheless, there was more interest in specialized landing-craft, especially by the USA, than there had been during the Great War. The Japanese, who used amphibious attacks in their war with China from 1937, made the most progress, both in developing types of landing-craft and in building a reasonable number of ships. Their *Dai-Hatsu* had a ramp in its bows, and this was to become the key type of landing-craft.

Shallow-draft boats played a role in wars in the 'Third World' in the 1920s and 1930s, being significant for operations in both coastal waters and on rivers. Each sphere of operations was important in China. In December 1920, Sun Yat-sen established his position in Guangzhou (Canton), his arrival backed by the navy's First Fleet. Five years later, Guomindang gunboats bombarded mercenary positions in fighting outside Guangzhou. In March 1926, three warlord gunboats attacked the Dagu forts, while other warships escorted transports landing 5,000 troops nearby.[47] The following spring, the defection to Jiang of the Fujian Naval Fleet gave him control of the Yangzi River and he reached Nanjing on one of his new warships.

Japanese pressure was also brought to bear in China using the navy, as in 1928 when warships were sent up the Yangzi and marines were landed at Wenzhou. In 1931, Japan sought to intimidate China during its occupation of Manchuria by holding naval exercises in the Yangzi and sending ships up the Whangpoo River. In 1937, naval gunfire played a major role in stemming the initial Chinese attack on the Japanese positions in Shanghai. The following year, Japanese warships sailed up the Yangzi and directly engaged Chinese positions. The Japanese employed only a portion of their navy in China, and, notably, few of their aircraft carriers, but had fleets on the Yangzi and off China.

The Japanese navy built up its amphibious capability by developing units that specialized as *rikusentai* (landing parties). They were given infantry training and, by the late 1930s, the navy had permanent landing units that were based ashore and armed with heavy weaponry including artillery. In one respect, this development represented a type of jointness in that amphibious capability was enhanced, but it also reflected the extent to which the Japanese army and navy in part fought separate wars, including with separate air forces, a process that was to be greatly accentuated in 1941 when Japan attacked the USA, Britain and the Dutch. At the same time, there were joint Japanese army-navy amphibious operations in the western Pacific in the late 1920s.

With far more expertise than other powers, the Japanese developed an amphibious doctrine and practice. They put the emphasis on attacking at night or at dawn, and on landing at several points simultaneously and then concentrating on land. Their experience was to stand them in good stead in 1941–2, notably in their rapid conquests of Malaya, the Philippines and the Dutch East Indies.

Supporting empire

Not only the Japanese deployed warships in support of imperial operations. In June 1920, Italian naval bombardment led the Albanian irregulars that had entered the port of Valona to withdraw. The Spaniards responded to the disaster at Annual in 1921 by dispatching several warships to Moroccan waters. The following year, a Spanish blockade of the Moroccan coast was announced. China was a major site of naval activities. Eight foreign warships were deployed off Guangzhou in 1925 at a time of anti-foreigner demonstrations. Two years later, the British, American, Japanese and French commanders on the China Station considered responding to Guomindang actions against foreign interests by sending warships up the Yangzi, sinking the Guomindang fleet, destroying their arsenals at Hankou and Guangzhou, and possibly preventing Guomindang forces from crossing the Yangzi.[48] In the event, these steps were not taken.

The French navy was used in support of imperial control, for example in North Africa and Syria. In December 1929, 350 American marines were sent on the cruiser *Galveston* from the base at Guantanamo Bay in Cuba to support American operations in Haiti. In April 1931, the Sandinista siege of an American-held position near the Caribbean coast of Nicaragua led to the dispatch of American marines from the Panama Canal Zone on the *Asheville* while the light cruiser *Memphis* was sent from Guantanamo Bay.

Conclusions

The Royal Navy also showed the flag in the empire. This role, however, was not its principal one. Instead, the Royal Navy focused on preparation for conflict with the fleets of rival powers. Despite its strengths, Britain lacked a navy capable of fighting Germany, Italy and Japan simultaneously. That was the product of the stop on capital ship construction under the Washington Naval Treaty, as well as the lack of sufficient British industrial capability and fiscal strength; but also of the build-up of the strength of these three powers.

However, to expect the arithmetic of naval power to provide for conflict at once with all three states was to anticipate a margin of superiority that was unreasonable given the state of the country and the fact that the potential enemies were well apart, but also one that diplomacy sought to avoid the need for.[49] Allowing for the significance and consequences of serious rivalries between the views of the key ministries, the Treasury, Foreign Office and Admiralty[50], British naval strategy planned that, if necessary, operations against threats arising simultaneously would be conducted sequentially in separate theatres. This strategy assumed that operational flexibility could help lessen the constraints posed by tough fiscal limits.[51]

In addition, war was likely to bring Britain the support of allies. A report by the Chiefs of Staff for the Cabinet drawn up in February 1937 suggested that, in the event of war with Germany, Japan and Italy, it would be necessary to rely on the French to deal with the last.[52] Indeed, the improvement in Anglo-French relations in 1938–9 led to a degree of cooperation, notably with the allocation of primary responsibility for particular waters, for example with the Mediterranean divided. This cooperation helped both powers. Although the loss of French naval support in the aftermath of German conflict in 1940 was unexpected, Japanese entry into the war in 1941 led to a British alliance with the USA that proved crucial both to the security of Australasia and to the maintenance of control over the Atlantic. The naval history of the Second World War thus demonstrated the extent and unpredictability of the political dimension of warfare. This element proved more significant, notably in 1939–41, than the lessons learned from differing weapons systems competing at sea.

6

Air power

'They are likely to rely for their military power still more on the mechanized weapons of the future, such as tanks, big guns and, above all, military aircraft'. Sir John Simon, the British Foreign Secretary, had no doubt of the threat posed by the Nazis. In March 1933, he informed the Cabinet that 'aviation offers to Germany the quickest and easiest way of making her own power effective . . . Against military aircraft the extensive fortifications of the French frontier [the Maginot Line] cannot avail . . . civilian populations must be organised and drilled in preparation for air bombardment and gas attack'.[1]

The belief in air power

The role of air power in the Great War had led to major interest in developing its potential, which accorded with a more general fascination with futurology, technology and technological change, the transforming character of flight, and the role of air power in modernization.[2] Each state used their wartime experience to interpret air power in a different fashion[3], albeit within a context in which they were unsure of its place in an altered and still dynamic strategic environment.[4]

The creation of air forces was a major institutional change in the organization of war. The RAF (Royal Air Force) was created in Britain on 1 April 1918, and was committed to a bold view of the potential of air power, although it was drastically reduced in size after the Great War. An independent air force was established in Italy in 1923, and, by 1926, it had 800 planes, second only

to France, where the air force achieved independence in 1933. Air forces insti-
tutionalized a commitment to air power, that, in turn, was a cause of heavy
expenditure. As a result, there was pressure in Britain from the army to end
the independence of the air force and, instead, to give both army and navy
their own forces.[5] The latter was the pattern in Japan.

Air power was seen by its advocates not only as potent tactically, but as
a war-winning tool, and also as the best way to avoid the drawn-out attritional character of conflict on the ground that had been suffered in the Great
War. Fear of stalemate in any future conflict and concern about the costs of
large-scale ground operations led to an emphasis on air power rather than
on appreciating the extent to which 1918 had shown the value of effective
artillery-infantry cooperation. In 1919, the British Admiralty, in a paper
for the War Cabinet, noted 'as aerial aggression develops into a distinctive
form of warfare such, for example, as bombing raids on industrial centres
by forces operating from distant theatres, the strategy and operations of our
aerial defence would appear to be the responsibility of the Air Ministry.'[6] A
sense of potent possibilities was captured by Orson Welles in his 1938 radio
production of *The War of the Worlds* in which the alien tripods using heat rays
proved deadly both against troops and planes[7]; the heat rays had been in the
original novel of 1898 by H. G. Wells.

While critics were sceptical about the time that victory through strategic
bombing would require and, instead, emphasized combined-arms operation;
advocates, such as Guilio Douhet and William Mitchell, claimed that wars
could be won through air power. In his *Il Dominio dell'Aria* [*The Command
of the Air*] of 1921, Douhet, who had been appointed head of the Italian
Central Aeronautical Bureau in 1917, claimed that aeroplanes would become
the most successful offensive weapon, and that there was no viable defence
against them. He saw bombers as the best way to overcome the impasse
of trench warfare and to deliver the effective total war that was required.
Douhet pressed for air forces to be independent, rather than under army or
naval command, and argued that air power could be used to attack enemy
communications, economies and populations, rather than the enemy fighting
forces. Emphasizing the value of a strong first strike and of wrecking enemy
morale and creating a demand for peace, Douhet advocated the use of gas and

incendiary bombs against leading population centres. However, his influence on the development of strategic bombing was marginal, not least because exiguous Italian resources did not provide the basis for the necessary air capability.

His expectations for strategic bombing left Douhet with little interest in air power as a means to support land or sea operations.[8] The same was true of British airmen, who played a key role in developing the concept of strategic bombing. It was seen as offering many of the traditional advantages of naval blockade, but in a more devastating and interventionist form. British assumptions were based on optimism, institutional need or at least preferences (in the shape of air force requirements), and the wish to have a Great Power capability in European and overseas warfare without having to incur the grievous casualties seen in the Great War or to introduce conscription. The belief in deterrence was coupled with the idea that defence could be had without the need to pay the blood tax charged by military operations of the type of those in the Great War. The strength of the British aeronautical industry was also significant.

There have been attempts to offer a less critical reading[9], and to emphasize the complexity of RAF doctrine.[10] Moreover, the Air Ministry was more moderate in its claims than independent air enthusiasts.[11] However, it is apparent that British assessments of strategic bombing were not based on a sufficiently informed analysis of the impact of bombing in the Great War, nor of subsequent developments in capability. British airmen argued that bombers would be able to destroy opposing economies and, more particularly, that large bombers would be able to fight off fighter attack and, thus, not require fighter escorts.[12]

As a consequence, the RAF had twice as many bombers as fighters for most of the inter-war period. Moreover, the specifications of the bombers increased over time. The Vickers Vimy that came into service in 1919 could drop nearly 2,500 pounds of bombs. In turn, the Handley Page Hyderabad, a heavy night-bomber wooden biplane that entered service in 1925, was succeeded by the Handley Page Hinaidi that came into service by 1929. The performance of fighters also improved. Thus, the Bristol Bulldog, which was in service from 1929 to 1937, took off quickly and had a higher rate of climb than its predecessors.

Improvements in fighter quality did not bring complacency. Bombers were seen not only as likely to be effective offensive weapons in war, but also as an essential deterrent against attack. In a paper of December 1936 for the Cabinet, urging investment on the RAF and Royal Navy rather than army, Neville Chamberlain, then Chancellor of the Exchequer, observed 'Unless we are to be at the mercy of a sudden knockout blow from a Continental Western Power we must have a strong Air Force. Further, such is the power of attack from the air that it is only by building up an Air Force capable itself of dealing a powerful attacking blow, and therefore affording a strong deterrent against any attack upon us, that we can ever hope to provide a real measure of security for these attacks'.[13] Priorities were not changed toward fighters until 1938, and deliveries of fighters to the RAF only became greater than those of bombers in February 1940. During the Second World War, precision daily bombing proved less successful than its pre-war advocates had claimed it would be. Not only was it highly inaccurate much of the time, but very costly in aircrew and aircraft.

Brigadier-General William (Billy) Mitchell, Assistant Chief of the Army Air Service, 1919–25, had been the senior American air commander in the Great War, and was to be the leading American air theorist in the inter-war period. His three books, *Our Air Force: The Key to National Defense* (New York, 1921), *Winged Defense* (New York, 1925), and *Skyways* (Philadelphia, 1930), made successively greater claims for air power. Again the emphasis was on strategic bombing, not on support for land or sea operations. Strategic bombing was seen as the best way to harm an opponent's ability to wage war, and the Americans developed plans for large, long-range bombers. Prototypes of what became the B-17 Flying Fortress joined squadrons from 1937. There was confidence, even complacency, that deploying B-17s in the Philippines would give the USA a vital advantage in the event of war with Japan.

Mitchell was also interested in large-scale aerial operations at sea. He claimed that air power had made battleships obsolete, and, to try to prove his point, sank the former German dreadnought *Ostfriesland* in 21½ minutes' bombing in 1921, although the value of this demonstration was lessened as the battleship was anchored and therefore an easy target. Moreover, in Britain, David, Earl Beatty, the First Lord of the Admiralty, argued in 1923 that anti-aircraft weaponry would enable battleships to see off air attacks.[14]

Mitchell's emphasis on air power led him to press for an independent air force, and he became critical of aircraft carriers as he feared a strong naval air arm would block his plans to wage a unified air war under a single air command.[15] The National Defence Act of 1920 had placed air power under the Army Air Service, which in 1926 became the Army Air Corps, but naval aviation was kept separate.[16]

The American Air Corps Tactical School developed a policy of high-flying daylight precision bombing designed to damage an opponent's industrial system. This later greatly influenced American policy in the Second World War, but, in practice, precision was to be difficult to achieve and bombing did not have the intended decisive strategic effect.[17]

It was claimed and widely anticipated that attacks on civilian targets would play a major role in future conflict. The major impact on public morale of German raids on London in the Great War seemed an augury. Fuller predicted that air attacks on London would lead the people to demand that the government surrender. In 1923, the Steel-Bartholomew plan proposed a coordinated system of fighter bases, anti-aircraft ground defences, and an Observer Corps to protect London against possible French attack. The Salisbury Committee recommended that year that Britain have a home defence air force sufficiently strong to provide protection against the strongest air force within striking distance.[18] French air power, which was emphasized by the *The Times* in 1922, was used to justify a build-up of the RAF.

The French air force was also a source of concern in Italy, notably when the latter considered war with France's ally Yugoslavia. The equations of air power played a prominent role in 1928 when war was considered. Italian planners noted that French bombers could outperform Italian fighters, notably by flying higher. It was also believed that Italian industry lacked an ability to replace losses of planes sufficient to maintain combat strength.

The British, meanwhile, feared an aerial 'knock-out-blow'. In 1928, the RAF conducted air raid manoeuvres over London. In John Galsworthy's novel *A Modern Comedy* (1929), Sir Lawrence Mont wonders how the English nation could exist with 'all its ships and docks in danger of destruction by aeroplanes'. In practice, there was no genuine danger in the 1920s.

In contrast, Hitler, who became German Chancellor in 1933, could be readily presented as a direct threat to Britain. As a result of the Versailles peace settlement, Germany had not been allowed an air force. Pilots, nevertheless, were trained and aircraft developed by the German army and navy in the 1920s, with the civilian air industry serving as the key cover. Once Hitler came to power, the development of German air power was rapidly pressed forward.

This development fed into a situation of mounting concern. In the 1930s, it was believed, in the words of the ex- and future Prime Minister, Stanley Baldwin in 1932, that 'the bomber will always get through'. Air Commodore L. E. O. Charlton developed these themes in *War from the Air: Past-Present-Future* (1935), *War over England* (1936), and *The Menace of the Clouds* (1937). The destructiveness of bombing was also the theme of *Flying* (New York, 1933) by Major-General James E. Fechet, former head of the American Air Corps. The British government anticipated large numbers of casualties in any German attack, in part because they believed that the Germans would pursue the all-out air assault on the civilian population they themselves planned for. In practice, the RAF lacked the capacity to carry out these plans.[19] The threat of German air attack led to British interest in protecting the airbases of nearby Belgium and the Netherlands from German conquest.[20]

Innovation in the 1930s

Air defence came to be a general concern in the 1920s and 1930s, with its own doctrine, technology and organization. Under Hitler, the Air Defence League both trained Germans and took part in the militarization of society. Similarly, in the Soviet Union, as part of the total mobilization of society, preparations were made to handle the civilian reaction to air attack.[21] The French, who failed to match this effort, had a serious lack of anti-aircraft guns, but did create a separate organization for *défence antiaèrienne du territoire* (D.A.T).

The increasing size of planes also led to interest in the use of airborne troops. A number of powers, especially the Soviet Union and Germany, trained parachute and glider-borne units. There were also developments in air transport: in 1935, the Soviets moved a 14,000 strong rifle division by air from near Moscow to the Far East, while, in 1937–8, they practised dropping artillery and tanks by parachute.

The potential of air power was investigated in other ways in the inter-war period. Airships, which had played a part in the Great War, appeared to have a potential, and there was interest in their cooperation with planes. In 1926, two Gloster Grebes, British fighters, were launched from an airship as an experiment. However, accidents, notably the crash of the Dixmude airship in Italy in 1923, the British R101 in 1930 and the *Hindenburg*, helped end interest in airships other than for limited roles. More centrally, they were too vulnerable to aeroplanes and lacked the manoeuvrability of the latter.

There was a growing interest in jet aircraft, rocketry and space flight, especially in Germany, where the *Verein für Raumschiffahrt* (Space-Flight Society) was founded in 1927, and, in the Soviet Union, Konstantin Tsiolkovsky (1857–1936) developed a theory of rocket flight which encouraged the use of liquid propellants for rockets. Other work led to the development of the Soviet Katyusha multiple rocket launcher.[22]

Far-reaching innovation was also seen in other fields. In 1930, Frank Whittle, a British air force officer, patented the principles that led to the first gas turbine jet engine, which he first ran under control in 1937. His innovation was rapidly copied, and the Germans, in 1939 and the Italians, in 1940, beat the British jet into the air. In 1938, the Germans began development of radio-guided bombs, which became operational in 1943.[23]

More significantly for the short term, there was an improvement in the flying performance and combat characteristics of planes in the inter-war period. The Ministerial Committee on Disarmament dealing with Air Defence noted in July 1934 that 'development in aircraft design and construction is rapid in these days' with consequent risks of obsolescence.[24] This improvement was particularly so for fighters in the mid and late 1930s, as wooden based biplanes were replaced by all-metal cantilever-wing monoplanes with high-performance engines capable of far greater speeds, for example the German Me-109. The significance of wind resistance led to an emphasis on retractable undercarriages.

The range and armament of fighters, and the range, payload and armament of bombers all increased.[25] The American B-17, Flying Fortress, was the first effective all-metal four-engined monoplane bomber. The Handley Page Heyford, which served from 1933 to 1937, was the last of the RAF heavy bomber biplanes. The Blenheim I, a fast monoplane bomber, first entered service in 1937, in which year the Miles Magister entered the RAF as its first monoplane trainer. The Air Ministry issued specifications for a four-engined bomber in July 1936, followed in September by specifications for a twin-engined all-metal medium/ heavy bomber.

A series of new planes entered British service in the late 1930s. These included the Wellington, the first model of which flew in December 1937. Until the arrival of the four-engined bombers, the Wellington played a key role in Bomber Command's force. Its airframe offered more resistance to opposing fire than earlier models, as it was made with a geodetic metal 'basket weave' or lattice construction. The Hampden I, which entered service in September 1938, was a twin-engined monoplane while, that year, the Short Sunderland I was the first RAF monoplane flying boat, replacing earlier biplanes. It was to be important to Coastal Command in the Second World War.

The idea of a death ray, which was considered in 1935 by the new British Aeronautical Research Committee, was not viable although a variation looked toward the very different idea of radar. While more mundane, the range of advances in the 1930s was still impressive and included flaps, variable pitch propellers, stressed skin construction, and high octane fuels.[26] The French development of power-operated turrets for bombers strengthened hopes that they would be able to beat off fighter attacks. These innovations spread. The Boulton Paul Overstrand, which began service in 1935, was the first RAF bomber with a power-operated turret.

Improvements ensured the obsolescence of existing planes and the need for fresh investment. Thus, in Britain, the Hawker Fury I, a biplane fighter with a maximum speed of over 200 mph that entered service in 1931, was made obsolete by the introduction of the Hurricane. Whereas, prior to the mid-1930s, despite the bold claims made by the protagonists of air power, its effectiveness was very limited, in contrast, from then to the early 1950s, aero-technology was relatively inexpensive, but potent enough to produce an age of mass industrial air power, provided investment was forthcoming.

The Soviet TB-3 was the first mass-produced, four-engine, all-metal bomber. Andrei Tupolev also produced the SB light bomber which, with Nikolai Polikarpov's I-16 fighter, entered service in large numbers in 1934, being among the most advanced aircraft in the world. However, they quickly became obsolete. Among the 409 Soviet planes sent to Spain by June 1937 were 76 I-16s, but they were no match for the early variants of the German Me-109 (B and C) which they encountered there. In response, the Soviets pushed forward the production of new aircraft, notably the I-22, I-26 and MiG-1 fighters, and the TB-7, DB-3 and Pe-2 bombers, but the fighters were not a match for their German counterparts.

More generally, in the late 1930s, improvements in fighters began to undermine the doctrine of the invincibility and thus paramountcy of the bomber. Thanks to the Rolls-Royce Merlin engines developed from 1932 and part of the major British advance in aero-engines[27], British fighters, by 1939, could intercept the fastest German bombers. The introduction of radar on the eve of the war was another blow to the bomber's claims.

Air power around the world

The inter-war use of air power, however, had already suggested that it might be less effective than its protagonists claimed.[28] Nevertheless, air power brought advantages and the use of planes in conflict became common. Air power was used in the Chinese civil wars of the 1920s, but with scant effect. In 1921, the Guomindang air force, supporting the defence against an Guangxi invasion, consisted of only a few biplanes that, in the absence of bombs, had to drop logs. A report in *The Times* on 26 September 1924 noted:

> The few bombs dropped hitherto on the front [at Shanhaiguan] have done practically no damage and have killed only a few civilians, because ill-directed from a great height and weighing only about 15lb. The earlier explosions made holes in the ground only 3 ft across, but when trying to damage the railway bridge larger bombs were used, making a crater 10 ft

across. The prospect of bombing has caused some flutterings in Beijing, where foreigners are resident all over the city, but none so far have thought it worth while to remove outside.

Planes were also important for reconnaissance.[29]

The potential of air power in China improved as more sophisticated planes were supplied. The Soviets shipped planes to Guangzhou (Canton) in the mid-1920s. Air power played a more significant role in China in the 1930s because of the strength of the Japanese air assault. In early 1932, when the Japanese deployment of troops to Shanghai met resistance, a Japanese air assault killed numerous civilians. It did not, however, end the resistance. However, when Japan was not involved, the Guomindang government was able to use air power against its opponents, as in December 1936 when forces advanced on Xi'an in order to free Jiang (see p. 158).

In 1937, Japan deployed about 1,500 planes at a time when only 87 of China's 300 planes were able to fly. Air power was used from the outset of the Sino-Japanese war, with the University of Tianjin, a prominent source of opposition to Japan, bombed in July 1937. The Soviet Union delivered 297 planes to China in the winter of 1937–8. Flown by Soviet pilots, they began operating in defence of Nanjing. However, Japanese air power was greater and this advantage proved important to Japanese advances in China. Moreover, there was heavy aerial bombardment of positions at a distance from the battlefield. In 1939, once winter clouds and fog had ended, Chongqing, Jiang's capital, proved the prime target. With no effective anti-aircraft support or air cover, the city was badly damaged by a series of heavy raids. This attempt to break Chinese morale, however, had no strategic or political effect.

Planes were used around the world, and from the outset of the period. The Yugoslav invasion of northern Albania in 1920 was accompanied by the bombing of the towns. The following year, the outbreak of violence linked to labour problems in the coalfields of West Virginia, led the Governor to ask for troops and aircraft. The government response included the dispatch of three DH-4B bombers, personally led by Mitchell as commander of the 1st Provisional Air Brigade. He told newspaper reporters that the Army Air Service could end the unrest by dropping tear gas on the miners. In the event, the immediate crisis passed and Mitchell left, but fighting in early September saw the local opponents of the miners use civilian aircraft to drop homemade bombs filled with nails and metal fragments. In response to the escalating crisis, 25 aircraft were ordered to West Virginia, although mechanical and other problems ensured that only 14 arrived. They were used for reconnaissance missions rather than for the bombing for which they were prepared. The concurrent deployment of troops led to the end of the crisis, although Mitchell of course claimed much of the credit.[30] American aircraft and pilots were also used further south, bombing Mexican rebels in 1923. In January 1927, two American 'free-lance airmen' working for the Nicaraguan Conservatives bombed Liberal positions.[31]

Meanwhile, independent non-Western states developed air power. In March 1922, ten planes were sent by the Atatürk government to the Anatolian front for reconnaissance activity against the Greeks. Moreover, the French handed over 14 scout planes as part of the peace agreement. The Atatürk government also bought 20 planes from Italy, equipping them with machine guns from old German fighters. A delegation sent to Germany bought 20 planes which were sent to the Black Sea via Russia, but only two arrived fit for service. The Turks were able to use their planes to support their surprise attack on the Greek positions on 30 August 1922 and, in the end, were successful in preventing the Greek planes from attacking and reconnaissance. In the Hijaz, in 1925, Ali bin Hussain, the opponent of Ibn Saud, had an air force of two drunken pilots and two planes. Although they managed to bomb Mecca, they achieved little either with this bombing or with other operations.[32]

The Italians provided the Iman of Yemen and the king of Afghanistan with planes, while the latter also received them from Britain and the Soviet Union, while Britain supplied them to Ibn Saud of Arabia. Planes were a currency of influence. The Afghans, however, were handicapped by a shortage of mechanics.

In 1929, the future Haile Selassie of Ethiopia owed success over his rival, Ras Gugsa Wolie, in part thanks to his use of an aircraft, flown by a French pilot who made bombing runs, causing panic. The city of São Paulo was bombed in the Brazilian civil war of 1932, demonstrating the strength and determination of the government forces, although the effectiveness of the bombing was limited. Nevertheless, it was regarded as demonstrating superiority and as a clear mark of sovereignty.

Reconnaissance was also an important capability of air power. In Persia (Iran), observation planes helped in operations against the hostile tribesmen, while in 1920 aerial reconnaissance and intelligence reports warned of the likelihood of further raid on Palestine from Bedouin tribes from east of the River Jordan.[33] In 1927, the Chiefs of Staff recommended the use of Shanghai-based planes to gather military information in China.[34] In 1930, the French used aircraft to guide police columns toward rebel concentrations in Vietnam. Reconnaissance was the prime use of the RAF in opposing the Arab Rising of 1937–9 in Palestine, although there was also bombing and strafing, with the Fairey Gordon, a light day-bomber, being used.

However, the conflicts of the 1920s and 1930s offered only limited guidance because they did not happen between equally balanced air forces, and rapid technological developments soon outdated experience. There was an air dimension in the Anglo-Italian crisis of 1935–6 over Ethiopia, although, in the event, there were no hostilities between the two powers. Nevertheless, the crisis showed the greater extent to which air power played a role in planning for war. Reflecting the dependence of strategic bombing on nearby aerodromes, the RAF proposed to bomb the industrial centres of northern Italy, such as Turin, from bases in southern France, assuming that France joined Britain. There was also a need to protect British colonies from neighbouring Italian colonies, and, in turn, to permit attacks on the latter, the RAF moved planes to Egypt (against Libya), British Somaliland (against Italian Somaliland and Eritrea), and Malta (against both Libya and Italy).

Spanish Civil War

In addition, it is not clear that the conflicts that did occur were adequately analysed. For example, the spectacular terror bombing of civilian targets, such as Madrid (1936), Guernica (1937), and Barcelona (1938), by German and Italian planes sent to help Franco's Nationalists in the Spanish Civil War did not actually play a significant role in the result of the conflict. The

German destruction of Guernica on 26 April 1937 was intended to de
the morale of the Republican Basques and thus weaken their resistance to
the Nationalist advance. Concerned about the world response, the Germans
and Nationalists sought to deny responsibility. The terrorized Basques did
not mount any resistance when the Nationalists moved on to take Bilbao in
June. The bombing of refugees became an Italian speciality, notably with those
fleeing Malaga in February 1937 and fleeing toward Barcelona in the winter
of 1938–9.

Yet, the impact of the bombing was exaggerated, and terror bombing
captured the imagination of many, sowing fears that the bombing of civilian
targets would be decisive in a future war. This affected British thinking at the
time of the Munich crisis in 1938. British intelligence exaggerated German air
capability. The resulting concentration on air defence was crucial for Britain
in 1940, but some of the preparations for air attack led to a misapplication of
scarce resources. As the Second World War was to show, Douhet and others
had exaggerated the potential of bombing (as well as underestimating the size
of bomber forces required), and underplayed the value of tactical air support.

At the same time, British observers in Spain did not only see German and
Italian air power in terms of the attack on civilians. Returning to Britain, the
British diplomat G. H. Thompson produced a report that was circulated to
the Cabinet:

> the Nationalist air forces that smashed the iron ring of defences round
> Bilbao were almost entirely made up of German machines piloted by
> Germans. The final attack was launched by eighty of these bombers in the
> air at one time, and they created havoc. The German aviation groups have
> continued to play a leading part in the present Asturian campaign, both in
> bombing attacks on cities and in co-operation with ground troops.[35]

Germany

The Germans prioritized their air force once Hitler came to power, and
spent accordingly in line with a materialist thread within Nazism. Air power
appeared to offer both a counter to German fears of vulnerability and a way to

embrace a modern technology that promised victory. Already, in March 1935, Hitler had told British ministers that his air force was the same size, a false claim but one that indicated his drive. That October, the ambitious existing *Luftwaffe* programme for expansion was stepped up.

However, the German air industry did not develop sufficiently to support an air force for a major conflict. The Spanish Civil War also suggested to the Germans that large long-range bombers were not crucial: they used dive-bombers there, instead, and developed dive-bombing tactics. Seeking a strategic bombing force that could act as a deterrent, Germany had initially led in the development of the four-engine bomber – the 'Ural' or 'Amerika' bomber – but produced only prototypes. The capability to produce the engines necessary for the planned heavy bombers was lacking. Nevertheless, the Germans expected to have the four-engined He-177 in production by 1940–1.[36] It did not become operational until late 1942 and was weakened by over-complicated engineering.

More generally, there were problems with the availability of aviation fuel for the *Luftwaffe*, and with its training programme, and also a preference for numbers of planes as opposed to a balanced expenditure that would include investment in infrastructure, for example logistical provision, especially spares. This preference owed much to the poor quality of leadership.

Hermann Göring, a veteran of the air struggle during the Great War, became Minister of Aviation in 1933 and Commander in Chief of the *Luftwaffe* in March 1935. He, however, was not interested in the less glamorous side of air power, and this helped to weaken the *Luftwaffe* in the subsequent war. He was also less than careful in his appointments. Ernst Udet, whom he made Technical Director, was overly interested in dive-bombing. Göring's concern for plane numbers helped to lead, in 1937, to the postponement of the four-engined bomber programme, as it was easier to produce large numbers of twin-engined bombers. Furthermore, the Germans concentrated on the search for a force structure that would make combined operations focusing on a rapid attack a success. This system, later described as *blitzkrieg* (lightning war), was necessary to satisfy Hitler's preference for quick wars and the state of the German economy, but resulted in a lack of support for strategic bombing which was seen, instead, as a long-term solution in warfare. *Blitzkrieg* entailed no obvious requirement for a strategic bombing force.[37]

Instead, the Germans became increasingly committed to air-land integration, with the *Luftwaffe* designed to provide both close air support and interdiction in order to enhance the possibility of obtaining a decisive victory, and thus a successful strategic outcome. Wolfram von Richthofen, Chief of Staff and then commander of the Condor Legion dispatched to help the Nationalists in the Spanish Civil War, pressed for close coordination in both space and time, and used the war to test and improve relevant techniques. The practice and philosophy of jointness was very important to what was later called *blitzkrieg*.[38] Aircraft suitable for this practice were developed. First flown in 1935, the Ju-87, or Stuka, was more accurate than most planes, remaining stable in near-vertical dives, which increased its accuracy against moving tanks, although, in practice, fighting the Poles, the *Luftwaffe* in 1939 understandably proved most effective against static units. Organizationally, the *Luftwaffe* benefited by avoiding the RAF's division into functional commands, namely the separation into Bomber Command and Fighter Command in 1936, and, instead, created *Luftflotten* (Air Fleets), each of which contained different types of aircraft.[39]

Air power and the approach to the Second World War

Elsewhere, the ability to learn lessons about air support from the Spanish Civil War was limited by inter-service rivalry and the nature of air force culture, especially in Britain where there was still a major commitment to strategic bombing as a way to break the will of an opposing population.[40] In 1932, Stanley Baldwin, the previous (and next) Prime Minister, had argued that 'the only defence is in offence, which means that you will have to kill more women and children more quickly than the enemy'. In 1936, when he resigned, Montgomery-Massingberd wrote:

> I feel that the biggest battle that I have had to fight in the last three years is against the idea that on account of the arrival of air forces as a new arm, the Low Countries are of little value to us and that, therefore, we need not maintain a military force to assist in holding them . . . the elimination of

any army commitment on the Continent sounds such a comfortable and cheap policy . . . especially among the air mad.

Instead, he claimed, correctly as it turned out, that a war on the Continent would still be decided on land.[41]

In particular, advocates of stratiegic bombing resisted the possibilities of ground-support operations. Indeed, RAF bomber crews were not trained to operate in the battlefield. The drive for institutional independence drove air power advocates towards strategic bombing. However, the need to provide fighter escorts for bombers was not appreciated by the British or the Americans until they suffered heavy casualties in the Second World War.[42] The American B-17, Flying Fortress, was heavily armed in the belief that they could defend themselves, but the reality proved otherwise. German day fighters learned to attack head-on because the top turret could not fire forward. B-17s were supposed to fly in box formations of four to provide mutual fire support, but, once the box was broken, the aircraft became easy targets. Diving steeply on to the formations or attacking from above and behind gave the fighters the edge.

The focus on bombers offers a parallel to attitudes towards the inappropriate reliance on tanks alone in mobile warfare, rather than on mixed-armed forces. A key point is the value of jointness. The history of air power suggests that much of its capability rested on being part of an integrated fighting system with an operational doctrine that relied on cooperation between arms and sought to implement realizable political goals. The same was true of the impact of mechanization on land warfare. However, cooperation between ground-attack aircraft and tanks was limited because such cooperation required effective radio communications. Moreover, both ground-attack aircraft and tanks tend to work independently if they aim to play to their strengths.

Lessons were also not drawn from the Sino-Japanese War. For example, the battle of Shanghai in 1937 showed that Chinese losses made during the day could be regained at night when Japanese air power was less effective. The vulnerability of ships to air attack was apparent, but these were isolated ships in confined waters. Having taken Shanghai, Japanese planes sank an American gunboat on the Yangzi.

In France and the Soviet Union, the stress in the late 1930s was on tactical doctrine and a related force structure. Instead of stressing strategic bombing, the French put the emphasis on reconnaissance aircraft and ground support.[43] The Soviet Union lacked an independent air force, but, despite weaknesses in relevant industrial capability, had, thanks to the build-up of its aircraft industry from the late 1920s, the largest number of planes in the 1930s.[44] Moreover, the Soviets had an interest in strategic bombing. The TB-3 was intended as a deterrent against Japan. However, Stalin's purges which were linked to a move for the air force from strategic capability to army support, hit the air force hard. The Italians suffered from political favouritism in procurement.

Both the British and the French devoted attention to fighter defence in the late 1930s, seeing this as a necessary response to German power, although the British Air Staff possessed scant evidence to support its belief that the Germans had plans for an air assault.[45] Concern about the *Luftwaffe* ensured that the French air force won a bigger share than the navy or, still more, army in the increased defence expenditure in 1934–5. Nevertheless, the weakness of the French air force was a contributory factor to vulnerability at the time of the Munich crisis.

In March 1934, Baldwin told the House of Commons that Britain would not accept inferiority in air power, and, that July, a large majority voted in the Commons for a major increase in the size of the air force by 1939. The British developed two effective monoplane fighters, the Hawker Hurricane and Supermarine Spitfire. In November 1934, the Air Ministry had issued specifications for a fighter with improved speed, rate of climb and ceiling, and with eight, not four, machine guns. The prototype Hawker Hurricane was ordered in February 1935 and made its first flight in November 1935. In December 1937, the Hawker Hurricane I entered service, beginning a new period of eight-machine-gun monoplane fighters that could fly faster than 300 mph. In March 1936, the prototype Supermarine Spitfire made its first maiden flight, and the plane entered service in June 1938.

Alongside early-warning radar, these planes were to help rescue Britain in 1940 from the consequences of devoting too much attention to bombing. At that stage, Britain had a numerical superiority over Germany in single-engined fighters. The Munich crisis had further encouraged an emphasis on air power in British rearmament and, by September 1939, the RAF had replaced its biplanes. In response to the German threat, new RAF air bases were built in East Anglia, Lincolnshire and Yorkshire, and squadrons were moved there from elsewhere in Britain. This emphasis extended to the USA where President Franklin Delano Roosevelt, increasingly conscious of the importance of air power, proved willing to support the provision of planes to the European democracies.[46] The French were keen to buy American planes and in 1939 purchased Martin and Douglas bombers.

With its capacity for long-distance detection of movement, radar rapidly developed. In 1904, Christian Hülsmeyer had first used radio waves to detect the presence of distant metallic objects. Thirty years later, the French CSF company took out a patent for detecting obstacles by ultra-short wavelengths, while, in 1935, Robert Watson-Watt published *The Detection of Aircraft by Radio Methods* and the Air Ministry decided to develop radar. The following year, the American Naval Research Laboratory demonstrated pulse radar successfully. The *Détection Electromagnétique* was developed to protect French naval bases in the Mediterranean and also the French border from Belgium to the Alps.

In 1940, the British benefited from an integrated air-defence system founded on a chain of radar early-warning stations built from 1936 to 1939, but still incomplete at the time of the Munich crisis. These stations, which could spot planes 100 miles off the south coast, were linked to centralized control rooms where data was analysed and then fed through into instructions for fighters. No other state had that capability at that stage. The weakness of anti-aircraft defences enhanced the importance of this system, and this weakness led to the formation of Balloon Command in November 1938.

Ethics received little attention in strategic debates on the part of the military. There was some uneasiness about the ethical nature and practical consequences of strategic bombing against civilian targets. Ethical concerns, or lip service thereto, were one factor behind the American emphasis on precision and on careful selection of economic targets rather than the broader attacks on civilian morale. However, other air power advocates focused on the idea of a 'magic bullet' promising victory without military casualties. In an undated memorandum that the catalogue suggests is from 1925–6, but which contains a reference to a document of March 1930, Field Marshal Sir George Milne, the Chief of the Imperial General Staff, brought ethical issues about air power into organizational questions. He wrote of

> the highly organised and unscrupulous propaganda of the Air Staff... the separation of the Air Staff from the General Staff which prevents problems of defence being considered as a whole, and with a proper sense of proportion as to their cost . . . the Air Staff have found it necessary, in order to find support for their separate and independent existence . . . to devise a special form of so-called air strategy . . . there appears to be two principles or catch words upon which it is based . . . attack against the nerve centers of an enemy nation . . . and the moral effect of the air arm. In dealing with problems of war on a large scale against civilized countries the former term is usually employed. The objectives of such strategy are the centres of production – nominally of munitions, which, be it marked, is a term of very wide significance. In effect this new form of strategy takes the form of attack against civilian workers, including their women and children. The hitherto accepted objectives of land and sea warfare have been the armed forces of the enemy, and whether or no we as a nation are justified morally in adopting a military policy which is so totally at variance with the accepted dictates of humanity, there is no doubt that we should be the first to suffer if the next war were to be waged on such principles.[47]

7

The 1930s: economic context

Policy choices were affected by economic possibilities, notably in terms of both strategic tasking and weapons procurement. The massive public deficits that had followed the Great War hit military expenditure, as did deflationary policies and balanced budgets. Although economic recovery eased the situation in the 1920s, the early 1930s provided fewer options than the 1920s. The overheating American economy collapsed as a result of a bursting speculative boom in share prices in New York in October 1929, the Wall Street Crash. This bursting of an asset price bubble became far more serious as the inexperienced central bank cut the money supply. The tightening of the financial reins, including the calling in of overseas loans, caused financial crisis elsewhere.

At the same time, the 1930 Smoot-Hawley Act put up American tariffs and depressed demand for imports. Other states followed suit, leading to a worldwide protectionism that had dramatically cut world trade by 1932. Similarly, American devaluation of the dollar in 1933 was followed by competing devaluations elsewhere.

The USA was not the sole source of the crisis. There were also separate sources of financial crisis in Austria and Germany. Far more than the mismanagement of financial and trading systems, however, was involved in causing the Slump and the Depression. There was also a more systemic problem, of the weaknesses of liberal and international economic practices, now referred to as globalization, as a result of the political and ideological potency of nationalist economic views. This nationalism emerged in response to the economic crisis as states sought individual security through protecting prosperity.[1]

As export industries were hit, unemployment rose substantially across the industrial world, underlining the value of remaining arms exports. In the USA, the unemployment rate rose to nearly 32 per cent in 1932, by when manufacturing was at only 40 per cent of capacity. The worldwide decline in consumer and business spending hit industrial production, although, under dictatorial control, the Soviet Union followed a different trajectory, with production increasing as did military spending. However, across most of the world, the pressure to deal with public finances hit arms production, and disarmament had a significant economic dimension, as in 1931 when the League of Nations backed a halt in arms spending. France's economic crisis in the early 1930s, combined with a determination to balance the budget in order to maintain the franc on the Gold Standard, led to a major fall in defence spending.[2] In turn, this encouraged a focus on the defences of the new Maginot Line, which may, however, also have been in some senses a job-creation scheme. In Australia, defence expenditure fell from £7.8 million in 1927 to £3 million in 1933, in large part due to the establishment of a Labour government in 1929.[3]

At the same time, due to the Slump, the industrial world's imports of raw materials declined, affecting commodity producers both in the industrial world (for example British coalfields) and elsewhere. Production and prices fell. This fall in commodity earnings brought serious economic and political problems throughout the developing world, for example in Latin America and Australasia, although the contrasting amount of political violence in these states indicated that there was no inevitable course of civil conflict. Governments were affected by falling tax income. In addition, these producers were now less able to finance imports. Indeed, at the same time that it led to the attempt to strengthen imperial economies through protectionism, the Depression of the 1930s also did much damage to the relationship between homelands and colonies, gravely weakening imperial links. This lasting damage to imperial links was not undone by the subsequent experience of the Second World War.

The Slump and the subsequent Depression destroyed the liberal economic order; led to a collapse of confidence in capitalist structures; undermined democratic governments so that, with the exception of Scandinavia, there was only one democracy, Czechoslovakia, east of the Rhine by 1938; and resulted in a marked deterioration in the peacefulness and stability of the international system.

It became more difficult to obtain capital and technology from abroad, while, as a result of the economic crisis, governments increasingly thought and planned in national (including imperial), rather than international, economic terms. This tendency led to a measure of corporatism, as governments sought to direct both labour and capital, and this corporatism was conducive to a closer integration of economies and national policies.

In the case of empires, 'national' meant the imperial, as efforts were made to find economic safety through existing political links. The economic manifestations included currency blocs, and imperial preference in trade, as well as, in the case of Germany and Japan, ambitions for territorial expansion. Such expansion was designed to provide resources and markets. In a paper for the Cabinet, Sir Francis Lindley, British Ambassador in Tokyo, in May 1933 observed 'With her population of 60 million expanding at the rate of close on 1 million a year, and the continuous raising of tariff walls by most of the countries of the world, it is not too much to say that the market of China is a vital necessity to Japan, and she will not allow it to be closed against her without a struggle.'[4] Four years later, Japan launched an attempt to settle one million households in Manchuria. Italy meanwhile sought to develop the agricultural potential of its colonies of Libya and Italian East Africa.[5]

As a consequence of the closer integration of economies and governments accompanying the decline of the liberal economic order, economic possibilities could be altered by political action. This process was clearly seen in Germany where, under Hitler from 1933, there was a major shift toward military expenditure. The German economy had not suffered fundamental losses as part of the Versailles Peace Settlement, and the reparations it paid were not too serious a burden. Indeed, Germany received more in loans, which were never repaid, than she paid as reparations for the wartime damage she had inflicted. As a consequence, despite serious limitations, the German economy could serve as the basis for a new war effort, although the problems of moving from industrial capacity to effective weaponry were underplayed both by Hitler and by foreign commentators. The attempted militarization of the economy, or, at least, of economic planning, led to a stress on national self-sufficiency. This policy encouraged an interest in the production of synthetic substitutes for imports. Germany's Four-Year Plan, introduced in 1936, developed production of synthetic oil, rubber and textiles, while Japan stepped up synthetic oil production in 1938.

In the Soviet Union, in large part in pursuit of the military build-up pressed by Marshal Mikhail Tukhachevsky, industry was boosted everywhere, and industry in the Urals and Siberia increased in the same proportion as in other regions. This increase, however, had clear strategic consequences, as the already-strong metallurgical industry in the Urals served as the basis for an expansion of industrial production that proved to be beyond the range of German air attack. Major new industrial capacity was also developed near Novosibirsk in south-western Siberia, while new plants were built in Soviet Central Asia. Nevertheless, the extent of the German advance in 1941–2 was not anticipated, and the speed of this advance affected earlier evacuation plans.[6]

Stalin's determination to keep control of the process of preparation led him to clash with the military leadership. Indeed, Tukhachevsky was a danger to Stalin because he displayed the habit of elevating military necessity to the point of demanding the subordination of the whole economy to the army. More generally, the overlap of the Soviet Terror with the acceleration of the European arms race in the 1930s and, even more, late 1930s, was no coincidence. Following the war scare with Britain in 1927, Soviet defence spending had risen[7], but it was to rise far more from 1931 in response to Japanese expansion into Manchuria. A 'great tank programme' was adopted, but it proved difficult to fulfil unrealistic plans about military expansion. In 1933, to the anger of Tukhachevsky, Stalin cut back plans that he saw as overly optimistic but, nevertheless, already by then, there had been a massive increase in the availability of tanks (4,700), planes (5,000), artillery (17,000), and machine-guns.

Such production, much of weaponry that was soon obsolescent and outclassed, could only be achieved by transferring resources from other economic sectors and by squeezing living standards. The ability to do so, and thus help jump-start Stalin's new Soviet economy, rested on the government's control of the means of force, and the two combined in the mass deportations that accompanied the collectivization of agriculture. Unlike Germany and Japan, the Soviet Union also benefited from producing large quantities of oil.

In Britain, confidence in peacetime economic planning was limited until the Second World War. In part, such planning was discredited for conservative British politicians by its association with the Five-Year Plans of the Soviet Union and its command economy, but, more generally, it was unacceptable to the powerful financial community whose views were central to British economic strategy until 1940. There was concern, notably in the influential Treasury, that a large rise in defence expenditure could cause insurmountable fiscal strain.[8]

In the USA, the welfare and economic reforms known as the New Deal, introduced by Franklin Delano Roosevelt after he became President in 1933, led to greater federal economic intervention, although without a recovery in production to the level of the late 1920s. The New Deal was also central to the growth of federal soft and hard power vis-à-vis states and local communities. In response to the Second World War, this capability was to be readily transferred to a military build-up unprecedented in American history.

As a reminder of the difficulties of judging policy choices, notably toward expenditure on armaments, the Depression gave rise to a critique of the traditional belief in 'sound finance', which had meant a balanced budget and low expenditure and taxation. These policies had hit defence expenditure, as with the Geddes Axe in Britain in 1922. This belief was criticized by John Maynard Keynes in his *General Theory of Employment, Interest and Money* (1936). He called for public spending to be raised in order to cut unemployment, and was ready to see very low interest rates and to tolerate inflation, a departure from conventional monetary policy. Rearmament was a central form of public spending.

It is far from clear, however, that such a policy was bound to work. Keynesian monetary policy really required a closed economy with very little liquidity. Moreover, pump-priming public spending designed to stimulate the economy, such as that in the USA and Sweden, still left unemployment high. Unemployment only fell below 15 per cent in the USA in 1940, although, by then, GNP per capita was $954 compared to $615 in 1933.

In some countries, there was a measure of economic recovery in the late 1930s from the depths of the Depression. Government borrowing and rearmament, driven by Hitler's determination to reverse the verdict of the Great War, revived German economic activity. However, the strains of the German proto-war economy caused serious problems and the rate of projected rearmament was unsustainable. The British economy was helped by the combination of loose monetary conditions (following departure from the Gold Standard in 1931) with orthodox fiscal policy, by low commodity prices, and by consumer demand from the prosperous section of the country. Public works played only a minor role in Britain as they were seen as likely to crowd out the private market. However, economic policy brought scant relief to the British heavy industrial sector, which did not grow appreciably until rearmament in the face of the German threat, a rearmament that left Britain in a good state to confront Germany. There was a marked relaxation of fiscal restraint in the late 1930s and the government proved capable of supporting a powerful military-industrial complex, one that was to make Britain a formidable opponent for Germany.[9]

It is unhelpful to imagine that there was a readily apparent fiscal policy for national power, let alone military effectiveness. Moreover, fiscal policy was bound up with the self-image of governing élites, not least thanks to the totemic resonance of terms such as sound money or prudence. Therefore, it is necessary to give due weight to the role of perception, especially as an aspect of the extent to which best practice was a political concept and choice, one requiring and leading to both support and confidence. This was true for fiscal and other aspects of policy. There was a parallel with military policy, with, again, self-image and the role of perception playing a role.

8

War in the Far East

The decision to expand the conflict into a struggle for the complete overthrow of Chiang [Jiang] is likely to involve the Japanese in an unlimited effort . . . from pitched battles the Japanese war on China will in future shift more and more to a less spectacular but no less deadly struggle between the political cohesion of China and the economic staying power of Japan.

HERBERT ROSINSKI, JANUARY 1938[1]

The standard focus for the 1930s in Euro-American scholarship is on the consequences of the rise of Hitler to power in 1933 and subsequent moves toward the outbreak of the Second World War in Europe in 1939. However, prior to that, there was already large-scale conflict in the Far East, and that must come to the fore because of the Far East's significance for much of the world's population and its importance for more general trends in military and political history.

As discussed in Chapter 3, China had a narrative of its own in the 1920s, that of the struggle towards unification and some economic growth. China was generally less subject to external intervention (excepting the armed presence and continuing extra-territorial rights of some foreign powers) than in the 1900s and 1910s, and the Guomindang (Nationalist Party) had brought a measure of consolidation and stability.[2] As a reminder of the potential consequences of military action, the Northern Expedition had been followed by major improvements in economic output and public finances. The stronger government was better able to dictate the terms of its partnerships with surviving warlords and, indeed, those in the south and south-west were to be suppressed in 1935–7.

In 1936, an alliance of warlords, notably the Guangxi Clique and the warlord of Guangdong, turned against Jiang Jieshi, the Guomindang leader, but bribery, as well as military action, quickly dispersed the challenge. That December, the Young Marshal, Zhang Xueliang, also turned against Jiang, in the hope that, by allying with the Communists, rather than fighting them as he was doing for Jiang, China would be able to turn its military against the Japanese and free Manchuria. He cooperated with the Communists to seize Jiang at the city of Xi'an, but then lost his nerve and subsequently was imprisoned while Jiang regained power. Zhang's army was brought under the latter's control, but was not employed to any useful purpose.

Guomindang versus Communists

The Guomindang government, now that it was a government with some wider authority, was also better able after the 1920s to fight the Communists. Nevertheless, the Communists proved more intractable foes than the warlords for the Guomindang, both militarily and politically. Communism had a political and ideological strength which distinguished the Red Army from the warlord forces. China thus witnessed the ideological conflict that was so important to the nature of war during the century, and that, in East Asia, was far from being a 'cold war' or confrontation short of large-scale conflict, either before or after the Second World War.

Founded in 1921, small, urban and intellectual-dominated, the Chinese Communist Party faced the problem of deciding how far and how best to align with the Guomindang, which, as a reforming movement opposed to foreign imperialist influence, had important features in common with it.[3] Direction from Moscow was a key issue, as it led the weak and marginal Communists initially to cooperation, in pursuit of what the Soviets saw as a united-front movement. Stalin favoured this policy, whereas Trotsky preferred revolutionary integrity. However, in 1926, Jiang, who distrusted Soviet influence in the nationalist camp and suspected the Communists, turned against the latter and had their influence in government curtailed. The Communist presence among China's growing industrial workers was significant, most notably in Shanghai. Once Jiang had taken over the city in 1927, the labour movement was brutally suppressed by the army in cooperation with the local underworld.[4] This 'White Terror' was seen across the Guomindang zone, with action against peasant radicals in Hunan countered by the Autumn Harvest Uprising, which was defeated.

This anti-Communist repression made it easier for Britain to accept Jiang, but led Stalin to change policy. In June 1927, he instructed the Chinese Communists to form a Red Army, embark on rural revolution and try to take over the Guomindang. The latter then completely dispensed with the Communists, who, in turn, began a rebellion. It started at Nanchang, the capital of the province of Jiangxi, but lacked sufficient troops or supplies, and was rapidly crushed. The survivors captured the port of Shantou where they mistakenly hoped that they would receive Soviet help. Instead, the Communists were swiftly defeated. That December, the Communists rose in Guangzhou (Canton), but much of the working class did not provide support and troops quickly restored a bloody order with many executed in the streets, including women and children. Like Zhang Zuolin in northern China, the Guomindang broke off relations with the Soviet Union which strove to direct the Communist struggle in China.

At the same time, the challenge from the Communists in China was affected by serious divisions over strategy among the Communists, while these divisions, in turn, were influenced by military developments. Leading Communists, such as Li Lisan, Secretary-General from 1928 to 1931, followed the traditional interpretation of Marxist-Leninism, seeking to exploit the revolutionary potential of urban workers. In contrast, a number of leaders, including Mao Zedong, more correctly perceived that the real potential in China, very differently from the Soviet Union, rested with farm labourers. However, in considering Mao, it is necessary to appreciate the degree to which his reputation was subsequently enhanced.

Initially, the Red Army suffered from a policy of trying to capture and hold towns; this only provided the Nationalists with easy targets. In 1927, in particular, the Communists in the province of Hunan were defeated when they attacked Changsha the provincial capital. They captured Changsha in 1930, only to be rapidly driven from it with heavy losses. Jiang, moreover, proved adaptable in recruiting support. In Shanghai in 1927, he used the criminal Green Gang to support the army against the Communists, and he gave its leaders high military ranks.[5]

The Red Army was more successful in resisting attack in rural areas, especially if in the traditional hideouts of social bandits, namely remote and mountainous areas, such as the Jinggang highlands on the Hunan-Jiangxi border. There, Mao managed to build up a force from defeated Communist units and local opponents of exploitative landlords. Mao regarded the rural base as an essential part of his revolutionary strategy. Without a base, it was impossible to develop a fighting force or to implement the revolutionary programme to obtain the support of the rural population. Drawing on his own ideas, on the traditions of the rural outlaw world, and on the experience of Guomindang brutality, Mao used violence for political ends from the outset in order to terrorize others and destroy potential rival leaders of the rural population. Under Guomindang attack and short of arms, however, Mao re-located into southern Jiangxi in January 1929, where he was able again to build up his local strength. He also pressed hard for the politicization of the Red Army, emphasizing the need for political officers.

In 1930, Mao took part in the attack on cities ordered by Li Lisan and the Communist Party. Changsha briefly fell, but other attacks failed, while a second attack on Changsha, in which Mao was ordered to take part, was defeated, not least thanks to the Guomindang use of aeroplanes and artillery. In Jiangxi, in contrast, and in a preview of what was to come after 1937, the Red Army could trade space for time and harry its slower-moving opponent, especially as the urban-centred Guomindang lacked much peasant support. This weakness led to the failure of Jiang Jieshi's successive 'bandit extermination campaigns'. In the first, launched in late 1930 and mounted with about 45,000 troops, Mao benefited from fighting on territory that favoured the defensive and this helped in mounting ambushes. As a result, the attackers took heavy casualties. Mao also staged a ruthless purge of the Party in Jiangxi, slaughtering the original local Communist leaders but also many thousands who had done nothing other than appear not to be on his wavelength. He alleged that opponents were Guomindang infiltrators. Although the scale was very different, there was a parallel with Stalin's purges later in the decade.

In February and May 1931, other Guomindang campaigns were launched against the Fourth Red Army, led by Zhang Guotao in the mountains of southern Hubei. Again, terrain and local knowledge helped thwart the attacks. As with Mao, there was also a brutal purge by Zhang of rival Communists.

In April 1931, there was yet another drive on Mao's Jiangxi position, this time with over 100,000 troops deployed under He Yingqin, the Minister of Military Administration and Chief of Staff. Initial failure was followed, in July, by direct intervention by Jiang who also brought reinforcements. The Communists were driven back with numerous casualties, but escaped destruction, in part because of the Guomindang's need to respond to the Japanese invasion of Manchuria (see pp. 164–5).

In 1932, after the battle for Shanghai was over (see p. 165), Jiang attacked the Communists anew, deploying about 400,000 troops and benefiting from the advice of Hans von Seeckt, the former head of the German army. Attacking Zhang Guotao's Fourth Red Army, Jiang used a scorched-earth and blockade strategy that destroyed the economic basis of the opposition.[6] Having exposed themselves to defeat through positional battles, the Fourth Red Army staged a break-out from August 1932, leaving a guerrilla force that maintained opposition in the mountains. Zhang's Fourth Red Army retreated to Sichuan, losing many men on their long march.

Jiang also attacked Mao in Jiangxi in 1932, deploying 250,000 troops. The Communists were put under heavy pressure, but again escaped destruction, not least because of a lack of determination on the part of many Guomindang units. It was the ability to survive, regardless of losses, which was to play such an important part in the later success of the Red Army, and indeed of guerrilla forces in other conflicts.

For the 1933 campaign against Jiangxi, launched in October with possibly about 750,000 troops, the Guomindang forcibly moved peasants in order to deprive the Communists of local support, especially of food and information, and also sought to control the countryside through the establishment of large numbers of blockhouses, with new ones built to accompany the advance. By 1934, 14,000 blockhouses had been built. Moreover, roads and landing strips were constructed. Serious pressure was brought to bear. The Communists tried, and failed, to thwart this strategy by conventional warfare, rather than resting on the defence and mounting ambushes. Their forces were increasingly affected by desertion.

Jiang, however, failed to focus on the campaign, in part because he went on a long trip to north and west China and in part because of his concern about relations with Japan. In accordance with instructions from Stalin, the First Red Army meanwhile, in October 1934, launched a break-out from Jiangxi, beginning the so-called Long March across several thousand miles of difficult terrain to Shaanxi; in which most of those who set out fell by the wayside. Local warlords, for example Long Yun of Yunnan, tended to let the Communists move on because they did not want trouble or intervention by Jiang, and because they were liberally bribed with Mexican silver dollars supplied by the Comintern in 1933–4. However, at the Xiang River north-east of Guilin in December 1934, an attack by the autonomous Guangxi general Bai Chongxi inflicted heavy losses while the Communists were in an exposed position.

This epic defeat, however, helped Mao regain influence, and then power, from Moscow-backed leaders who favoured more conventional warfare. Mao's return led to the revival of a coherent guerrilla strategy. Guomindang blockhouses were bypassed while its air attacks proved unable to stop the Communists. After crossing even more difficult terrain, Mao moved to the bare mountains of northern Shaanxi, which he reached in October 1935. After Mao and Zhang had decided to go their separate ways, Zhang's Fourth Red Army was largely destroyed by Guomindang and warlord forces in separate campaigning in Sichuan.

In his new rural base, Mao was more remote from the urban centres of Guomindang power. In 1936, an attempt to invade Shanxi in order to create a supply line to Soviet-run Mongolia failed. Nevertheless, funded and provided with arms by Stalin, Mao became a factor in the complicated negotiations of power in China, while the Red Army, capitalizing on its survival despite all of the Guomindang's assaults, became larger.[7]

In 1937, Mao published *Guerrilla Warfare*, a pamphlet in which he argued that, in response to opposition, unlimited guerrilla warfare offered a new prospect that was more effective than what was presented as more primitive guerrilla warfare:

In a war of revolutionary character, guerrilla operations are a necessary part. This is particularly true in a war waged for the emancipation of a people who inhabit a vast nation . . . the development of the type of guerrilla warfare characterised by the quality of mass is both necessary and natural . . . We consider guerrilla operations as but one aspect of our total or mass war . . . All the people of both sexes from the ages of sixteen to forty-five must be organised into anti-Japanese self-defence units.[8]

Operationally, the emphasis included words and phrases used to describe conventional warfare in the period, such as 'mobility, and attack . . . deliver a lightning blow, seek a lightning decision'.[9] Yet, general revolutionary wars were seen as very different to conventional warfare, being defined in terms of:

the whole people of a nation, without regard to class or party, carry on a guerrilla struggle that is an instrument of the national policy . . . All these struggles have been carried on in the interests of the whole people or the greater part of them; all had a broad basis in the national manpower, and all have been in accord with the laws of historical development.[10]

Thus historical development assumed a long-term conflict. In the short-term, of course, the Communists had failed to overthrow their opponents or even hold Jiangxi, and the Guomindang were in a dominant position. In 1933–4, Hans von Seeckt, Commander in Chief of the German army in 1920–6, played an important role in increasing the effectiveness of the Chinese army, being followed by Alexander von Falkenhausen, a retired German general.[11] Western, particularly German, arms were purchased; by this point, Germany was China's largest supplier of arms. Relatively well-off in arms, the one area where the Guomindang force still fell behind to the Red Army was in its commitment to a cause.

Foreign intervention, 1929–36

However, the prospect for stability in China was fatally compromised by foreign intervention. This was not the case of action again by Britain and France, which, indeed, were far more afraid of developments in Europe (and within their own empires), and had less of an impact on China in the 1920s and 1930s than they had in the mid-nineteenth century. In fact, unlike during the Opium Wars, Britain could do little to protect its extensive commercial interests. Whereas in 1860 British and French forces had occupied Beijing, in October 1929 Soviet forces attacked Manchuria. This was in response to the seizure of the Soviet share in the Chinese Eastern Railway. Well-trained, and using modern artillery, tanks, and, in particular, planes, they rapidly defeated Zhang Xueliang, the Young Marshal, the son and successor of the warlord Zhang Zuolin, inflicting heavy casualties. The Chinese backed down and returned the Soviet share in the railway.

The General Depression from 1929 also played a major role. Hit by a collapse in vital exports, and mass unemployment, Japan became more bellicose in the 1930s, breathing 'an atmosphere of gun-grease'.[12] In part this bellicosity arose because sections of the military followed autonomous policies ignoring civilian restraint, and in part because the military supported a militarism that challenged civil society and affected government policies, leading to what was called, by some, 'government by assassination'.

In 1930–1, Japanese officers, angered by what they felt was the failure of the government to defend national interests, planned a coup and the creation of a military government. Instead, they found it easier to seize control of Manchuria where they were concerned that Japan's existing leased rights were under threat. On 18 September 1931, Japanese soldiers of the Kwantung Army blew up part of the South Manchurian railway near the city of Shenyang (Mukden). This incident served as the basis for taking over Mukden and for an advance north and west from the Kwantung Leased Area, the established Japanese sphere of influence in southern Manchuria. Japanese forces moved forward along the railways and seized major positions. The railways were particularly important in campaigning due to a lack of motor transport.

Zhang Xueliang, the Young Marshal, and local warlord, commanded 200,000 troops on paper but was suffering from drug addiction. Crucially, he and Jiang did not respond to the Japanese move as they, particularly Jiang, hoped that the Western powers would compel Japan to abandon its action. Instead, Jiang initially endorsed the appeasement of Japan while concentrating on the destruction of the Red Army. Partly as a result, Jiang did not send

Zhang his well-trained divisions: Manchuria fell to Japan in a five-month campaign after an ineffective resistance.

The Japanese increased pressure on China by attacking the Chinese section of Shanghai from late January 1932. After early hesitation, there was strong resistance with German-trained divisions fighting well against the Japanese in a large-scale conflict to which the Japanese eventually committed over 50,000 troops as well as 200 planes and warships. The devastation caused by Japanese bombardment and bombing was very great, while the landing of a Japanese amphibious force up the Yangzi River outmanoeuvred the Chinese who fell back from Shanghai. In part, the operation arose from the determination of the Japanese navy to compete with the army.

In the end, under international mediation, China accepted the demilitarization of Shanghai while Japanese troops were pulled back from Chinese areas of the city. This attack had been a particularly blatant instance of the process by which the unequal system of treaty ports and foreign intervention in China that had begun with Britain in the late 1830s was now very much a means to increased Japanese control. Japan's commitment to intervention in China rested on a concept of its security and national interest that was not matched by the other imperial powers, bar the Soviet Union to an extent.

The Soviet Union had hitherto been the dominant power in north Manchuria, but, feeling vulnerable, it proved willing to cede its interests before the Japanese advance, and this willingness was important to the consolidation of the Japanese position in Manchuria. So also was the failure of Britain and the USA to cooperate. The League of Nations criticized Japanese policy, which led to Japan leaving the League in 1933 in its most public abandonment of internationalism, but no other effective consequences.[13] In 1935, the Soviets withdrew from Manchuria to the frontier on the Amur River, selling Japan their stake in the Chinese Eastern Railway, although relations between the two powers remained tense. Renamed Manchukuo in 1932, Manchuria was nominally placed in 1934 by the Japanese under the formal rule of Aisin-Gioro Puyi, the last Qing (Manchu) emperor, but the emperor was very much a Japanese client.

After the civilian government in Tokyo had failed to support illegal acts by the army in the 'Manchurian Incident' in 1931, a young naval officer assassinated the Prime Minister, Inukai Tsuyoshi, on 15 May 1932, and a cabinet of 'national unity' including military leaders and bureaucrats was formed. Conflict of opinions within the army in Japan also led young officers to stage a revolt in Tokyo on 26 February 1936 that, however, was suppressed by other military units. The assassination of officers by younger officers, however, served to quieten voices of reason and caution among both civilians and military in Japan. Although there has been controversy about the extent of change and militarism in 1930s' Japan, and there was little to match the violent mobilization in the Soviet Union, nevertheless, party politics, which continued through the decade and beyond, became less significant from 1932. Moreover, the impact of the Depression, and the popular relief at what was seen as decisive action in Manchuria, clearly hit Japanese internationalism.[14]

The creation through force of Manchukuo did not suffice to guarantee Japan's security and satisfy its ambitions. Japanese expansionism in northern China led to the seizure of the province of Jehol (modern Hebei) which was added to Manchukuo in 1933. Jehol was poorly defended, and the Japanese were able to use their artillery and planes to demoralize the army of the local warlord, Tang Yulin, who had failed to take defensive advantage of the mountainous terrain. His poorly led army collapsed, and the Japanese advanced to the Great Wall, threatening Beijing and Tianjin. Zhang Xueliang was sacked as coordinator of the defence of the north, but Jiang continued to use his troops to fight the Communists in Jiangxi. Meanwhile, the Japanese sphere of influence in northern China grew, with the Chinese agreeing, by the Tanggu treaty of 21 May 1933, to leave northern Hebei demilitarized and, in effect, under Japanese control.

A conviction that large-scale war between Japan and the USA or Soviet Union was inevitable had developed in Japanese military circles and led to pressure for the strengthening of the military, the state and Japanese society, with the latter two seen in an authoritarian and militaristic perspective. China was regarded as a base for vital resources necessary for preparing for this conflict. To develop these resources, Manchuria was heavily used as a colony for Japanese emigrants who, as well as producing economic wealth, would act as defenders of what was a strategic asset against the neighbouring Soviet Union.[15]

In contrast, civilian views became less significant in Japan. The cabinet of

Admiral Saitō fell in July 1934 and the attempt to restore party cabinets in a time of crisis was unsuccessful. The Japanese were disturbed by the expansion of Guomindang power and pretensions in China, notably the build-up of the German-trained divisions of the Central Army. In practice, Jiang proved willing to accommodate Japanese demands in 1933–5, in large part because he wished to strengthen and unify China, not least by destroying the Communists. Jiang saw this as a necessary step before confronting Japan.

Some in the Japanese army were inclined to despise their opponents and to exaggerate the ability of their will (and military machine) to overcome the problems posed by operating in China. These problems were not simply a matter of the ratio between Chinese space and Japanese resources, but also the determination and fighting quality of the Chinese. These Japanese were misleadingly confident that China would fall rapidly, although others in the army knew better. In fact, conquest turned out to be an impossible goal: the amphibious-based expeditions of the Western powers in the nineteenth century were a more realistic response to the nature of the military balance between China and outside powers, and to the problems of campaigning in China.

Alongside discussion of Japanese policy in 'rational' terms, there was both a social basis for militarism in what remained mainly an agrarian society[16], and a sense of imperial mission, a sense that for some, but far from all, was linked to a radical Shintō ultranationalism, and, in particular, a belief in a divine providential purpose of Japanese superiority and expansion.[17] The attitudes and impact of Zen Buddhism have been a source of controversy, but one school of scholarship emphasizes their bellicosity.[18] Hirohito, who became emperor in 1926, proved a supporter of the military, although the emperor was not expected to voice an opinion or make decisions on military matters. Instead, the expectation was that he would accept the advice of his professional officers and officials. Only when they came to a complete impasse, as in the 1936 uprising, was there space for the emperor's intervention.[19] The 1936 attempted coup, although unsuccessful, not least in the face of the emperor's imposition of martial law, resulted in the fall of the government and the rise to power of Prince Fumimaro Konoe who became Prime Minister in June 1937. In November and December 1938, he issued declarations that outlined a New Order for East Asia, ending Western imperialism and Communism there.[20]

The Japanese had already tried to incorporate their colony in Korea. General Minami Jiro, formally commander of the Kwantung Army and ambassador to Manchukuo, who was appointed Governor-General in 1936, banned the Korean language and literature from school in 1937. Conscription began the following year.

After the violence of 1930–6, it is difficult to speak of moderates in the Japanese governments. Whether they were army officers like Senjuro Hayashi or civilians like Konoe, minsters generally agreed that Japan could not afford to compromise in international relations and that a war between Japan and either or both of the USA and the Soviet Union was probably unavoidable. In this, they were persuaded by the ideological opposition of Japan and the Soviet Union, and by the long-burning hostility between Japan and the USA over the Pacific. The powerful Imperial Way and Control factors in the army were divided in large part by their emphasis on spiritual myth (the Imperial Way) versus the rational plan approach (the Control faction), but both were convinced that Japan was heading for war with one of the USA or the Soviet Union. They differed in how to prepare for it.

War between China and Japan

In part, the Sino-Japanese War that broke out in 1937 can be seen as an unintended conflict, but one born from ideas of national prestige; and, with them, what a modern nation could no longer accept. The unplanned incident between Chinese and Japanese troops near the Marco Polo Bridge outside Beijing on 7–8 July during Japanese night exercises occurred at a time when many leaders in Tokyo, including some influential generals, were convinced that Japan should concentrate on the preparation of her army for war with the Soviet Union. Indeed, Stalin had been trying from 1935 to improve relations with China and get Jiang and the Communists to cooperate. The attack Jiang had ordered on the Communists in Shaanxi in late 1935 had failed, in part because Zhang Xueliang, to whom it was entrusted, was unenthusiastic (preferring to fight Japan), while the forces sent were weak. Jiang refused to release his key divisions for the campaign.

Ideally, it was felt in Japan that, in order to prepare for conflict with the Soviets, China should be persuaded to accept her fate as a junior partner of Japan, and the ensuing diplomacy was designed to show Jiang he had no alternative. It was Jiang's uncooperativeness that prompted Tokyo to try to give him a short sharp lesson. Jiang's attitudes reflected a recent strengthening of Chinese nationalism as well as the marked improvement in the German-trained Chinese army. He moved divisions north across the Yellow River into the part of China that in 1933 had been left demilitarized by the Chinese Central Army.

In turn, while not wanting war in China, the Japanese felt the nation's honour had been challenged by the Marco Polo Bridge incident and sent fresh forces to the region, which Jiang, obviously more concerned now than in 1931, saw as a reason for war. The Chinese refused to yield to Japanese pressure to withdraw and, instead, Jiang, confident in his army, proved willing to fight and eager to assert Chinese sovereignty. Large-scale conflict broke out toward the end of July as the Japanese moved large numbers of troops into the area. In the event, Beijing, which was surrounded, was abandoned by its defenders. The Japanese occupied the city on 29 July, capturing Tianjin on the 30th.

The Chinese proved far stronger in the Guomindang heartland of the lower Yangzi valley. Japanese positions in and near Shanghai were attacked from mid-August as Jiang sought to use his élite units to advantage, not least in order to counter Japanese success in northern China. A General War Directive of 20 August called for a war of attrition designed to stop Japan from winning rapidly. The Japanese navy's attempt to seize Shanghai in August was firmly resisted by the Chinese, and the Japanese army had to intervene in strength to provide assistance. Bitter fighting led to the destruction of the best Guomindang units (and, with them, some of Jiang's best officers), which had been German-trained. Once a Japanese amphibious landing had threatened to cut off the Chinese forces, the conflict also led to the fall of the Chinese sector of Shanghai on 11 November. The Japanese air assault had been very damaging, but the Japanese also lost heavily in the house-to-house fighting. Aside from his losses, however, Jiang had failed to gain the international intervention he had anticipated.

The Japanese Central China Expeditionary Force then advanced on the Guomindang capital, Nanjing, which fell on 13 December after a heavy air attack and the breaching of the city walls by artillery. The subsequent slaughter of civilians, which, in part, was a deliberate step to crush resistance, made a compromise peace unlikely. The Chinese military headquarters was moved up the Yangzi to Wuhan. The Japanese also overran the northern provinces of Hebei, Shanxi and Inner Mongolia, defeating badly led but numerous opposing forces.

The ports of Xiamen (Amoy) and Guangzhou (Canton), which fell on 21 October, as well as the Yellow River valley, and Wuhan and other cities on the middle Yangzi, all followed in 1938, and the island of Hainan in February 1939. The Japanese 1938 campaign overran Shandong and, although delayed by Jiang's deliberate blowing open of the dykes on the Yellow River in June (which covered large areas with floodwaters and wrecked local logistics), linked the Japanese positions in northern and central China. The Japanese also gained important commercial positions, but it proved impossible to encircle and destroy the principal Chinese forces. Wuhan, a major industrial centre, fell in October to converging advances supported by air attacks. The firm defence that had been promised collapsed.

The 1939 campaign added important coastal positions, the island of Hainan and the port of Shantou, as part of an attempt to separate China from foreign links. This was the situation in which Ethiopia had found itself when attacked by the Italians (see p. 191). The 1939 campaign reflected Japanese naval strength and amphibious capability which had earlier been seen in Shanghai. Japanese-ruled Taiwan proved a useful local base for operations against the Chinese eastern coast.

The Japanese were helped by the extent to which many Chinese did not fight. Some warlords were unwilling to risk their troops. On a number of occasions, German advisers prepared defensive positions only to find that their Chinese defenders fled when the Japanese approached. More generally, there was a lack of coherence in the Chinese response that reflected the still-strong local ties of warlords and most troops. There were various armies in 1930s China, but no real national army.

In operational terms, as a comment on debate in the West, the Japanese showed that it was not necessary to introduce mass mechanization in order to conquer large tracts of territory. Lacking raw materials and industrial capability, which helped explain the strategic importance of Manchuria, Japan was technologically behind the Western powers in many aspects of military innovation, such as the use of tanks and motorized transport. On the other hand, the Japanese made extensive use of air attacks. The aeroplane manufacturer Mitsubishi was relatively advanced in fighter technology. These air attacks helped in the capture of cities such as Kaifeng.

A lack of *matériel* and the limited use that could be made of what was available led to a greater stress on 'spirit' over material, for example with an emphasis on the use of bayonets and swords in attack. These tactics echoed those of the Russo-Japanese War (1904–5) when 'spirit' played a key role in Japanese assaults, but it acquired greater emphasis during the Sino-Japanese War. 'Spirit' and offensive tactics combined at the tactical and operational level to help defeat the numerically stronger Chinese. Developed for use against the Red Army, this warmaking led to the conquest of large areas of China.

'Spirit', however, did not suffice in China not least because, ironically, the Japanese underrated the extent of nationalist determination in China, a state where unification and a broader sense of nationalism had gathered pace with a growing mass media and transport network in the 1920s. The Japanese also exaggerated the practicality of a protracted war strategy. The army was greatly expanded in numbers, and, by the end of 1937, 600,000 troops were involved in campaigning in China; but the Japanese, like any other foreign would-be conqueror in the modern age, lacked the manpower to seize all of China. The capital had been moved to Chongqing, which the Japanese army could not reach. Moreover, greatly affecting the situation further south, the Japanese felt it necessary to deploy large numbers of troops in Manchuria, both to deter Soviet intervention and to counter continued and growing guerrilla activity, especially from a warlord, Ma Zhanshan; local outlaws; disbanded Chinese soldiers; and Communists. The Japanese were also affected by resource shortages, as well as by logistical deficiencies, notably the problems of transporting sufficient food as Chinese forces cleared the countryside of supplies. There were also long-standing problems with Japanese army logistics.[21] Thus, in November 1938, the Japanese advance toward Changsha in Hunan was stopped by supply problems. Fighting then ended for the year.

In addition, resistance continued. The Guomindang military had been badly affected by successive defeats, losing well-trained units and equipment; and most of what was left was indifferently trained and led badly. The Chinese military also lacked equipment, especially adequate artillery, let alone motorized transport and air supply. Nevertheless, Japanese advances were resisted successfully, for example that on Changsha in September 1939; the city was not captured until 1944. By September 1939, the Japanese had lost half a million troops killed or badly wounded, and, with attrition an increasingly apparent factor[22], it no longer seemed possible, even at this early stage, to conquer China. Already, that January, Konoe Fumimaro had resigned as Prime Minister having come under attack for failing to settle the China conflict.[23] In 1940, Saitō Takao, a veteran conservative politician, told the Diet that the war was pointless as well as expensive, a view that led to his being banished from the Diet.[24]

The parallel between Japanese failure and the far more complete failure of the Germans in the Soviet Union suggests a comparison. Recent work offers a positive re-evaluation of the Soviet forces, and it is probable that something in that direction can be attempted for the Chinese. For example, in March 1938, defending Chinese inflicted heavy casualties on Japanese troops ambushed in the town of Taierzhuang. As in Shanghai in 1932, the Japanese found their firepower less valuable in town-fighting.

Nevertheless, the first-rate Chinese troops lost in 1937 could not be replaced, and the large numbers raised in 1938 and 1939 were worse trained. There was no time to train them, while corruption among the officer corps became more significant. The Central Army also suffered from the Japanese conquest of many of its recruitment areas. In contrast, the warlord regions in southern China were not conquered and, as a result, the warlords were able to continue recruiting, and their forces became proportionately more significant. While tension continued with Jiang, the Communists took a major role in the resistance to the Japanese behind Japanese lines, although some Communists sat out the war with Japan. This resistance led the soldiers of the conquering Japanese army to become terrified of being isolated outside of their fortified positions.

Even within occupied areas, which in theory covered about a quarter of the country, and held about a third of the population, Japanese control outside the cities was limited and episodic. The British Chiefs of Staff noted in December 1939 that 'Japanese authority in China is limited to certain main centres and to lines of communication, and Chinese guerrilla forces continue to take considerable toll of Japanese garrison posts'.[25] It proved far easier to destroy the Chinese navy in 1937 and to deploy overwhelming force against cities, the nodes of the transportation system, than it was to fight in rural areas. There, the ratio of strength and space told against the Japanese, particularly when their opponents, most notably the Communists, employing guerrilla tactics, moved into the rural areas of northern China and hit Japanese communications. Japanese military leaders were surprised and frustrated by their failure, despite committing much of the army and air force to achieve victory. The western provinces of China were totally beyond the Japanese, while much of the area in the Japanese zone of occupation was not in fact under control. In a stalemated strategy, 34 divisions were bogged down by 1939, which made any large-scale Japanese conflict with the Soviet Union unlikely.[26]

The Japanese also failed to win over sufficient Chinese support. The Japanese had added territory to Manchukuo in 1933 and 1935, and also established the 'Provisional Republic of China' in north China in 1937, and the 'Reorganised National Government of the Republic of China', based at Nanjing, in 1938. These various bodies organized their own forces, but the Japanese found them of limited value and treated them with suspicion.[27] Across China, there was both collaboration, especially from peripheral members of local élites, and resistance, as well as the full range of each.[28]

Japanese conquests in China indicated a lesson that Hitler would have done well to consider before attacking the Soviet Union in 1941: that high-visibility gains did not necessarily lead to overall victory and that conflicts could develop an insuperable complexity. Ishiwara Kanji, Chief of the Operations Section of the Japanese General Staff, had warned that an invasion of China would result in an intractable commitment, with victory unobtainable and withdrawal impossible. However, more aggressive views had prevailed. He was transferred from the General Staff in September 1937, and the attempt he encouraged to secure German mediation[29] was abandoned in January 1938 when, on the 16th, the Japanese government announced that the Guomindang was not an acceptable participant in peace talks. This was a sign that they intended to create their own puppet government in China, although, throughout, there was a lack of clarity about Japanese goals. On 22 January 1938, the Japanese Foreign Minister, Hirota Kōki, told the Diet that a 'new order' in Asia was Japan's goal.

1938 saw greater militarization and government control in Japan, not least with the National Mobilisation Law passed that year.[30] The corporatism of the economy became more pronounced as government powers were extended. The government attempted, often without success, to rationalize production and favour industry over agriculture. Intellectuals and others participated or compromised as nationalist themes were voiced more stridently.[31]

The Japanese lack of agreement and clarity on policy toward China and its implementation helped to thwart possibilities for peace or winning support. In particular, the peace initiative towards the Guomindang in late 1937, an attempt to make the Japanese successes in the recent campaign a decisive victory, suffered both from Jiang's refusal to recognize Manchukuo and from the lack of Japanese agreement on policy. The latter also affected the attempt to benefit from the defection, in December 1938, of Wang Ching-wei, a long-standing rival of Jiang for leadership of the Guomindang and the head of its radical wing. After difficult negotiations, he eventually became the President of the Nanjing-based 'Reorganised National Government', which claimed to govern most of central and south-east China. However, the Japanese could not decide how much power to allow Wang: caught between accusations of betrayal and ineffectiveness, his government was quickly discredited.[32] The Japanese hope that China would cooperate in a Japanese-led East Asian economic bloc was not feasible. Instead, Jiang, now preserving his forces, counted on eventual war between Japan and the Western democracies to liberate China.

Japanese campaigns in China also showed that brutality did not work: a lesson that their racialism prevented the Japanese from learning. The massacre by Japanese troops of large numbers of civilians after the capture of Nanjing in December 1937, including using people for bayonet practice, as well as mass rapes, was the culmination of barbarous Japanese conduct during their advance up the Yangzi. This brutality did not break Chinese morale, but testified to an emerging immoral and callous attitude within the Japanese military and to its failure to provide any other answer to the quagmire of its own making.

The memory of war

After the Second World War, this Japanese brutality became a highly contentious issue, and one that is significant for this book as it is an important instance of the lasting impact of the conflict of this period. From the 1970s and, even more, the 1980s, when Sino-Japanese economic relations were of increasing importance, there was a shift in approach in China, with an emphasis on a new, more specifically targetted (rather than generally anti-capitalist and anti-imperialist) nationalism designed to help counter the strains created by economic and social transformation, as well as the political challenge posed by American-led pressure on human rights. Commemoration of the Sino-Japanese War as an acute form of the imperialist aggression in China that was repeatedly condemned by the Communists, played a major role in this Chinese nationalism. This condemnation linked the critique of nineteenth and early twentieth century Western and Japanese exploitation of China, with a defensive hostility towards Japan's strong and persisting post-war alliance with the USA and what seemed to some as a greater conservative nationalist activism in Japan from the 1970s. Partly as a consequence, there came to be stronger emphasis in China on the Nanjing Massacre of 1937 by Japanese troops. This had been less emphasized earlier in so far as the massacre took place in the Guomindang capital.

The eventual Chinese Communist wooing of Taiwan in the 1990s and 2000s in pursuit of unification also played a role in this greater stress on wartime Japanese aggression and brutality. As a result of the emphasis on Chinese nationalism, the war with Japan ultimately came to loom larger than the Civil War in Chinese consciousness.

In Japan, in contrast, the brutal wartime conduct of its forces was actively contested in public memorialization. Nationalists, Marxists and liberals were each able to define different and competing interpretations of the national past. Silenced during the war years, left-wing scholars were very influential in the early post-war decades. Their approach was broadly Marxist (though by no means inaccurate as a result) in terms of seeing a conspiracy, prior to 1945, between the military and big business, supported by conservative governments and the newly created urban bourgeoisie, both to repress the masses at home and to exploit surrounding nations, especially China, which, from 1949, was a Communist state. The most common terms in this historiography were *gunkoku-shugi* (militarism in politics and society) and *tennō-sei* (the Emperor system: a system of repression using the symbol of the monarchy in education and propaganda to keep the masses docile and supportive of the military and expansion).

From the late 1960s, the now dogmatic Marxist critiques of aggression by Japanese élites were accompanied by a greater range of scholarly writing. Indeed, conservative Japanese historians, especially from the 1960s era of economic resurgence and the global respect accruing from the Tokyo Olympics of 1964, tried to defend aspects of the authoritarian and bellicose Japan of the 1930s and early 1940s, especially in terms of Japan's ideology of pan-Asian liberation. This ideology existed at least from the 1880s but developed in the 1930s to justify a policy of conquest and control that, in reality, rested on an explicit Japanese nationalism.

The contrast between the fate of the wartime leaderships is important, with Emperor Hirohito continuing to reign until his death in 1989, albeit as a constitutional monarch who, after 1945, had renounced his divinity (enshrined in the earlier Japanese constitution of 1889); whereas Hitler and Mussolini had a very different fate. There is a scholarly view in Japan which criticizes the Allies for 'letting off' Hirohito, and also blames Hirohito for allowing himself to evade responsibility for the war, while others, such as General Tojo, were executed as war criminals.

In contrast to the general German willingness among scholars and public to accept responsibility for the Second World War, there was a widespread reluctance, in both government and public in Japan, to highlight Japan's role in beginning the conflict with both China and the Western Allies, and to take primary responsibility for what had happened during the war, notably atrocities towards Asian and Western civilians and the mistreatment of prisoners. Instead, there was an increasing determination from the 1960s, by some Japanese politicians and commentators, to accept nothing that might compromise both nationalist pride and, more charitably, the creation of a modern patriotic citizenry. This tendency was accentuated by conservative activists who, in part in response to an increasingly materialistic society, sought to emphasize Japanese heroism, idealism and sacrifice during the war.

In practice, the Japanese military reacted to the impasse in China, particularly the impossibility of controlling such a vast territory and the persistence of opposition which made Japanese intervention an intractable commitment, by becoming even more brutal after 1937. This violence of Japanese forces in China even in 1937, however, testified to an increasing brutalization in conventional war, and long before the German invasion of the Soviet Union in 1941 which some have seen as a turning-point in wartime brutality. Violence was given official Japanese sanction in the 'kill all, loot all, burn all' campaign launched in 1942, a campaign, to terrorize the Chinese into submission, whose inhuman methods simply strengthened Chinese resistance.[33] In 1942, the Japanese killed at least a quarter of a million Chinese in a savage offensive that included the use of biological warfare. In this campaign, the Japanese employed cholera, dysentery, typhoid, anthrax, plague and paratyphoid germs.

From the 1960s, high school textbooks dealing with Japanese atrocities in China were a *cause célèbre* in Japan and then more widely. Cases brought in the Tokyo District Court in 1965, 1967 and 1984 pitted the Ministry of Education against the historian Ienaga Saburō. The descriptions, in Ienaga's projected high school textbook *Shin Nihon shi* [*New History of Japan*], of the Nanjing Massacre in 1937 and of biological warfare experiments in China by the Japanese army's Unit 731 had attracted the attention of the ministry's censors. The ministry won cases in 1989 and 1993, but, in 1997, Ienaga narrowly gained a favourable decision from the Supreme Court.

From the 1980s, particular controversy focused on the Nanjing Massacre, which, by this time, had become a key point in dissenting recollections of the war between China and Japan, and also within Japan itself. There were heated arguments over both the number of Chinese civilians killed, which was in fact very large, and over the extent to which massacre was an integral aspect of Japanese warmaking in China. The post-war Tokyo War Crimes Trials treated Nanjing as a serious atrocity, and Hirota Kōki, Japan's Foreign Minister, was convicted and executed for his inaction when informed about the war crimes at Nanjing, establishing a precedent that a civilian could have responsibility even though not in the military chain of command.

Some Japanese nationalists, however, became more open in rejecting responsibility for the Nanjing Massacre (some even claiming that it had never taken place), and indeed for Japanese policy as a whole. In the mid-1980s, there was an infamous case (exposed by the *Asahi* newspaper of Japan) of a Japanese writer who took the army's record of the death toll, and, in his published version of it, crossed out a nought on every figure e.g. turning 10,000 into 1,000. The *New History of Japan* (2001), produced by the Society for History Textbook Reform, adopted a crudely apologist, if not jingoistic, account that led to formal protests from both China and South Korea. Rumours that the 2005 edition of *The New History Textbook* would not even refer to the Nanjing Massacre led to demonstrations in China, while there were also boycotts of Japanese goods.

The government and observers in China proved critical not only of Japanese nationalists, but also of signs of official tolerance of their views. Thus, in 2002, the Chinese Foreign Minister protested when the Japanese Supreme Court refused to consider any appeal by Azuma Shirō, a veteran who had been found guilty of libel in 1996 by the Tokyo District Court for allegedly attributing an atrocity to his platoon in the journal about Nanjing he had published in 1987. In June 2007, ultra-nationalist Japanese MPs claimed that only 20,000 people had been killed at Nanjing, a figure that is far too low, only to meet with a response from the Chinese Foreign Ministry of 300,000, a total, in contrast, at the highest end of the range of suggested figures.

The visual media also entered the fray, and again with governmental encouragement and interference, and to a degree not seen in Europe since the close of the Cold War. In 2007, the Chinese Foreign Ministry responded critically when Mizushima Satoru, a nationalist Japanese film-maker, proposed to make a documentary, *The Truth about Nanjing*, that was intended to deny claims of Japanese atrocities, not least by challenging the evidence. This documentary was designed to counter the Chinese film *Nanjing 1937* (1995), which had provoked nationalist demonstrations in Japan.

City of Life and Death (2009), a major Chinese film about the Nanjing Massacre, notable for the technical excellence of its reconstruction and the artistic excellence of its cast and crew, was on the whole well received and took $10 million in its first week, although the response was also complicated by the favourable portrayal of an individual Japanese soldier, an unexpected approach in a Chinese film. As a result, the director, Lu Chuan, while gaining praise from many, also had to put up with death threats and with claims that he served the cause of Japanese revisionism. The same year, *John Rabe*, a co-produced German-Chinese film focused on the activities of a German businessman in Nanjing who sheltered about 650 refugees and provided valuable evidence of the atrocities.

Academic scholarship plays a role. There have been numerous conferences bringing together Chinese and Japanese historians to discuss the legacy of the Sino-Japanese War. If the situation outside the world of scholarship is often less positive, Japanese students and the public, nevertheless, for all the experience of reactionary nationalism in Japan, are readily able to explore alternative readings of national history, and the most active critical participants in the debate about Japanese actions are Japanese. Moreover, the media has confronted difficult issues, as in the special programme, including testimony by participants, on the Nanjing Massacre broadcast by *TV Asahi*, a leading Japanese network, on 15 August 2002, the anniversary of Japan's surrender. For Japan, this is the key commemorative anniversary for the Second World War.

Focusing on this controversy serves as a reminder that the period covered by this book contains many episodes that have remained, or become, important to attempts to define identity through collective memory, and notably grievance. Thus, the Arab Rising of 1937–9 was not simply a case of resistance to British imperial rule, but, also, an aspect of the competing Arab and Israeli public myths. Similarly, the Waziristan campaigns of the late 1930s are part of the collective memory of opposition to outsiders that is so potent in the North-West Frontier province of Pakistan.

Confrontation and the Far East

Returning to the 1930s, war and confrontation in the Far East encouraged a drive to build up military capability. Investing more capital in Manchukuo than the British had in India over the previous century, the Japanese

developed Manchukuo as a military and industrial base effectively outside
civilian control, although there was also considerable local cooperation.[34] The
build-up there of coal-and iron-based heavy industry served as the basis for
a powerful military-industrial complex. The complex reflected the greater
understanding outside the West (compared to previous centuries) of the need
for industrial capacity as a basis for warmaking, as well as Japanese military
concern about the potent industrial capability that already existed in America
and the Soviet Union. The War Ministry established the *Kokusaku Kenkyukai*
(National Policy Research Association), a consultancy, to prepare five-year
plans and advise the army on economic matters.

This industrial capacity was used to support expansionism in China and
to strengthen Japan in the event of war with the Soviet Union, a possibility
greatly feared, and anticipated, in Japanese army circles. Historical rivalry
looking back to the 1850s had been exacerbated by the clash of ideologies
following the Russian Revolution in 1917 and was greatly strengthened by
competition over China. In response to encouragement, labour needs and
an ideology of expanding to avoid overcrowding in Japan, a million Japanese
emigrants moved to Manchuria.

In turn, Japanese expansionism affected Soviet preparedness. Military
industry there was already growing due to its having a highly placed patron
in the shape of the Red Army to push for investment and resources, as well
as the presence of Communist military thinkers who recognized the need
for a comprehensive peacetime organization for war as part of a process of
continual conflict and inevitable war. This was a drive that was not restricted
by meaningful pressures limiting investment such as concern for consumer
well-being. Military industry was also encouraged by an ideology of hostility
to foreign powers that characterized even Communist moderates; and by
the extent to which Stalin's rise to power was supported by a military high
command concerned by the efforts of the fiscally conservative Communist
right, such as Nikolai Bukharin, to resist the increase in military spending. All
these together contributed to an extensive development of military industry.[35]

The catalyst for full militarization was Japan's invasion of Manchuria
in 1931 which brought forward long-standing Soviet, and earlier Russian,
concern about Japan as a strategic threat in the Far East and a rival in China.

The Japanese had occupied much of the Soviet Far East from 1918 to 1922. In December 1931, Japan rejected the Soviet offer of a non-aggression pact. Soviet concern provoked not only the expansion of bases, forces and logistical infrastructure in the Far East, a measure pushed by the Committee of Defence in January 1932, but also a full-scale industrial mobilization that entailed retooling the heart of Soviet heavy industry for armaments production.

The cost was immense, but levels of production far ahead of anything else in the world were achieved. For example, tank production rose from about 1,000 annually until the end of 1931 to 4,000 a year. Aircraft and artillery production also rose greatly and these rises were accompanied by a degree of specialization by type. The extent of production was such that large numbers of particular types of weapons could be produced. There was never any meaningful retreat from that level of production.[36] Despite massive economic dislocation caused by German advances in 1941, and allowing for the major help provided in 1941–5 by the Western Allies, for example British heavy tanks in the Battle for Moscow in 1941, this economic growth was to sustain a large-scale Soviet military effort in the Second World War.

Japanese policy continued to encourage Soviet preparedness because Japan came to look to Germany for a strategic partnership designed to counter both the hostility of Britain and the USA to Japanese expansion against China, and the challenge posed by the Soviet Union to both Japanese and German ambitions and ideologies. Soviet preparations in the Far East and the more general build-up of the Red Army were well covered by Japanese intelligence, not least the development, by the end of 1935, of a 170-strong long-range Soviet bomber force able to reach Japan. In the Far East, the latter was heavily outnumbered in planes and tanks by the Red Army, and Soviet planes threatened Japanese communications with Manchuria.

This situation encouraged pressure by proponents of a still larger Japanese military build-up, but Takahashi Korekiyo, the Finance Minister, who had already supported a more than doubling of the military budget from 1931 to 1935, resisted this further increase as the imports required to manufacture armaments put great strain on the balance of payment. Takahashi, however, was murdered on 26 February 1936 during an unsuccessful army coup and his replacement, Baba Eiichi, agreed to raise army spending, even though the increased imports required for the production of more weapons helped exacerbate both the adverse balance of payments and inflation. Germany faced the same fundamental problem in its rearmament.

Reports in late 1935 about an Anti-Comintern Pact, which Japan, in fact, was to sign on 25 November 1936, led Soviet strategists to fear a war on two fronts as opposed to their previous confidence that they would be able to fight on one front at a time. As a result, the Soviets, who, due to Japanese expansionism, now had a long frontier with Japan, built up their forces in the Far East. This increase, in turn, encouraged Japanese concern about the Soviets and, thus, strengthened the case for cooperation with Germany. In January 1936, Marshal Tukhachevsky pressed the Central Committee of the Communist Party on the need to confront the danger of simultaneous war with Germany and Japan. Similarly, the British were increasingly having to confront the possibility of war with Germany, Italy and Japan.

Concern about Japanese intentions towards neighbouring Mongolia led the Soviet Union to sign a pact of mutual assistance with Mongolia and to warn Japan against expanding there. Signing a non-aggression pact with China on 21 August 1937, and supplying Jiang with arms and over 3,000 advisers, were steps taken by Stalin to divert Japan from Manchuria and Mongolia into a new, intractable commitment in China.[37] The plentiful arms supplied to Jiang by Stalin helped keep the opposition to Japan viable and also affected the availability of Soviet arms for the Spanish Republicans. In turn, in the summer of 1938, responding to repeated Japanese pressure, Hitler recalled Germany's advisers from China even though the General Staff had wished to keep them there.[38]

In the late 1930s, the Soviets displayed their capabilities in two clashes on the uncertain new frontier with Japan's expanding power. At Changkufeng in August 1938, the Japanese suffered from poor coordination between armour, infantry and artillery[39] while the Soviets deployed a larger force, although it did not fight well and Vasily Blyukher, the commander of the Red Banner Far Eastern Army, was recalled and imprisoned. Stalin had been ready to fight because he knew from military intelligence that, despite the bellicosity of the Japanese Kwantung Army's leadership in Manchuria, the Japanese government and military leadership in Tokyo did not want another conflict to add to the war in China. A limited war served Stalin's purposes.

Clashes between the Japanese forces in Manchuria and the Soviet Union, both directly and thanks to the Soviet dominance of Mongolia, escalated from May 1939. The previous month, the Kwantung Army command, on its own initiative, had instructed its commanders to take an active role in settling border issues, including staging temporary invasions. On 11 May, a small Manchukuo-Japanese unit attacked a Mongolian post on the contested border. This fighting escalated swiftly, not least because the Kwantung Army wished to consolidate its position on the border and also saw the Red Army as greatly weakened by Stalin's purges. Both sides launched major air raids with aircraft involved in aerial battles in numbers: over 150 in individual battles. In July, Japanese forces twice invaded Mongolia, but were stopped.

Concern that this action might result in a Japanese advance into Siberia that would cut the Trans-Siberian railway led Stalin to appoint General Georgi Zhukov to command a counter-offensive into Manchukuo by the newly organized First Army Group. In the subsequent battle of Khalkhin Gol (Russian) or Nomonhan (Japanese), begun on 20 August 1939, Japanese forces were seriously beaten by Soviet forces ably led by Zhukov. A Japanese dividion was encircled and destroyed by 31 August. Casualty figures are contentious, but over 10,000 Soviet dead and 25,000 Japanese are the figures given by Amnon Sella. The Soviet success reflected numerical superiority in troops and planes, the availability of effective tanks (T-35s) and artillery (though not shells), and Zhukov's skill in combining the different arms, including air-land cooperation, and winning and sustaining operational advantage.[40] By 1 September 1939, 30 per cent of Soviet military personnel was stationed in the Far East. At a larger scale, Khalkhin Gol underlined the lesson of Changkufeng and revealed that Japanese confidence about the impact of the purges was seriously misplaced. The Japanese were out-fought.

These battles increased the concerns of the Japanese army about Soviet intentions, as well as suggesting that the purges of its military leadership launched in 1937 had not destroyed the fighting effectiveness of the Red Army, although it had been compromised. Moreover, the Soviets had ably risen to the serious logistical challenge of deploying large numbers and fighting in this remote region. The conflict closed on 16 September 1939. It contributed to the diplomatic and political realignment of the period which

included the Molotov-Ribbentrop (Soviet-German) Pact, the fall of the
Japanese government, and greater Japanese interest in a non-aggression treaty
with the Soviet Union. The confidence of the Japanese army that a policy of
success in China, military superiority over the Soviet Union and alliance with
Germany would ensure a positive future was cruelly exposed by the failure
of the advance on Changsha in September, Khalkhin Gol, and the Molotov-
Ribbentrop Pact.

Meanwhile, Japanese expansionism against China had overthrown British
and American views and policies about the latter as well as seriously compro-
mising their interests there and more widely. Concern over Japan became
more significant in the military planning of both powers. It has been argued
that there was a tendency, due in large part to racial stereotyping, to under-
estimate Japanese strength and resilience, and thus the threat posed by
Japan,[41] but there is also evidence of considerable concern. The British were
willing to threaten naval pressure on Japan, but the USA proved unwilling to
take part in the simultaneous naval demonstration the British pressed for in
December 1937.

Instead, the Americans took a defensive stance, concerned primarily about
a potential challenge to their position in the Philippines. They expected to
protect the islands with naval strength, although air power also played a part.
Similarly, for Britain, the building of a major naval base at Singapore, which
opened in February 1938 after work was authorized in October 1932 and had
resumed in 1933, aimed to provide a support for British power and influence
in East Asian waters, and to protect the axis of British imperial power across
the Indian Ocean from the Suez Canal via India to Australia. In each case, the
specific purpose was to provide a counter to Japanese naval strength and a
deterrent to Japanese expansionism.

France's focus on European security ensured that it could not hope to
protect its Indo-China colonies of Vietnam, Laos and Cambodia and, instead,
was reliant on Anglo-American deterrence.[42] In 1937, the French yielded to
Japanese pressure to prohibit the transit of arms supplies to China. France's
priorities ensured that the new base at Camranh Bay was not supported by
a naval deployment while Indo-China proved vulnerable not only to the
Japanese but also to the threat of Thai attack in pursuit of a border dispute.[43]

Although the British ability to send ships to Singapore depended on the challenge in Europe, this was scarcely a military prospectus determined only by the rise of Nazi aggression. Nevertheless, Germany was part of the wider algebra of Japanese power as its rise played a major part in the calculations of international power through which the Japanese advanced and debated policy. Germany appeared a deterrent for the Soviet Union, Britain and, less certainly, the USA; but, as part of their failure to plan jointly, the Japanese army and navy each interpreted this deterrent capacity in a different way. Such deterrence was seen as necessary if Japan was to be able to pursue a China policy, although the latter itself was subject to debate.[44]

The Molotov-Ribbentrop Pact was followed in September 1939 by war over Poland which left France and Britain exposed to German attack. As a result, both powers became vulnerable in the Far East which gave opportunities to the Japanese navy and its political supporters.

9

Conflict and the Western Empires in the 1930s

Italy conquers Ethiopia

The rise of Hitler, also in the 1930s, scarcely set the agenda in the case of the imperial dimension outside the Far East. Instead, there the principal source of aggression and expansion was Mussolini's Italy, albeit not at the scale of Japan in the Far East. Italy had failed humiliatingly when, in pursuit of its ambition to dominate the Horn of Africa, it had invaded Ethiopia in 1896, with its greatly outnumbered army heavily defeated at Adowa. Once he had subjugated Libya, Mussolini saw an opportunity to gain fame by reversing this humiliation. He had been thinking about revenge and taking over Ethiopia since at least the mid-1920s, although rivalry with Yugoslavia was a higher priority. However, French strength acted as a deterrent against war with Yugoslavia.

Mussolini became committed to war with Ethiopia by at least late 1933, and he planned that the war would begin in 1935. Preparations began accordingly. Ethiopia represented opportunity as it was the only part of Africa not under European rule, with the exception of the West African state of Liberia which was under a form of American protection. Although expansionism was the key note, war also seemed necessary in order to consolidate the Italian colonial position in neighbouring Eritrea and Italian Somaliland, as well as to thwart the regional ambitions of Britain and France or what Mussolini feared might be their ambitions. Moreover, Haile Selassie, the ruler of Ethiopia, had been trying to strengthen his country in order to protect it, not least by improving the army, and this policy, notably the assertion of Ethiopian sovereignty, seemed to challenge the Italian desire for hegemony. Italy had long sought to limit Ethiopian sovereignty and to prevent its direct representation in international bodies.

The conquest of Ethiopia in 1935–6 was a brutal one in which advanced weaponry was used alongside native auxiliaries: Eritreans bore much of the fighting, and the Italians thus benefited from the long-standing antipathy between them and Ethiopians. The latter had a large army, albeit a far smaller one than that Italy deployed, but most of their rifles and artillery were antiquated, and there was a lack of standardization as well as of ammunition. However, on the pattern of non-Western states modernizing their forces, for example those of Persia (Iran), there was an élite Imperial Army that was better equipped and that had been trained by Belgian instructors.

In contrast, the Italians deployed motorized columns including about 250 tanks, supported by about 350 planes, while large quantities of mustard gas were also used. As a reminder of the savagery covered by such remarks, it is appropriate to cite the eye-witness testimony of Captain Brophil, who had organized the Ethiopian Medical Corps. His ambulance received its first victims of mustard gas bombs in the last week of December:

> In nearly all cases those brought to the ambulance for treatment were civilians, the greater proportion being women and children burned in the exposed parts of the hands and face, blinded, choking, and gasping for breath. Many of these cases did not reach the ambulance until days after they were first burned, as they could only be brought for treatment at night, or early in the morning, on account of the constant bombing by Italians.[1]

On the one hand, Montgomery-Massingberd saw the invasion as demonstrating the inability of a strong air force to ensure an early victory[2], and that despite serious Ethiopian weaknesses in planes and anti-aircraft guns. On the other hand, the new technology compensated for Ethiopian bravery, for the ineffectiveness of much Italian generalship, and for the logistical problems of campaigning in the very difficult mountainous terrain. The last forced the Italians to devote much energy to road building, and led commentary on the campaigning to focus on the availability of good roads that could be used for mechanized columns.[3]

The Italians invaded Ethiopia from their colony of Eritrea to the north on 3 October 1935, and from Italian Somaliland to the south-east early in 1936. The latter was a much more difficult and lengthy axis of advance, with fewer supplies available locally. Mussolini wanted a quick victory to deter international intervention, but the poorly organized initial advance made little progress and Mussolini had to replace General Emilio De Bono, the Minister of Colonial Affairs, who had been entrusted with the planning. De Bono proved hesitant once campaigning started, but the Italians also suffered from poor communications and the failure to engage the Ethiopians in a pitched battle. The British were unimpressed, the War Office reporting on 17 January 1936:

> The failure of air bombardment to produce a decisive effect on the moral of the Ethiopians has been a further surprise and disappointment to the Italians . . . Owing to the check on the Tembien plateau and the delay in starting construction of weather-proof lines of communication, it now seems improbable that the Italians on the northern front will be able to advance much further, or secure a decisive success, before the opening of the wet season in April puts a stop to active operations for a period of about five months . . . short of killing the Emperor of Ethiopia or engaging in large scale gas warfare from the air, it is difficult to foresee what other major success the Italians can now hope to achieve.[4]

However, in place of De Bono, Pietro Badoglio, the Chief of the General Staff, was given command of the Italian forces in Ethiopia in November 1935. During the winter of 1935–6, Badoglio regrouped the army and Mussolini sent over 150,000 reinforcements as well as authorizing the large-scale use of gas in breach of the 1925 Geneva Gas Protocol.

The main thrust of the Italian offensive resumed in the spring of 1936. Fortunately for the Italians, the Ethiopians chose to meet them in battle, rather than to avoid engagements and rely on guerrilla tactics. Thus, mistaken native strategy, which owed much to Haile Selassie's determination for Ethiopia to act like a developed state, as well as superior Italian weaponry, notably the firepower, especially bombing, Badoglio emphasized, played a major role in Italian success. In the end, this success proved easier than British and French military commanders had anticipated. The Italians also benefited from superior intelligence that owed much to the interception of telegraphic messages. The intelligence dimension was important as it was necessary to fix the location of Ethiopian forces. Reconnaissance planes played a major role in gathering intelligence.

The force from Eritrea fought its way through the province of Tigre, and in March and April 1936 delivered powerful blows against the main Ethiopian defence. The Ethiopians were defeated at the battle of Mount Aradam, and the Ethiopian capital, Addis Ababa, was captured on 5 May. Mussolini annexed Ethiopia on 9 May, and officially declared the establishment of the new Italian empire which now had nearly 12 per cent of Africa's territory. As in Morocco in the 1920s, numbers were also important. The Italians deployed nearly 600,000 men. Italians killed in action, seriously wounded or missing numbered 3,964, along with 5,142 Ascaris or local troops.[5]

Addis Ababa had never previously fallen to European forces, and its capture therefore represented a highpoint of Western expansion. In many respects, however, this capture was very different in type to that represented by the American occupation of Tokyo in 1945, as the Italian advance represented the last stage of the 'Scramble for Africa', which was essentially a nineteenth-century enterprise. Looked at differently, the 'Scramble' continued into the twentieth century, not least with the accentuation of the British grip on Egypt, and Mussolini's enterprise was only to appear anachronistic from the perspective of post-1945 decolonization.

The Italians were greatly helped by the failure of other Western powers to act on the League of Nations' condemnation of the Italian invasion. Under Article 10 of the League's Covenant, member states agreed 'to respect and preserve . . . the territorial integrity and existing political independence of all members' while Article 16 provided for immediate economic and social, and possibly military, sanctions against any aggressive power.

Reality proved otherwise. The support of the French and of the British Foreign Secretary, Sir Samuel Hoare, for a settlement of the dispute at the expense of Ethiopia, was seen as appeasement and led to Hoare's enforced resignation. Hoare, however, had been authorized by the Cabinet to accept Italian conquests. The British government then considered oil sanctions against Italy, as well as closing the Suez Canal to Italian resupply ships. The latter step would have greatly harmed Italian logistics for which the Mediterranean-Red Sea was the key axis. Italy lacked oil, whereas Britain controlled the production of oil in Iraq and Persia (Iran), as well as its shipping.

France, however, was only willing to cooperate if Britain undertook to guarantee the continued demilitarization of the Rhineland in the face of Hitler's revisionist demands, a step which Britain was unwilling to take. Indifferent to the fate of Ethiopia, the British government wanted to keep Italy true to the Stresa Front against Germany; did not want to provoke Italian attacks on British shipping and bases in the Mediterranean, not least as losses might harm Britain's other strategic interests; and sought to avoid antagonizing the Americans by stopping their tankers.[6] Fear of inter-European conflict prevented any moves against imperial gains, as it had also done prior to 1914. Concern about Italy's position in any clash with Germany helped ensure that its expansionism was accepted and was also to affect the response to Italy's intervention in Spain. On 6 April 1936, Stanley Baldwin, the Prime Minister, told the Cabinet that closing the Suez Canal 'would involve war with Italy, which . . . he was unwilling to envisage in the present state of Europe'.[7]

At the same time, the international dimension played another role in helping explain why the Italians were far more successful in 1936 than they had been 40 years earlier. Whereas Menelik II had received French and Russian arms in the 1890s, and had used them to considerable effect, there was no comparable support in the 1930s. Also, there was no comparison to the German and Soviet arms that China received when attacked by Japan in the 1930s.

Moreover, the pace of Italian advance was far quicker than in the 1890s. This enabled the Italians to retain the initiative. The high tempo enjoyed by the Italians owed much to their mobility and to their ability to apply their firepower. At the same time, the conflict compromised Italian military effectiveness as experience was bought at the cost of exhaustion of manpower, *matériel* and finances.

Once established, Italian rule in Ethiopia proved harsh and this harshness, which owed much to racism, led to a resistance movement. This was a resistance of ambushes and surprise attacks on precarious Italian supply routes, which the Italians countered by building forts and by the recruitment of local troops. Developing from 1937, the Ethiopian guerrilla campaign had some effect, and the Italian response was savage. Rodolfo Graziani, who had succeeded Badoglio as Governor-General in May 1936, had already proved a harsh repressor of the Senussi tribesmen in Libya. From their colony of French Somaliland (Dijbouti), the French provided some help to the rebels. Ready Italian control had not been established and when Italy entered the Second World War its position was challenged by rebellions in Ethiopia. With the help of invading British forces, Haile Selassie was restored in 1941.

Nevertheless, despite the weaknesses of Italian control, Ethiopia had proved far more vulnerable than China. The latter was far larger and more populous, whereas Ethiopia had only a single centre of authority and also suffered from the lack of international support from over its frontiers. All comparisons invite caveats, but this one is instructive for both wars. So also is the contrast between Ethiopia and Libya. The latter proved easier for the Italians to control, as the population was more concentrated than that of Ethiopia and the terrain better for aerial surveillance. The Italians also benefited from the length of their presence in Libya.

The conflict in Ethiopia was also accompanied by a mobilization of Italian opinion, which was coordinated by a propaganda ministry established in 1935. This ministry sponsored favourable accounts, hindered unfavourable ones and sought to manage the flow of information. The war was also used to make the Fascist system seem necessary and superior, and to legitimate both Mussolini and militarization. The serious financial drain of the conflict was ignored.

In practice, Italy could not afford its heavy military commitments to Ethiopia and, subsequently, Spain, nor its general military build-up. However, Mussolini was not interested in limits while potential international opponents failed to appreciate Italian weaknesses. Indeed, in the late 1930s, as Mussolini planned an invasion of Egypt, the British anxiously considered how best to defend their position there, not least as it protected both the fleet base at Alexandria and the Suez Canal. The British were also concerned about the Italian naval presence in the Red Sea, Italian dealings with Yemen and the possibility of Italy winning over Ibn Saud of Arabia.[8]

France and the USA

None of the other Western powers launched comparable expansionist operations, but they were involved in military activity in order to preserve their position. The French crushed a nationalist uprising at Yen Bay in Vietnam in February 1930 and a peasant uprising between May 1930 and September 1931 in central Vietnam, the Nghe-Tinh Soviet movement. Labelling anti-colonialism as criminal, harsh French action involved the killing of people and livestock as well as village burnings and crop destruction.[9] The French also pacified the tribes of the Moroccan Atlas by 1933. In 1937, a Kurdish uprising in Syria was suppressed.

In some colonies, political concessions alleviated discontent. In 1936, Syria gained autonomy, but French control over military and foreign affairs continued. Moreover, troops were used to support the police, as in March 1939, in response to the threat of a general strike in Damascus, when West African troops as well as armoured cars and cavalry were deployed. West African troops were also employed in March 1937 to break strikes in the iron and phosphate mines of southern Tunisia, while, that September, demonstrations about water supplies and policing in the Moroccan city of Meknēs led to the use of cavalry.[10]

Although the decline of international trade ensured that its empire became more important to the French economy in the 1930s (as also happened for the British), the focus of French defence on the homeland meant that little help was given to developing colonial defence. For example, few planes were sent to the colonies, while the emphasis for the colonial forces was increasingly on a role in defence of France in Europe.[11] This emphasis had implications for the defence of the colonies as the French focused their concern there on protecting the ports through which North African troops would be transported to France, notably Oran and Bizerta.

In contrast, the American withdrawal from Nicaragua in 1932 and Haiti in 1934 owed much to a sense of the intractability of the local situation. The Americans were unwilling to devote resources comparable to those deployed by the British and French, and lacked the same sense of mission, but the American ability to leave the situation to supposedly friendly national governments and militaries was also important. Moreover, America's regional strength provided an opportunity to intervene anew if required.

The British Empire

The most far-flung empire, that of Britain, faced the most serious opposition. Alongside problems stemming from the Depression came rising nationalism. The two were linked, not least in opposition to taxation and expenditure cuts which pressed hard on indebted societies. Thus, in Nigeria, there were rebellions against taxation as well as strikes and a marked rise in crime. In response, the government launched tax raids and made many arrests.[12] In the Mediterranean, there was hostility from the Nationalist Party in Malta, as well as Greek-Cypriot nationalist riots in 1931 which were countered with British troops flown from Egypt. Most seriously, there was large-scale resistance in the Arab Rising in Palestine in 1937–9. There had been disorder in 1936, but it gathered force in 1937 after the Peel Commission, which had been established to tackle the linked issues of Jewish immigration and the violently hostile Arab response, recommended the partition of Palestine between Arab and Jewish states.

This report was rejected by Arabs and led to the rising. In 1938–9, the British used 50,000 troops to suppress this rising, an instance of the need to deploy large numbers of troops in order to maintain the imperial position, and one that challenged Britain at the time of the Munich Crisis, after the end of which further reinforcements were sent. Concern about Palestine was accentuated by Mussolini's attempts to exploit Arab nationalism as an aspect of his drive for Mediterranean hegemony, a drive that entailed the overthrow of the British position.[13] There was also anxiety about the response of Ibn Saud.

Initially, the Arab Rising posed a serious problem for the British, not least as, in response to sniping and sabotage, and short of information about the rebels, they were unable to maintain control of much of the countryside. However, the opposition lacked overall leadership and was divided, in particular between clans. Moreover, recruiting Jewish auxiliaries, the British also developed an irregular capacity of their own, notably Orde Wingate's Special Night Squads. Faced with a firm opposition from about 3,000 guerrillas, the British used collective punishments to weaken Palestinian support for the guerrillas and also adopted active patrolling. In addition, partition as a policy was abandoned in September 1938 while, in the winter of 1938–9, significant reinforcements were sent and a more energetic stance led to the reoccupation of rebel strongholds. The Rising was essentially over by March 1939, and two months later a White Paper [government proposed legislation] outlined a new policy: independence in ten years and Jewish immigration limited in the meanwhile.

The need for large numbers of troops was also seen on India's North-West Frontier. In 1936, rebellion broke out again, under the Faqir of Ipi, who drew both on tribal opposition to the British presence and on Muslim *jihadi* sentiment. In 1937, the British deployed over 60,000 men to crush the rebellion. The Faqir's peak strength was only 4,000 men and, although his men had good rifles (which was an instance of the shrinking arms gap in hand-held weapons between Western forces and their operations), they lacked artillery and machine guns. Nevertheless, British success in subduing the region owed as much to tribal rivalries and financial inducements as to superior numbers and firepower.

Technology had only limited value, although it could be helpful. The British deployed about 50–60 armoured cars, which were used mainly to escort road convoys, and proved quite effective in that particular role. More generally, armoured cars were important in the inter-war period due to their usefulness for imperial policing, not least thanks to their all-terrain specifications. During the Second World War, their lack of protection and vulnerability to tank fire, led to armoured cars playing a smaller role, which has led to a failure to appreciate their earlier importance. Armoured cars came into their own again in the 2000s as American and British forces in Iraq and Afghanistan struggled to protect troops while maintaining their mobility.

A handful of light tanks also went for an occasional trundle on open ground on the North-West Frontier in the late 1930s, but could get nowhere near the kind of mountainous terrain on which the principal engagements took place. The campaign also revealed the weaknesses of Western communications, not least because the tribesmen cut telegraph lines. As wireless was still in its infancy in the British forces, most signalling below brigade level was carried out using old-fashioned coloured flags, and by heliograph (signalling using the sun), and despatch riders. Only the largest bases and headquarters had reliable wireless communications. British success was consolidated by new roads, but guerrilla opposition in Waziristan continued until 1943. This very much reflected continuities of conflict in the region that were to be seen anew there in the 2000s and 2010s.

At the same time, the Waziristan campaign was, like the Arab Rising in Palestine, a contained struggle. The Waziristan risings did not spread to the many Muslims elsewhere in British India, while the British did not respond to their difficulties by invading neighbouring Afghanistan, in which the Faqir of Ipi was apt to take refuge. However, the fighting effectiveness of the British Indian Army against the Japanese in Malaya and Burma in 1941–2 was affected detrimentally by the extent to which its recent experience of warfare was largely in the arid, unforested uplands of the North-West Frontier.[14] Moreover, the expense of the campaign ensured that less money was available for capital expenditure on new weaponry.

There were also problems for the British in Burma where, in the Saya-San rebellion of 1930–2, politico-religious opposition to British rule was exacerbated by the effects of the economic depression on the colonial economy, helping to cause a rebellion in the Irrawaddy delta region. Religious identity and anger played a role in the rebellion.

However, it is the strength of the imperial military system that emerges most clearly. Much of the empire was vulnerable to external attack by a well-armed state, as was to be revealed in the Second World War. In the early 1930s, Malta had only 12 anti-aircraft guns, and they were old and increasingly obsolete, while 'the fuelling stations on the route to Singapore (particularly Trincomalee) are inadequately defended', according to the ministerial committee reporting to the Cabinet in 1934.[15] The defences of Burma and Ceylon (Sri Lanka) were to be cruelly exposed by the Japanese in 1942, but these land and air defences in fact depended on British naval superiority. A land invasion of Burma was not anticipated and one of Ceylon could only occur if the Japanese were able to defeat the Royal Navy.[16]

Yet, the empire was not without resources for such a challenge and, moreover, was still strong against more traditional opponents. Indeed, much planning focused on how best to protect Britain's position in the Far East. Alongside the emphasis on moving the fleet to Singapore came the idea of moving additional planes and, to that end, developing an air reinforcement route thither as well as an additional air base at Singapore.[17]

As far as more traditional opponents were concerned, the Saya-San rebellion was defeated, while the British were able to deploy substantial forces to deal with both the North-West Frontier and Palestine. The size of the Indian Army, a volunteer force, was the key factor. As a result, there was no need to raise large numbers of troops in Britain, and thus no conscription there until April 1939 when it was introduced in response to the rising crisis in Europe.

India was also under a reasonable level of control, and the government sought to adapt policy in order to keep India in the empire. The resulting legislation was a central aspect of British policy and strategy. The Government of India Act of 1935 passed by the National Government, a Conservative-dominated coalition, moved India towards self-government, but was also designed to ensure British retention of the substance of power.

Seeing this legislation as a move towards the abandonment of empire, a section of the Conservative Party, led by Winston Churchill, then out of office, bitterly opposed the Act. However, if the bitterness of the parliamentary rebellion against the Act was a testimony to the pull of empire in Britain, it was also a product of their failure. After 1918, there was a more general sense that empire had to change, and that reform of the government of India was, alongside Imperial Trade Preference and more equal relations with the Dominions, the best means to give the empire a future. It was to that end that Leo Amery, an ardent imperialist, supported the legislation in 1935, while Lord Irwin, the Viceroy of India, backed eventual Dominion status for India.[18]

The extent to which the Act represented a long-term solution was unclear, not least because the Indian National Congress did very well in the provincial elections of 1936. Nevertheless, the British authorities were able to work with the 'parliamentary' wing of Congress and there was scant sense that India represented a source of strategic weakness and military need.

Moreover, for most of the 1930s, Egypt, Iraq and Persia (Iran) did not pose Britain the difficulties faced in 1919–21. Relations with Iraq were regularized anew in 1930 when a new treaty restricted British powers while, at the same time giving Britain the strategic assets it sought: sovereign rights in two bases and the right to use all Iraqi military facilities in the event of war. Iraq became independent in 1932. The bases provided the RAF with an important regional presence as well as serving as part of its wider network in Asia. Egypt also provided Britain with vital bases, but the focus there was on naval capability both in the Mediterranean and as part of the wider network linked by the Suez Canal.

Empire represented a key commitment for Britain. The Chief of the Imperial General Staff, in a report circulated to the Cabinet by the Secretary of State for War in October 1932, pressed for neutrality in Europe, 'the consolidation of the Empire and the safety of Imperial communications'.[19] The Committee of Imperial Defence responded to its critics in 1934 by arguing that 'it would not be possible to organise a larger mechanized force than the one we recommend below without upsetting the whole system by which our forces overseas [in the empire] are maintained by the Home Army'. The committee proposed a tank brigade as part of an expeditionary Field Force designed to be sent to the Continent in the event of conflict, but also argued that imperial tasks cannot 'be met by the creation of a highly specialised "robot" army at home, even if that were the best system for a Continental war'.[20] In December 1936, the War Office reported to the Cabinet that progress on mechanization of the cavalry and on the reorganization of the infantry required the close cooperation of the military authorities in India.[21]

When, in the Munich Crisis in 1938, war with Germany seemed possible over the future of Czechoslovakia, the British Chiefs of Staff urged caution, although, looked at more critically, they failed to provide the Cabinet with sufficient options. Uncertain about the possibility of Italian and Japanese intervention on behalf of Germany, dubious about French strength, and conscious of numerous British global commitments, including Palestine, they warned about the dangers of becoming entangled in major military action on the Continent.[22] Under the plan approved earlier that year, the expeditionary Field Force was 'to be organised primarily with a view to reinforcing the Middle East'.[23]

It might have seemed necessary to invest in tanks in order to confront the possibility of a Continental war with Germany, but, as far as the threat environment was concerned for Britain, there was also the prospect of naval action against Italy in the Mediterranean, as well as the need for troops to protect Egypt, Sudan, Kenya and British Somaliland in the event of such a conflict from the large Italian forces in the region. War with Japan over

China or as a result of Japanese expansion against the British Empire was also possible; while the Arab rising and Waziristan campaigns were large-scale current obligations.

Far from there being any tradition of appeasement, military-diplomatic policies involved competing tasks and were, therefore, an issue of prioritization, as had earlier been shown in 1918–22. A lack of clarity about allies and enemies made it difficult for Britain and other powers to produce effective strategic plans.[24] For example, in considering how best to deter Japan, British policymakers factored in China, the Soviet Union and the USA, in order to create a shadowy, 'virtual' alliance to maintain their position in the Far East, but the value of this 'no-bloc' policy was very unclear and it was to prove inadequate.[25] Japan was to be brought down by these powers in 1945, but, in the meanwhile, the British Empire had suffered terrible damage and a crucial loss of prestige.

Planning did not take place in some sort of bloodless, rational fashion. Suppositions were also significant, including those subsequently described in terms of strategic culture. Racist views were present in pre-war British intelligence assessments of Japanese capability, but they did not dominate the analysis. Inter-service biases and rivalries proved more significant.[26]

Conclusions

There were no such imperial commitments for Germany, while the emphasis for France was very much on preparations for war in Europe, and not in the empire, for example against Japan in South-East Asia. The ongoing Soviet policing of the Central Asian border and the maintenance of Mongolia as a puppet state look quite similar to things that the formal imperial powers did, but the Soviet Union did not repeat its 1929 demonstration in Manchuria and its focus was very much on war with Japan and Germany.

Imperial conflict and capability were important in the 1930s, not only for what occurred, but also for what they entailed about the ability to act elsewhere. This was particularly the case for Britain due to its wide-ranging commitments. With the benefit of hindsight, it is possible to point to serious flaws in the decisions taken by British policymakers, but it is also worth underlining the difficulties of assessing links between challenges and commitments. In particular, the issues of prioritization between commitments and the linkage of challenges both posed serious problems. The British concern with empire reflected the experience of the Great War when the empire had provided crucial support, in men, money and supplies, in Europe. Thus, the empire was both a source of weakness, through over-extension, and strength.

10

The Third World in the 1930s

Warfare in the Far East and conflicts of imperial expansion and defence were not the sole forms of warfare outside Europe. Instead, there were many independent states, principally, but not only, in Latin America, which had a military history that it is all-too-easy to overlook. Attention focuses on conventional warfare and this focus ensures that these states are generally underappreciated. The exception is the Chaco War between Bolivia and Paraguay in 1932–5, although that is frequently neglected, or considered, like the Spanish Civil War (1936–9), only in terms of what the conflict appeared to suggest about the likely nature of a future European war. As an instance of neglect it is striking to consider that the inter-war volume in the prestigious series on total war does not consider the Chaco War.[1] It was, in fact, the largest-scale international conflict of the early 1930s. After assessing that war, we will consider how politics and local culture affected military events and developments, both in Latin America and in independent states in the Third World.

The Chaco war

Long-standing competing territorial claims in the sparsely populated Chaco region that separated Bolivia and Paraguay had resulted in clashes in 1921 and 1927 and had nearly led to war already in 1928. That year, Colonel Rafael Franco, a Paraguayan colonel, acting without orders, seized and destroyed a

Bolivian fort that had been built inside territory claimed by Paraguay. He was sacked, however, as neither government yet wanted war, nor was ready to fight it, in particular lacking sufficient armaments. However, both powers actively prepared for conflict.

In June 1932, there was a clash over a water source in Chaco, an important site as water was in short supply in the region, but one that could have been settled by negotiation or allowed to simmer. Instead, in a new departure, Bolivia escalated the dispute and turned to the attack. In July 1932, war broke out. Daniel Salamanca, the determined president of landlocked Bolivia wished to advance to the Paraguay River, which would provide a route to the sea and make Bolivia more of a regional power, as well as subjugating Paraguay. The route to the sea was a key geopolitical issue as it would enable Bolivia to export its minerals, especially tin, without being reliant on intermediaries who might refuse permission, change high transit duties, and stop movements at time of war. Bolivia thus sought to compensate for the loss of its Pacific coastline to Chile in the War of the Pacific of 1879–83.

In the Chaco War, Bolivia spent nearly twice what Paraguay could afford, and was also more populous and had the latest weaponry, including planes. In contrast, Colonel (later Marshal) José Estigarribia, the Paraguayan field commander who had been educated at St Cyr, claimed that his men lacked sufficient arms, ammunition, medical supplies and men, and were reduced to oxen for transport.[2] Medical care indeed was poor, the League Commission reporting in 1934 that 'sick and wounded frequently receive inadequate attention.'[3]

Nevertheless, the Paraguayans were better led, militarily and politically, had a superior officer corps, benefited from better communications, and understood both how to operate in the humid flood plains and how to fight a war of manoeuvre in the harsh, largely waterless, scrub terrain beyond the flood plains. This environmental awareness was important to tactical and operational capability, and notably to manoeuvrability and logistics.

The Bolivian army was German-trained, like the best divisions in the Chinese army, but the Bolivians had a poor command structure, commanders unsuited to staff work not least logistics, and a weak officer corps. As Commander in Chief, Salamanca actively intervened in operational and tactical issues and blamed his generals for failures.[4] Bolivian morale was low, and, unlike

Paraguay which was supported (short of intervention) by Argentina, and also supplied via Chile, Bolivia lacked allies. Bolivian positions were encircled, and their supply lines over-long and reliant on poor communications, notably dirt roads. A British officer reporting from the Bolivian side noted:

> Paraguay, deriving advantage from her geographical position, is placed comparatively near the scene of operations, and her troops, supplies, and food are transported to the front by a combination of light railway, lorry, mule, and march methods. Bolivia, on the other hand, suffers a separation of 1,000 miles between her forces and her main base at the capital, of which only 500 miles are covered by rail. Over the remaining distance runs a narrow and broken road, at first over high rocky plateaux, and then over wooded mountain slopes down to the flat plains of the Chaco jungle. This is thick with dust in winter and often washed away in summer. Troops and supplies perform the 500-mile trek by lorry and donkey, while in the opening stages of the war, when transport was extremely short, some of the regiments were compelled to march most of the way on foot, ankle deep in the dust and suffering torture from thirst and danger.[5]

In the desolate Chaco, the Bolivians lacked the water necessary for their larger army and its tactics of the mass offensive. These tactics proved highly inappropriate, J. W. Lindsay writing of 'the Bolivians being cut down by the Paraguayan machine guns'.[6]

Bolivian invading forces were defeated and pushed back into Bolivia in 1932 and 1933, a process aided by Paraguay fighting near its heartland. When the Paraguayans advanced in 1934, they, in turn, suffered from over-long supply lines and their advance was eventually checked. A report in the *New York Times* and *The Times* commented on charging troops being 'mowed down' by 'strongly entrenched Bolivian machine-gunners'.[7] Nevertheless, Paraguay now controlled the Chaco. This success led, in November 1934, to the overthrow of President Salamanca on a visit to the front. He quipped that it was the first military operation that the Bolivian high command had executed efficiently.

The war ended in June 1935 with an armistice in which Paraguay was left in control of the Chaco, although this was followed by a military revolt that overthrew the president, Eusebio Ayala: anger at the moderate peace terms was linked to opposition to his liberalism and his neglect of the military. The role of armies in replacing or threatening to replace their political leaders and commanders is a major theme in the military history of this period. Bolivia subsequently rearmed, which encouraged Paraguay to turn the armistice into a treaty in July 1938.[8] The settlement has lasted, and, indeed, there has since been no war on this scale in South America, which, in terms of international conflict, has been the most peaceful settled continent since 1935.

The war was on a different scale to anything witnessed in Latin America in the inter-war years. It saw both battles, notably Boquerón, Toledo and Nanawa, and the capture of fortified positions, such as the Paraguayan seizure of Picuiba. Like the Spanish Civil War, the mobilization and deployment of resources were crucial in the Chaco War, as was the linkage of political cohesion with military resilience. Bolivia lost maybe 60,000 dead, about 2 per cent of its population, and Paraguay 36,000 or 3.5 per cent. These percentages suggest that the war can be seen as a major struggle, albeit not on the scale of the Chinese-Japanese conflict, nor with the large-scale use of advanced weaponry and decisive results witnessed with the Italian invasion of Ethiopia in 1935–6. Each side in the Chaco War deployed nearly 400,000 troops, while military modernization was seen with the use of modern weaponry and with foreign military advisers, notably French, German and White Russian. The modern weaponry included planes, tanks, flamethrowers and automatic weaponry, Lindsay commenting on the extent to which the weaponry used was more modern than that in the Great War: 'This is . . . a war in which the highest civilisation – speaking in terms of warfare – is taking part'.[9] In 1926, Bolivia had used the wealth gained by exporting tin to agree a contract with Vickers-Armstrong, the key British arms-manufacturer. This agreement included the provision of 196 pieces of artillery, 750 machine guns, 12 planes and 36,000 rifles. Not all of these arms arrived, however, nor were of good quality, nor could be deployed to the Chaco.

In response to the war, Britain, followed by the USA stopped issuing licences for the export of *matériel* to the combatants, and Britain pressed the League of Nations to follow suit with an international embargo. However, neither Italy nor Japan were willing to cooperate. There was also the issue of even-handedness between the belligerents.[10]

The campaigning received relatively little international attention, in part due to the difficulty of reporting directly on what was happening in the Chaco, but, more generally, due to a failure to see the conflict as having much to teach. In part, this stance reflected a racial contempt for the combatants on the part of European and American commentators[11], but there was also a sense that the war was of limited consequence. The Spanish Civil War was to receive far more attention. It was relatively easy to report directly what was happening there, the conflict appeared important to European politics, it was possible for many to engage with one or other of the combatants, and the direct participation of several European powers encouraged an assessment of the campaigning in terms of its wider significance.

Contemporary neglect of the Chaco War has contributed to the later lack of attention. However, there was also some reason for this neglect. When governments and militaries went looking for 'lessons' or how to fight the next war, it is not surprising that they should have paid little attention to wars, like the Chaco War, whose military forces and infrastructures (if not their weaponry) were so poorly developed as to make any 'lessons' less than relevant for what was termed 'first-class' or 'European' war. The same was true of civil wars except in so far as the forces of major states intervened. This tendency to give little weight to some things, and not to others, has its precursor in the way that the American Civil War was largely ignored before the Great War in favour of the Franco-Prussian War.

Conflict elsewhere in Latin America

No other international war in Latin America was on the scale of the Chaco War. Chile, for example, took delivery of six modern British destroyers in 1929 and created an air force from the previous army and navy aviation branches the following year, but it did not fight its neighbours. However, there were some conflicts between states. The interaction of territorial disputes with a bellicose reluctance to climb down and compromise, was the key reason. On 1 September 1932, a band of armed Peruvians took control of part of Amazonia then under Colombian rule. They had been organized by rubber and sugar entrepreneurs who had lost land in territory recently ceded to Colombia. Backed by local Peruvian military units, this move was then supported by the Peruvian president, Luis Sánchez Cerro, a former colonel who had seized power in 1930 and become a populist leader.

In distant tropical rainforest, the sphere of operations was difficult for both powers. With Brazilian permission, Colombia sent a naval flotilla via the Atlantic and Amazon, reaching the territory in dispute in February 1933, a reminder of the extent to which naval power could also involve inland waters. Most of the territory was then recaptured, although there was no victory in battle to win fame. The League of Nations played a role in negotiating a settlement on Colombia's terms, which also owed much to the assassination (for other reasons) of Sánchez Cerro in April 1933. His successor, Oscar Benavides, did not have the same commitment to the issue.

The established interpenetration of domestic and international politics, which had been very common in relations between Latin American states in the nineteenth century, was seen in 1936 when the Peruvian opposition negotiated with the president of Bolivía, Colonel David Toro, seeking backing for rebellion in return for promising support for a Pacific outlet for Bolivía, thus addressing the issue of access to the Pacific. The plot, however, was terminated as a result of diplomatic pressure, and such schemes were far less common than they had been in the nineteenth century.

External intervention by both Latin American states and international powers played a smaller role in the 1930s than in the nineteenth century, although the Depression led to a competition by international powers for markets and raw materials. This competition was accentuated by the aggressive stance taken by Germany in Latin America and its linkage with ideological commitment and arms sales. German influence challenged the far more established positions of the USA and Britain, with the American influence increasingly dominant over that of Britain. It was claimed that foreign oil interests played a key role in the Chaco War, with Standard Oil of New Jersey competing with Royal Dutch-Shell, but the evidence for this view is slight; although the control of the Camiri oil field was significant in the closing stage of the war.

The military and politics in Latin America

The military also suppressed insurrections in Latin America. An army coup overthrew the peasant-backed government of El Salvador in 1931, and the subsequent peasant revolt was smashed with much slaughter in 1932. Moreover, the army was used against peasant opposition in Honduras in 1932 and 1937. In September 1938, artillery was employed to help end opposition in Santiago, the capital of Chile.

The military was central to the politics of coups, attempted coups, and threatened coups, and these became more common in Latin America in the 1930s, in part because the decline of the global economy hit commodity exporters particularly hard and thus wrecked the public finances of many Latin American states. In Chile, Carlos Ibánez resigned as president in July 1931 in the face of demonstrations caused by the fiscal crisis. The crisis of public finances affected the military and encouraged them to take a more active role in politics.

In the largest state, Brazil, the government was overthrown in 1930 when the federal army proved unwilling to resist a rebel army advancing on the state of São Paulo, the economic and political centre of the country. The rebellion, which began on 3 October, stemmed from an unwillingness to accept the verdict of the presidential election of March 1930, which had rewarded the dominant oligarchs of the state of São Paulo. Instead, claiming an overseeing right as custodians for the nation, the federal army seized power on 24 October before, on 3 November, handing it to Getúlio Vargas, the leader of the revolt, who was also the defeated candidate in March as well as the governor of the state of Rio Grande do Sul, the centre of the revolt.

In turn, federal forces suppressed the three-month-long 'constitutionalist' revolt against Vargas in 1932, which was supported by 40,000 troops largely from the São Paulo militia. As so often, this episode in Latin America is ignored in military history, even though the government deployed more than 75,000 troops, and also used air attacks. In comparison, the risings by pro-Communist troops in Brazil in 1935 were small-scale and rapidly suppressed.[12] In 1937, Vargas used troops to dissolve congress, declare a state of national emergency and establish the *Estado Novo* or New State, in which he enjoyed near dictatorial powers. This authoritarianism was frequently characteristic of states in which military power played a major role. Vargas was to remain president until 1945, returning to hold power in 1950–4.

Coups and interventions spanned the continent, although in Mexico, after the purges of 1923, 1927 and 1929, the military increasingly adopted a professional rather than a political role. In Chile, the air force played a role being used in September 1931 against a naval mutiny. About twenty planes of the Chilean Air Force failed to make any direct hits when bombing the warships and only caused three casualties, but the air attack combined with the government's uncompromising demand for complete surrender to cause an immediate and marked decline in the mutineers' morale. Thus, the bombing achieved its purpose. The mutiny ended. In 1932, the buzzing of the presidential palace played a role in repeated coups in Chile. Moreover, the election of Arturo Alessandri as president of Chile in 1932 was guaranteed by military action.

In August 1933, a coup in Cuba led to the resignation of the president. The following month, action by a group of sergeants led to a new president being chosen. In January 1934, the sergeants, now colonels, took power, putting in their choice of president. The 'Sergeants Revolt' entailed the overthrow of the conservative officer corps.

Coups included those in Argentina and Peru in 1930, Uruguay in 1933, Bolivia in 1930, 1934, 1936 and 1937, Ecuador in 1935 and 1937, the Dominican Republic in 1930 and Guatemala in 1931. The constitutional, but unpopular, liberal government of Hipólito Yrigoyen in Argentina was overthrown by General José Uriburu on 6 September 1930 when several hundred officer cadets marched from the garrison in Buenos Aires to seize possession of the centre of government, encountering opposition from only a few snipers. Thereafter, although only a small portion of the army was involved in the 1930 coup, force played a major role in Argentine politics. After a Radical revolt was suppressed in July 1931, most of the leading Radicals were arrested which, alongside electoral fraud, helped the army candidate, General Augustín Justo, win the election of November 1931. Becoming president the following February, he subsequently used the politics of appointments and promotions to maintain control of the army. This helped Justo contain the fascistic paramilitary *Legión Cívica*, which was sponsored by Uriburu and led by a retired general. Justo remained president until 1937.

In August 1930, Sánchez Cerro had seized power in Peru, both overthrowing the president and thwarting the attempt by General Manuel Ponce, the Chief of Staff, to lead a military junta. In this case, as in many others, a coup served to help a determined military leader to power, rather than providing an opportunity for the military as an institution to seize power.

In the Dominican Republic in 1930, the refusal of Rafael Leónidas Trujillo y Molina, the head of the armed forces, to support the president led the latter to resign, and Trujillo won the subsequent election, one in which he was able to intimidate with ease. Trujillo then ran the Dominican Republic until assassinated in 1961. In Uruguay, force also played a role in creating an authoritarian regime, but the coup of 31 March 1933 was carried out by the police, with the armed forces acting as spectators.

Military regimes claimed to be more stable and orderly than parliamentary constitutional government, but the reality was often very different. In Peru, the Minister of Government, Colonel Gustavo Jiménez, was dismissed in late 1930 for radicalism, only to seize power briefly in March 1931. Deported in 1932, he mounted an unsuccessful coup in March 1933. With Peru essentially under martial law in 1932, a Radical mutiny in the city of Callao was suppressed in May, and a Radical insurrection at Trujillo in July. In Bolivia, the military failed to establish a stable government after President Salamanca was overthrown in 1934, and, in a difficult political environment, this led to a succession of weak ministries.

Usually, the military avoided fighting each other at the time of coups, but, in August 1932, divisions over the Ecuadorean presidency led to the hard-fought Four Days' War. Military force played a leading role in Ecuador. In 1935, the oligarchic president, Velasco Ibarra, was overthrown by the armed forces when he tried to make himself dictator, the military going on to choose Antonio Pons (1935) and Frederico Páez (1936), before Páez was overthrown by General Alberto Enríquez Gallo in October 1937. The following year, a civilian president dissolved the Assembly and declared himself dictator, but with the support of the armed forces.[13]

At the same time, the Latin American militaries did not invariably oppose constitutional rule. Although there was a right-wing slant in the armed forces, there were also, as in Europe, important elements that were not right-wing, for example in Bolivia in 1936–9 after failure in the Chaco War.[14] In Latin America, nevertheless, the army frequently created the regime. A similar pattern was to be seen in some European countries, but there were also successful attempts there by dictatorial governments to enhance their control over the military.

To ignore Latin America in the military history of the inter-war period is to provide an account that not only neglects the Chaco War but that also dramatically underplays the military's role in politics. As such, the Latin American militaries serve as a reminder of the importance of political contexts and, on the world scale, of the variations in strategic cultures that it is necessary to consider. This perspective is important in its own right and also helps in considering the situation in some other states, notably China, for the interpenetration of politics and military activity seen there in the 1920s and 1930s had instructive parallels with Latin America. The habit of primitivizing or ignoring the latter because of the type of forces or military technology available is unhelpful.

Suppressing regional dissent

'Third World' governments tended to use their military forces more often for the suppression of regional opposition than for engaging in foreign war. This was even more so in South Asia than Latin America, and notably so in Iraq, a new state which had emerged from the ruins of the Ottoman Empire. Army expansion there was backed by nationalists as a way to integrate the state. In 1933, the tribes had about 100,000 rifles, the army only 15,000; but conscription was introduced in 1934, adding to troop numbers and broadening the social base of the officer corps. Army numbers rose from 3,500 and 11,500 men in 1932 to 44,000 in 1933.

The army was able to break the military power of its disunited opponents. In 1931, the RAF helped suppress a Kurdish rising. In 1933, the Assyrians (Nestorian Christians) were defeated, although looked at differently, this operation largely involved a massacre of unpopular civilians, a massacre staged by the army supported by Kurdish tribes. In 1935, in part with the support of the Iraqi air force, tribal uprisings were suppressed, providing the army with a new source of prestige. The uprisings owed much to opposition to conscription, a key issue in tension between state and tribes.

The following year, the Iraqi army staged its first coup and it thereafter played a central role in politics. General Bakr Sidqī, victor over Assyrians and the tribes, was able to force the resignation of the government in 1936, but, in turn, in 1937 his government was overthrown by the army. In a reminder of the central and intertwined nature of tribal and military politics, a long-standing theme, Bakr Sidqī was criticized for allegedly backing the Kurds and for failing to provide the army with the improved supplies he had promised.[15]

Other tribal risings had been overcome in Persia (Iran) in 1932, while in Ethiopia, Haile Selassie sought to increase central power as a key element of a modernization designed to resist Italian takeover[16], a modernization watched with concern by Mussolini. In Afghanistan, in the late 1930s, British-supplied light bombers were employed to help the ground forces of Zahir (r. 1933–73), suppress rebellion.[17] However, in contrast to his predecessor Amamullah's policy, there was no significant attempt to compromise the power of tribal or religious leaders. The Afghan army was built up in the 1930s, but the tribal levies remained important.[18] German influence increased from 1935.

The use of the military in Persia, Afghanistan and Ethiopia conformed to long-standing local patterns of military activity and thus serves as a reminder of the need to understand continuity in goals and tasking. This continuity helps explain the extent to which military developments were fed into pre-existing patterns of behaviour. The personal loyalty that was appropriate for a politics of repression was linked to an institutional conservatism and control, in which the army was the arm of the state, while the state, in some respects, was the arm of the army. New weapons and doctrine were very much subservient appendages to this process.

11

Politics and the military in the Europe of the 1930s

As in Latin America, the attitude of the military became more significant in the 1930s as the failure of democratic institutions to deal successfully with economic problems provoked authoritarian solutions and a decline in liberal democracy. The ineffectiveness of governments encouraged militaries to intervene as they saw themselves as the only effective institutions. Civil-military relations, coups and civil wars are not the same, but they contributed to the growing prominence of military matters.

The attitude of the armed forces was particularly crucial at the time of coups and seizures of power, for example those of Antonio de Salazar in Portugal in 1932, Konstantin Päts in Estonia in 1934, and King Carol II in Romania in 1938. There was also an army coup in Bulgaria in May 1934, which led to an authoritarian government, and the country became a Crown-backed military dictatorship under King Bōris in 1935. He took care to woo the army. Under General Ioannis Metaxas, a former Chief of the General Staff, Greece became a military dictatorship in 1936, bringing to a close a period of acute instability in which the military had played a central part. Unsuccessful republican military coups in March 1933 and March 1935 had led to the purging of the army and had helped bring about the restoration of the monarchy in late 1935.

These coups were mounted from within the structure of power, and essentially represented an attempt to monopolize authority. In Estonia, economic crisis strained the political situation, with the political parties challenged by the League of Veterans of the War of Liberation founded in 1929. With the latter likely to win the presidential election in 1934, Päts, as head of the government, declared a state of emergency, abolished the League, and arrested its leadership. After Parliament had approved this, it was dissolved and Päts ruled by decree. League members planned a coup in 1935, but it did not take place. The alleged threat of civil war was employed in 1934 as the excuse for a similar seizure of power by the Latvian Prime Minister, Karlis Umanis. In both Estonia and Latvia, the military supported the coups. In Latvia, the Minister of Defence, General Jānis Balodis, played a key role. In Poland, the militarization of politics and government under Pilsudski was followed, after his death in 1935, by the 'Rule of the Colonels', with the military running the government.

The military was also important in resisting coup attempts, as in Finland in 1930 and 1932, Spain in 1932 and Austria in 1934. The assassination of King Alexander of Yugoslavia in 1934 by the Croat separatist *Ustasa* (insurrectionary) movement did not lead to changes because his cousin, Prince Paul, who became regent on behalf of the young Peter II, was supported by the army. Alexander had dispensed with the constitution in 1929.

In Austria, force played a large part in the politics of the early 1930s. Economic problems multiplied and a banking crisis in 1931 brought down most of the financial system. Unemployment rose to nearly 40 per cent in 1934. This crisis was the background to an increase in the violence between left-wing and right-wing paramilitaries, which became more common after the 1927 killings in Vienna. An attempted coup by the right-wing paramilitaries failed in September 1931.

In March 1933, the response to the ongoing crisis by Engelbert Dollfuss, the leader of the Christian-Social government since May 1932, was to create an authoritarian Catholic state with Parliament abolished. Although threatened by the Nazis, Dollfuss chose to see the socialists as the main threat and, in February 1934, responded to a general strike by attacking the socialists. Backed by right-wing paramilitaries, the army overcame the left-wing *Schutzbündler*, using artillery in Vienna. The Social Democratic Party was abolished. In turn, a Nazi coup in July failed, although Dollfuss was killed in his office. Mussolini moved troops to the Italo-Austrian frontier in order to deter Hitler from intervening.

In Germany, the army made preparations for the declaration by Franz von Papen, the conservative Chancellor, of a state of emergency. This was a step, designed against Communist disorder, Nazi paramilitary activity, and a possible general strike, that might have stopped Hitler's rise to power. In the event, there was no such action and Hitler gained power in January 1933.

The military was also used in a number of states to overcome political and regional opposition and labour disturbances. In the Soviet Union, widespread opposition to collectivization increased from 1929. In response, the Soviet authorities, in what they saw as a war with conservative peasants, turned more to violence, including the extensive use of the Secret Police which was organized in an increasingly militarized fashion from 1934. There was a large-scale forcible resettlement of peasants judged unacceptable. Soldiers as Party members participated on an individual basis, but Red Army units did not intervene.[1] Nevertheless, the idea of a total mobilization of resources to pursue the cause of the Proletarian Revolution had bellicose implications for both foreign and domestic policy.

In Spain, the army and the Civil Guard were widely employed against strikers and anarchists in 1918–21 and in the early 1930s, while, in July 1931, artillery was deployed against anarchist strikers in Seville, and, in 1934, the army suppressed a coal miners' uprising in the Asturias region of Spain. The ability of the miners in 1934 to unite, seize weapons from depots and arms factories, and defeat the local police provoked a military response, partly planned by Franco, which was brutal. As later in the early stages of the Spanish Civil War, a key element was advancing in columns (although that risked ambushes) and the use of air power. The latter was particularly important as the rebels had neither planes nor anti-aircraft defences. The Spanish Air Force bombed and strafed rebel-held towns and positions and demoralized the defenders, although the actual destruction was more modest. The government forces also had naval support, with the 8-inch guns of the cruiser *Libertad* shelling the town of Gijon. The government deployed 26,000 troops against about 10–12,000 rebel fighters. The rebels fought hard and used machine guns and artillery as well as rifles, but they were very short of cartridges and the deployment of the Spanish Foreign Legion from Spanish Morocco ensured that they faced good, well-trained troops with high morale. The last was necessary for the room-to-room fighting required to retake the city of Oviedo. After the rebellion had been defeated, there was serious looting and widespread killing of prisoners as well as of civilians.[2]

In neighbouring Portugal, strikes in 1934 also led to the deployment of troops but, although Salazar's *Estado Novo* was authoritarian, it relied more on the *Policia Internacional de Defesa do Estado*, a very effective secret police force, than on the army.

In Britain, it was the police and the law, not the army, which were to contain both the Communists and the British Union of Fascists. The Public Order Act of 1936 banned political uniforms and paramilitary organizations, and controlled marches. The previous year, troops had been brought in to back up the police after sectarian riots in North Belfast claimed 11 lives. However, such assistance was not needed in Britain. Similarly, when, in September 1931, pay cuts imposed by the National (coalition) Government led to the Invergordon Mutiny, in which sailors of 15 warships refused to go on duty, the crisis was ended when the cuts were revised. The army had not been called in, no more than it had acted that year to organize, support or oppose the formation of a coalition ministry.

In contrast to many states, the British military was not an agency for political transformation and enforced modernization. Instead, the officer corps saw itself as a force for stability, and this view was not seriously challenged either from within the corps or from the ranks. An army report of 1938 was more generally true of the British military: 'The cavalry regiments . . . attract officers from families which in the past have preserved the feudal conception that the holding of estates carries with it a liability for the defence of the kingdom'.[3]

At a very different scale to the Soviet Union and Spain and far less murderously, the American army in Washington on 28 July 1932, nevertheless, bloodily dispersed veterans pressing for money, the 'Bonus Army' because they were seen as left-wing radicals and because they were unwilling to disperse from their encampments in Central Washington. Under Douglas MacArthur, its Chief of Staff from 1930 to 1935, the American army not only refused to accept a subordinate role to the police, ignored presidential instructions during the operation, and used excessive force against these demonstrators[4], but also complained bitterly about the level of fe_ expenditure in 1933. However, although President Franklin Delano Roosevelt thought MacArthur dangerous, a prescient assessment, there was no prospect of the general changing the political situation. In 1935, MacArthur, who had presidential ambitions, was sent to the Philippines to oversee its defences and he remained there until 1942. Violent strikes led to the use of National Guard units in 1934 and 1934–7, but Roosevelt refused to deploy federal forces.

In France, the emphasis was on the police to try to keep order at the time of the large-scale far-right Stavisky riots in Paris on 6 February 1934 when a large number of demonstrators unsuccessfully sought to storm the Chamber of Deputies. The French army had a far more ambivalent political position than its British or American counterparts. Yet, although its officer corps was right-wing and opposed both cuts to military service and budgets, it did not react to the democratic creation of a Popular Front government in 1936 nor to the factory occupations of that year. This stance owed much to the determination of the commander, General Maurice Gamelin, who did not see himself as a military dictator.[5]

Spanish civil war

The situation was very different in Spain. Opposed to the modernizing policies of the left-leaning Republican government and concerned about the possibility of a Communist seizure of power via the Popular Front after the narrow left-wing electoral victory in the hard-fought elections of 16 February 1936, a group of senior army officers, who called themselves the Nationalists, sought to seize power in a rebellion that began in Spanish Morocco on 17 July and on the Spanish mainland on 18–19 July. Their failure, and that of any attempt to reach a negotiated settlement, led to a bitter civil war which only ended on 28 March 1939 when the Nationalists seized Madrid.

The Spanish Civil War is commonly seen as a harbinger of the Second World War, and the ideological division between the two sides are emphasized and, indeed, the Nationalists depicted the Republicans as the servants of the Antichrist. Caution is required on the first head, while the ideological dimension was scarcely new. It had played a role in the civil war aspect of the Peninsular War of 1808–13, and even more in the Carlist Wars. Although there was a naval dimension, the Spanish Civil War was essentially fought in Spain. As a result of the nineteenth-century loss of most of the Spanish Empire, the overseas dimension of the rising was slight, although there was initial fighting in Spanish Morocco, with Republican resistance in the town of Larache having to be overcome after hard fighting.

As far as land conflict was concerned, the Spanish Civil War was different from the Western Front in the Great War, as well as from the initial campaigns in the Second World War. In contrast to the former, there was no density of defensive positions, so that, as a well-developed system, the front line was only episodic. This made it possible to break through opposing fronts relatively readily, but, in contrast to the German successes in 1939–41, it proved to be very difficult to develop and sustain offensive momentum. As a result, exploitation was inadequate; a pattern seen in the failure of Republican attacks in the battles of Brunete (1937), Belchate (1937), Teruel (1937–8), and the Ebro (1938), and of Nationalist attacks at Jarama (1937) and Guadalajara (1937).

This failure was a product of the nature of the Republican and Nationalist armies, which were poorly trained and inadequately supplied, but also of a lack of operational art, seen particularly in inadequate planning. This lack helped give an attritional character to the war, much of which did not have the more fast-moving manoeuvrist dimension of the Russian and Chinese civil wars of the 1920s. The mountainous relief of much of Spain contrasted with the relatively flat, open terrain in Russia where the fronts could move very rapidly. Moreover, the sheer physical size of Russia meant lower unit density and thus thinner lines, which ensured that once a line was broken it was difficult to reconstruct.

The attritional character of the struggle in Spain underlined the importance of resources, including foreign support. It also meant that much value accrued to the side that was better able to manage its economy, maintain morale, and retain political cohesion. On all three heads, the Nationalists proved more effective. The Republicans were particularly unfortunate in the timing of the conflict because, if it had occurred during the Second World War, the Western Allies probably would have provided them with support in response to the German backing for the Nationalists.

Instead, Britain was not willing to help while French military assistance was small-scale and, in 1937, the American Congress banned the sale of arms to either side. The British government did not like the idea of France having right-wing dictatorships on three of its borders, but was unclear what could be done without jeopardizing Britain's international position. The government, which was not only Conservative-dominated but also greatly concerned about Spain becoming a strategic partner of its Soviet supplier, tried to stop British volunteers taking part, a measure designed against the Republicans who benefited most from such volunteers. The Civil War also fed into the Left-Right ideological rivalry in British society.

The initial Nationalist rising was successful in some areas, but, elsewhere, Republican positions were preserved by workers or by loyal forces. The rebel generals had failed to carry the whole of the military. Areas of control were consolidated on both sides during July 1936 as flying columns sought to suppress local opposition. This suppression involved large-scale violence with those judged unacceptable murdered. In Republican areas, this had a quasi-revolutionary character, not least in the killing of clergy. The Nationalists also killed for their vision of order, and did so in a less disorganized fashion.[6] The British diplomat G. H. Thompson was to find 'the same repression, the same terror'.[7]

By the end of July 1936, Spain was divided into two zones, with the Republicans controlling the capital, Madrid, and the bulk of the population and industry, and backed by the navy and most of the air force; while the Nationalists, supported by most of the army's combat units, dominated the more rural areas. General Francisco Franco's Army of Africa was a particularly experienced unit, and the role of German intervention in helping him, from 29 July, transport close to 14,000 troops by air from Morocco was highly significant. The blockade by the Spanish navy was thus circumvented. The Nationalists also called up reservists where they could and organized the right-wing militias into army units.

The Republicans found it far harder to organize an effective army, partly because of political differences, but also because they, especially their militias, lacked the necessary planned organization and discipline. These issues compromised training and affected fighting quality. The militia were also short of equipment. The Nationalists, instead, favoured a more centralized army. Republican divisions became more pronounced in May 1937 when fighting began in Barcelona over the stance, within the Republican camp, of the anarchists who, in the event, were brutally suppressed. In a parallel to the purges in the Soviet Union, Stalin was determined to destroy alternative views and those holding them were murdered.

As a consequence of their difficulties, notably their lack of a striking force, the Republicans lost the initiative in the early stages of the war and were unable to capitalize on the early difficulties faced by the Nationalists. Instead, Franco used the Army of Africa to overrun western Andalusia and to link up with Nationalists further north, storming the city of Badajoz on 14 August 1936. The untrained worker militias were unable to mount effective opposition. Franco's success enabled him to gain predominance over his military colleagues and, on 21 September, he was made *Generalissimo* of the rebel armies, and, on 1 October, *Caudillo* or head of state.

However, although Franco was able to fight his way close to Madrid by early November, he was blocked, in the assault on 8 November, by the strength of the resistance around the capital. Subsequent frontal attacks conquered part of the city but were stopped. On 23 November, Franco called off the assault. This check resulted in the war becoming both longer and more wide-ranging in its intensity, which increased the likely value of foreign help, while also putting a premium on the resilience of the Spanish combatants. Under the pressure of necessity, both sides had proved able to adapt to circumstances. In his advance towards Madrid, Franco had successfully motorized his force, using buses and trucks that he had seized, and was therefore able to outflank larger Republican forces.

Conversely, helped by Franco's decision to move first, in late September, to relieve the besieged Nationalists in the *Alcazar* (fortress) of Toledo, the Republicans had been able to improvise an effective defence of Madrid, and, supported by larger numbers of troops, guns and armour, to block the Nationalist attack, before obliging the overstretched Franco and his tired forces to abandon it in late November. The Republicans controlled the air because Soviet aeroplanes went into action at that time. Despite its limitations, air power was important as aeroplanes served as a substitute for artillery.

Notwithstanding Franco's failure to capture Madrid, Germany and Italy recognized his government on 18 November, which committed them to

Nationalist victory. Ideological issues were coming to the fore in the international response to the conflict. In November, Hitler sent 12,000 men as well as tanks and aeroplanes, but he proved unwilling to do much more. In December, Mussolini agreed to dispatch two brigades of troops. In the end, Mussolini was to send 80,000 troops and Hitler fewer than 19,000.[8] This joint contribution greatly furthered the alliance between Germany and Italy, so that by the end of 1936 Mussolini was talking of a Rome-Berlin Axis.

Operations in Spain enabled the Germans and Italians to test out weapons, tactics and doctrine, notably of air attack. Lieutenant-General Walter von Reichenau, formerly head of the *Wehrmachtamt* (Armed Forces Office) and in 1938 Commander of the 4th Army Group, told a meeting of Nazi leaders, in a lecture circulated that July by the British Foreign Secretary to the Cabinet, that

> the experience of the Spanish war has made it easier for us to abandon the wrong path we were treading as regards tanks. The war in Abyssinia, where the Abyssinians lacked all means of countering tanks, had established the reputation of the light tank. This led us to launch ourselves upon the wholesale construction of these light and fast machines. We neglected the building of heavy armoured tanks. On the Spanish battlefields it turned out that it was precisely the heavy tanks with their steel armour plates that proved far away the more efficient.[9]

Once operational mobility had been lost, the Nationalists discovered the intractable nature of position warfare in the face of a numerous opponent. Attempts to recover mobility in November 1936 by outflanking Madrid only overstretched the Nationalists and exposed them to attack. Franco tried again in February 1937, when he sought to cut off Madrid from Valencia, thus rupturing a key supply route, but the larger Republican force thwarted him in the battle of the Jarama.

The nature of the war excited considerable foreign attention, being seen as a test-case for the changing character of war.[10] J. F. C. Fuller, then a retired British major general and a newspaper correspondent, displayed marked sympathies with Franco, but this does not detract from the value of his military observations. Having visited Franco's army, he sent a report to British Military Intelligence in March 1937 that drew attention to its deficiencies:

It is in no sense a great war, a trench war or even a guerrilla war . . . a city war . . . main strength of the Reds was in the towns . . . had Franco a highly organised army and plenty of transport he could take Madrid. But he has not. For instance, General Queipo de Llano told me himself that, when he launched his advance against Malaga, he had only 28 lorries . . . Nothing like the full manpower has been called up, in fact it cannot be, as the military organisation is not able to absorb more men.

Fuller also drew attention to the nature of the fighting sphere, and its relation to the limited tempo of the conflict:

though the nominal front is immense . . . its garrisons are minute . . . The front is totally unlike the fronts in the World War. Not only is it in no way continuous, but, generally speaking, hard to discover, and during my journey, so far as I know, at times I may have been in Red territory . . . The villages normally are natural fortresses, generally walled all round, and whichever side holds them "holds" the intervening gaps as well. Immediately west of Madrid, and of course in other places also, actual trenches do exist. I visited the Madrid ones which were very sketchy . . . Though I was in this frontline for an hour and a half only two Red shells were fired and a few rifle shots were heard.

Interested in tank warfare, Fuller was disappointed by what he saw:

Of tanks I saw few: on Franco's side the Italian light tank is an indifferent and blind machine . . . Tank tactics are conspicuous only through their absence. Machines are generally used singly, or, if in numbers, they split up over a wide front. The result is that they are met by concentrated fire . . . In fact, there are no tactics, no proper training or maintenance. One of Franco's officers told me that the largest number so far used in an attack was 15! I do not think we have to learn from either tanks or anti-tank weapons in this war, because the basis of tactics is training, and this is mainly a war of untrained men with a sprinkling of foreign mercenaries.[11]

Fuller's view was overly critical, not least because there were many experienced men in the armies. French observers emphasized the effectiveness of anti-tank weapons against tanks. People saw what their doctrine demanded. Fuller however was correct about the emphasis in the Spnish Civil War on infantry and the difficulties of developing effective mass armies given the lack of sufficient time, training and resources. There were similarities with the problems that had faced the British in 1915–16 and the Americans in 1918, but the context was far more difficult for both sides in Spain, not only because resources were lacking, but also because there was not a cohesive and effective state organization for either side.

In the absence of a rapid Nationalist victory, different strategies were proposed. The Italians, who had about 50,000 troops in Spain at this stage, as well as aeroplanes, sought to emulate their success in conquering Ethiopia in the spring of 1936, and proposed rapid advances. These included a converging drive on Valencia, the seat of the Republican government, from Malaga (captured on 8 February) and Teruel that would quickly have split the Republican zone into a number of areas. Victory would enable the Italians to redeploy their forces to pursue other opportunities. The Germans, who like the Italians had expected and wanted a quick war, backed the same plan, but Franco rejected it. He was more concerned to fit strategy and operations to force structure and, in particular, to adopt a cautious approach.

The deficiencies of motorized forces, which the Italians did not know how to use according to British and German theories, were displayed in March 1937. Then, an Italian advance east of Madrid towards Guadalajara became overly dependent on the few roads in the region, lost momentum and logistical support in poor weather, and was finally driven back in a successful counter-attack that began on 18 March. Franco had failed to provide the Italians with necessary support. He was opposed to the Italians playing an independent role as they had done both in the capture of Malaga and in the Guadalajara offensive. The outcome of the latter helped persuade Franco to decide not to resume his attack on Madrid.

Franco then turned north to conquer the Cantabrian littoral and its industrial resources, capturing the port of Bilbao on 19 June 1937. The divided and poorly commanded Republicans in the north were badly trained and lacked air power. To take the pressure off the north, the Republicans counter-attacked in the centre, especially in the battle of Brunete, west of Madrid, on 6 July. The Republicans broke through the weak Nationalist line, but Franco sent reinforcements including German and Italian aeroplanes. The Republicans proved unable to maintain their impetus, a general problem in military operations, and their troops lost more heavily. Brunete revealed their deficiencies, not least poor coordination between the arms and, related to this, an inexpert use of the available artillery and tanks. The Republicans also lacked sufficient air power. The Soviet decision in July 1937 to dispatch aid to the Guomindang in China greatly reduced the amount available to help Spain, while Stalin was increasingly uninterested in the Spanish struggle.

The intractability of the conflict, however, led Franco in August 1937 to press for Italian help against Soviet shipments of arms to the Republicans. Mussolini rapidly complied in the Mediterranean, and submarine attacks were soon launched.

Defeated at Brunete, the Republicans were unable to prevent the Nationalists capturing the port of Santander on the northern coast on 26 August, while San Sebastian fell on 13 September. The loss of ports reduced the possibility of obtaining foreign supplies and, indeed, of counting internationally. Similarly, a Republican offensive near Zaragoza in late August revealed the same problems as Brunete and failed to prevent the Nationalists overrunning Asturias in October. This success gave the Nationalists an important industrial zone, and freed their troops and warships to operate elsewhere against the divided Republicans. As in the Russian Civil War, the relationship between the fronts was readily apparent for both sides. So also was the cumulative nature of success.

The desire to gain the initiative was understandable, but repeated offensives had already weakened the Republicans and the next, launched on 15 December 1937, only did the same. The Republicans captured the city of Teruel. However, instead of this success leading to hoped-for-peace negotiations, an effective Nationalist counter-offensive regained the town on 22 February 1938 and inflicted heavy casualties in fighting in the bitter winter.

Foreign commentators continued to be critical about the character and quality of the warmaking. In April 1938, the British Assistant Military Attaché in Paris commented, after visiting Nationalist Spain:

Even a short visit brought out very clearly a number of singular features which characterise this war, a war in which the majority of the participants are almost entirely untrained, a war in which comparatively small forces are strung out on a vast length of front, a war in which modern weapons are used but not in the modern scale, and, finally, a war in which there have been more assassinations than deaths in battle . . . In view of these singularities, it will be obvious that the greatest caution must be used in deducing general lessons from this war: a little adroitness and it will be possible to use it to "prove" any preconceived theory . . . To anyone with experience of the Great War, the almost complete absence of warlike activities in all three sectors of the front visited was most striking . . . It seems that the battle only flares up intermittently, and then only on small portions of the front; for hundreds of miles the enemy is out of rifle shot . . . no attempt is made by either side to harass the other in his business of living and feeding . . . the paucity of the artillery when an action does take place . . . very soon the full fury of the fight dies down; and the end is either a stalemate in the same positions or rapid advances.

The Assistant Attaché went on to ascribe recent Nationalist successes principally to 'their ability to concentrate in secrecy a large preponderance of field artillery in the sector selected for the break-through'. He noted that, in general, tactics were 'largely based on Great War principles', with creeping barrages and trenches. He also commented on deficiencies, including 'an incomplete and ad hoc organisation', poor transport and roads, and the conduct of the war 'in an utterly haphazard way'.[12]

These strictures were overly harsh. Franco had followed up his success at Teruel, where the leading Republican units were destroyed, rather as the Guomindang ones had been in Shanghai in 1937, by overrunning the region of Aragon and driving to the Mediterranean, which was reached on 15 April 1938. The Nationalists benefited from superior numbers of artillery and aircraft, on the whole supplied when and where needed by Germany and Italy. Republican Spain was now divided in two and morale was low. Nevertheless, Franco did not exploit his success by turning on Barcelona, the Catalan capital, at once, despite German pressure to do so. Concern about the possibility of

French entry on the Republican side was a factor as was a determination to crush his opponents.[13]

Franco's delay gave his opponents an opportunity to regroup. Indeed, the ability of the Republicans to generate and deploy considerable forces was clearly demonstrated by their surprise counter-attack on the river Ebro in July.

However, this operation also indicated the problems of mounting break-through attacks, as initial Republican successes were contained by Nationalist reinforcements. The Republicans did not have the skills to profit by their early success. Ultimately, Franco's better logistics and supply of aircraft and artillery gave him the edge. The battle continued until November as an attritional struggle, with both sides suffering heavily. This was more serious for the Republicans as it was not easy for them to acquire fresh armaments, especially heavy guns. In contrast, Germany and Italy provided plentiful supplies to the Nationalists.

In late December 1938, the Nationalists turned against Catalonia with greatly superior equipment and numbers. Initially, but only very briefly, their attack was held, but the campaign showed the possibility of a rapid advance, as the Republican front collapsed, in part due to stronger Nationalist firepower. Many Republicans fled across the frontier into France. On 26 January 1939, Barcelona fell with scant resistance. On 27 February, Britain and France recognized the Nationalist government. Part of the Republican military leadership rebelled in March, determined to force through negotiations with Franco. He, however, insisted on total surrender and, at the end of the month, the Nationalists, meeting scant resistance, overran the remaining Republican areas, Madrid falling on 28 March. This led to the end of the republic. At least 300,000 Spaniards had been killed in the war.

Under Franco's dictatorship, large numbers suspected of opposition sympathies, let alone activity, were executed, with Franco signing many death sentences.[14] The military and paramilitary became the key defences of the regime. The Franco dictatorship, which lasted until his death in 1975, was Fascistic, but its key theme was a conservative authoritarianism led by a general enjoying military support.

The memorialization of the war was very important to the Franco regime. In the Valle de los Caidos (Valley of the Fallen), Franco spent two decades and about £200 million on building the basilica in which he was buried as well as a monastery and a towering crucifix. The vast edifice, visible 30 miles away, was designed as a monument to the Nationalist dead in the Civil War, Franco declaring, 'The stones that are to be erected must have the grandeur of the monuments of old, which defy time and forgetfulness'. Some of the ex-Republicans used as forced labour for the building died.

Post-Franco, the Civil War could be discussed more freely. Initially, there was a setting-aside of the war in order to help foster national reconciliation, but, from the 1990s, pressure built up to confront its true character. From 2000, there were exhumations of the mass graves of those murdered for holding unacceptable views. Under the Socialist government of 2004–11 there was a willingness to acknowledge the large numbers killed as the Nationalist forces repressed opposition and secured their position.[15]

Mussolini's Italy

The outcome in Spain at the end of 1939, was different to that in Italy where the dictator, Benito Mussolini, was less in control of their armed forces than Franco was. Mussolini had benefited from their failure, by deciding not to act in 1922 and 1924, to resist his seizure and consolidation of power, but, equally, did not feel a need to transform them. The Italian military had not suffered the traumatic experience of revolution, like those of the Russians and Hungarians, nor defeat and enforced reduction, like those of the Germans, Austrians and Hungarians. The armed forces were not brought under Fascist control, and continued to swear loyalty to the Crown. Although Mussolini was Minister of Marine for most of the period, and in 1938 appointed himself 'First Marshal' of the empire, with a military rank at least equal to that of Victor Emmanuel III (r. 1900–46), his control of the armed forces was limited and he had little power over senior appointments. In 1925, Mussolini felt it necessary to appoint Pietro Badoglio as Chief of the General Staff. Badoglio repeatedly thwarted Mussolini's desire for action and played a major role in his overthrow in 1943.

Furthermore, the armed forces were not circumvented. The Fascist programme of 1919 had called for the creation of a National Militia, which was to have been the basis of a popular army under party control, as well as for the nationalization of all armaments factories. The Fascist paramilitaries appeared to provide the basis for a new type of army. However, visiting the Italian forces invading Ethiopia in 1935, Fuller found that the general to whom he was attached commanded a:

> group of blackshirts [a Fascist militia], a curious collection of men who looked like brigands and enjoyed looking like it. Their discipline I should say was evil. For field purposes I cannot imagine them being of much use; but I should say that they would prove admirable in a street fight . . . a kind of Pirates of Penzance[16] business . . . this war is not a demonstration of soldiership but of Fascism: an officer is made second in command of 4,000 men, not because he is a good soldier but a Fascist poet.[17]

In the event the 1919 programme was not implemented, and the Fascists, despite the concern of military commanders, did not create a parallel military force. Indeed, Mussolini made the Blackshirts subordinate to the army. Instead, he sought to develop the existing professional armed forces. This won him support among them, as did his commitment to a national mobilization of resources and energy that the democratic system had lacked.[18] In 1923, a Supreme Defence Commission and a Subcommittee for the Preparation of National Mobilization were established. There was an attempt to develop industry and agriculture in order to make Italy self-sufficient and also pressure to raise the population.

Like many politicians and commentators in the period, especially, but not only, those on the Right[19], Mussolini was fascinated by new technology, seeing a focus on machines as an analogue for the powerful authoritarian progressivism he intended to introduce, a common trend among dictators. He believed that the adoption of advanced weaponry would serve to enhance Italy's international position and was particularly interested in air power, describing Italy as a natural aircraft carrier in the Mediterranean.

Mussolini readily used his military to support his goals. In 1923, the Greek island of Corfu was occupied in a successful attempt to make Greece back down in a quarrel over nearby Albania. This use of force pleased the military. In 1934, Italian troops were moved to the Austrian frontier during the crisis following Dolfuss's assassination in order to deter German intervention in Austria.

Moreover, Mussolini provided more troops than Hitler to support Franco in the Spanish Civil War. In November 1938, the Italian Chamber of Deputies echoed to calls for acquiring 'Tunisia, Corsica, Nice, Savoy', all French possessions. The following April, Mussolini invaded Albania, an independent state where Italian influence was already strong. It fell rapidly and Victor Emmanuel III was declared King of Albania.[20] Mussolini was not to join Hitler in 1939, but German successes in 1940 led him to attack Britain and France, ignoring the caution of the military.[21]

Reality, however, did not measure up to Mussolini's bombast, his talk of reviving the grandeur of ancient Rome and his ambitions at the expense of the British and French empires. Italy lacked the resources and industrial capacity to give weight to his hopes, as the Supreme Defence Commission made clear in 1929. In addition, the military mobilization that took place, although very expensive, was seriously flawed. The end result was armed forces that were to be found seriously wanting when Italy fought the Allies in 1940–3, not least poor equipment including the lightly armed CV-3 tank.

Mussolini was driven by a belief in the inherently competitive nature of international relations, and in the central role of force in this competition. These beliefs affected the full-range of his policies, cultural, economic, financial and social. For example, he saw emigration and declining fertility as challenges to his vision of a strong Italy, and this priority led him to adopt pro-natalist policies.[22] Consequences Mussolini envisaged included more men for the military and more colonists for the empire.

Mussolini's use of, and relationship with, the armed forces were typical of a number of inter-war autocratic regimes. In Hungary, the army was largely independent of political control. In contrast, in both Germany and the Soviet Union in the 1930s, dictators felt it necessary to seize a greater control over the armed forces, in order to ensure that they were loyal to them personally, rather than to any notion of national interests.

Hitler and the military

Hitler, who gained power in Germany on 30 January 1933, had not followed the advice of Ernst Röhm, who wanted to transform the Nazi *Sturmabteilung*

(SA) movement he headed into a militia-type army that would incorporate the professional military and remove their independence.[23] This form of Nazi revolution was unacceptable to both Hitler and the army.[24] Röhm, who had acted as an adviser for the Bolivians during the Chaco War, was murdered and the SA destroyed in the Night of the Long Knives. Hitler also used the violence of 30 June to 2 July 1934 to murder those suspected of involvement in a conservative conspiracy against the Nazis. This conspiracy had sought to exploit military unease with the SA but had failed to win the backing of President Hindenburg.[25] During the Munich crisis in 1938, Sudeten *Freikorps* mounted raids across the German-Czech frontier to the anger of the German army command, and Hitler felt it necessary to restrain them and bring their actions under army control.

Hitler, nevertheless, was resolved to control the army. After the death of President Hindenburg on 2 August 1934, Hitler combined the office of the President with that of the Chancellor which he already held, and thus, as head of state, became Supreme Commander of the armed forces. At the suggestion of the army leadership, who thought that it would bind Hitler to the army, an oath of unconditional loyalty to him as *Führer* (leader) of the German people was taken by every officer and soldier in the armed forces on 2 August. This oath was underlined in subsequent army education sessions. Moreover, the armed forces now addressed Hitler as *Führer* while the army's uniforms were altered to accommodate the swastika.

Hitler subsequently showed a clear determination to control the army, a goal that reflected his need for it to support his aggressive policies, his determination to tolerate no other views, and his dissatisfaction with the attitudes and reliability of his senior military advisers and of the army leadership in general. At the same time, Hitler promised the army a key role as the means to German greatness, and rearmament was pushed hard.

In 1933, Germany left both the League of Nations and the World Disarmament Conference at Geneva, and attempts to apply international pressure to stop Germany rearming failed. Anglo-French differences that preceded Hitler's rise to power were significant. The British had pressed for France to reduce its armed forces as a way to persuade Germany to accept limited rearmament, but were unwilling to provide France with the treaty for mutual defence that its government insisted on. In turn, the German government in 1932 was only willing to continue limitations if others moved in the same direction. Whatever his tactical positions, Hitler was not interested in limitations. A large arms budget was announced in March 1934. Conscription was re-introduced in 1935 and military service fixed at three years.

Hitler faced opposition on some points from the army leadership. General Werner von Fritsch, the Army Commander, Werner von Blomberg, the Minister of War, and other senior colleagues had been against the dispatch of troops into the Rhineland in March 1936, which had unilaterally abrogated the demilitarization of Germany's Western frontier provided for under the Versailles peace settlement and confirmed under the Locarno agreement. In 1937, both Blomberg and Fritsch made it clear that they were unhappy about Hitler's plans, specifically the risk of war with Britain and France, while Blomberg stressed the strength of Czech fortifications as a reason for caution in going to war.

In 1938, as war seemed likely as a result of the Czech crisis, Ludwig Beck, the Chief of the Army General Staff, prepared a coup in the event of war breaking out. Earlier that year, he had protested without success at the occupation of Austria. Due to Hitler's moves and their weaknesses, the military leadership did not back him up. Blomberg proved unable to defend army interests against Hitler and, in January 1938, he was summarily removed when he made a questionable choice of wife. The same month, Fritsch, falsely accused of being a homosexual, was interrogated by the Gestapo, obliged to resign, and tried by a military court: a dramatic display of the army's subordination. Although he was acquitted, Fritsch was not restored to his post. The opportunity was taken for a wider dismissal of commanders regarded as unsympathetic. Fourteen generals (six from the *Luftwaffe*) were dismissed and the position of War Minister was left empty.

The isolated Beck resigned on 18 August 1938: his plot for a coup on 28 September was not executed because of a lack of support from other senior generals, and because Britain and France negotiated the Munich settlement, so that there was no mobilization or war. Beck's emissaries to Britain seeking support had been rebuffed.

Hitler, meanwhile, acted to strengthen his position. In 1938, he not only removed Blomberg and Fritsch but also took effective control of the entire military high command. As Supreme Commander, Hitler carried out the functions of the War Ministry. Separate ministries were created for the three branches of the armed forces and they were coordinated by the new High Command of the Armed Forces, which would be easier for Hitler to control. On 20 February 1938, Hitler told the *Reichstag* that the armed forces were now 'dedicated to this National Socialist state in blind faith and obedience'.[26]

Stalin and the military

In the Soviet Union, the military was affected by the purge of all sectors of government and society as Stalin strove to crush any potential form of dissidence. Feeling it necessary to terrorize the armed forces, Stalin moved with far greater violence than Hitler. Claiming to discover a conspiracy between the Soviet and German armies, a belief fed by the German provision of forged information[27], he had his military heavily purged in 1937. The claim by the Soviet leadership that there were plans for a military coup is not without some basis[28], but also requires more evidence. Had such a coup occurred then it would have been one of the most dramatic instances of the role of military in politics in the inter-war period.

In the event, Marshal Mikhail Tukhachevsky, the talented and independent-minded commander of the Red Army, was shot on the night of 12 June alongside other senior officers. The purges continued until 1941. Over half the generals, including the vast majority of corps and divisional commanders, were killed, and about 23,000 lesser officers were killed or dismissed, including many of the most senior and experienced. An alternative basis of political power was thus ruthlessly crushed. At the same time, the purge of the military encouraged a new stage in the more general terror against perceived opponents of the Revolution. The NKVD acted as the shock-troops of this terror.

Party control of the armed forces had been pushed hard from the outset, especially by Mikhail Frunze and, after his death in 1925, by Kliment Voroshilov, a marshal close to Stalin. He became Commissar for Military and Naval Affairs in 1925, a post changed to Commissar for Defence in 1934. Party control was strengthened with the reintroduction, in 1937, of the system of dual control introduced in the Civil War. All military orders had to be countersigned by a political commissar. In 1938, military soviets, with a commander, chief of staff and a commissar, were created to provide trusted leadership at army and corps level. Political commissars, however, were not noted for their military ability. They also played a major, but harmful, role on the Republican side in the Spanish Civil War.

Stalin's drive for control had an impact on force structure and doctrine, although other factors were also important. For example, the purges did not discredit the cavalry, which had been built up in the 1920s and 1930s by Budënny, a protégé of Stalin, but the cavalry was in the process of being phased out in the late 1930s. Tukhachevsky, in contrast, had been committed to large-scale mechanized warfare and to seizing the offensive, and had been responsible for the creation of an armoured division in 1931 and of mechanized corps in 1932 (see p. 95). However, the corps were disbanded in 1939. Instead, the emphasis shifted from the large armoured formations advocated by Tukhachevsky, and his commitment to a 'deep' attack based on the rapid and far-flung operational exploitation of tactical successes, to smaller units integrated with the infantry. However, in part it was the experience of the Spanish Civil War, specifically the recommendation of General Pavlov, a Soviet adviser to the Republic, that tanks were better suited as infantry support that led to the disbanding of the mechanized corps, a decision that was reversed in 1940. Stalin, indeed, was an enthusiastic supporter of tanks, aircraft and modern technology.

As far as the purges affecting morale and the use of the initiative, this was in part unsubstantiated hearsay from the post-Stalin era, particularly by Nikita Khrushchev, who wanted to blame everything on Stalin. Soviet officers did not later claim this as an excuse when looking back on the war years. Nevertheless, it was widely believed by contemporaries that morale and cohesion had been affected by the purges. The German leadership was delighted, while the British General Staff assumed that the purges, alongside the reintroduction of Party control, 'must have had a serious adverse affect on the value for war of the Russian Army'.[29]

Conclusions

The interaction of control over the military with policy was important as, through a series of crises, Europe moved closer to war. None of the European states had a military outside civilian control and driving policy, as that of Japan became during the 1930s. At the same time, although different in character and intention from each other, the militarized nature of the German, Italian and Soviet regimes played an important role in helping increase the volatility of international relations. Rearmament in Britain and France, however, indicated that such militarism was not necessary in order to increase military effectiveness.

12

Preparing for war

Arguing purely from economic grounds, Germany is unlikely to embark on a war in which she cannot foresee a good prospect of gaining a decision in a short time.

BRITISH CHIEFS OF STAFF SUB-COMMITTEE, 12 NOVEMBER 1937[1]

The rise of Hitler did not initially lead to a widespread expectation of a cataclysmic war. Only with hindsight did the appointment of Hitler as Chancellor in January 1933 appear to make another Great War inevitable. Revolution and ideological radicalism in one country without such a conflict had already been experienced with the Soviet Union. The Russian Civil War had been followed by tension but not conflict. Moreover, there was a hope in Britain that Hitler's demands for a revision of the Versailles settlement could be achieved and Germany's integration into the international order sustained, rather as Napoleon III's pressure on behalf of France had been finessed in the mid-nineteenth century. In the winter of 1933–4, the Defence Requirements Sub-Committee decided that the German threat was in the future[2], while Japan was the immediate threat to British interests.

Very differently, the Soviet government saw the rise of Hitler as a way to advance its interests, distracting France and radicalizing Germany en route towards a proletarian revolution.[3] This approach rested on a misunderstanding of the situation within Germany and of the serious challenge posed by Hitler's opposition to Communism and to the Soviet Union.

Planning for war

In the meanwhile, speculation continued as how best to fight a future war, not least because disarmament had run out of steam. Indeed, the World Disarmament Conference of 1932–4 proved a total failure. The search for a doctrine of rapid victory focused on utilizing the operational possibilities of the new weaponry of tanks and aircraft, as this seemed at once the best way to respond to the apparent possibilities of this weaponry and also to avoid a recurrence of the devastation and prolonged struggle of the Great War. Thus, it was a search for a short-term warfare that could be effective, one that was limited not in means but in longevity, as opposed to what was presented as the ineffective, lengthy total war seen in the Great War. At the level of control, the emphasis on such operations suggested that war would be entrusted to trained, regular forces under military command, rather than to mass armies in whose direction civilian politicians played a major role. However, the Soviet Union was not expecting or planning in terms of limited war.

Increased concern about Hitler encouraged a stronger focus on military preparedness from the mid-1930s, and the willingness of first Japan and then Italy to launch wars that risked wider international crises, strengthened this process, although in 1933 the French government still put the emphasis on a balanced budget.

Under the pressure of growing German, Italian and Japanese strength, ambition and unpredictability, the other powers rearmed in the 1930s, although their ability to do so was affected by limitations in industrial capacity and capability, by financial problems, and by a lack of certainty over tasking and over appropriate force structure. A lack of clarity about allies and enemies made it difficult to produce effective strategic plans.

Despite the build-up in expenditure in the 1930s, there were still serious deficiencies in the armed forces of the major powers. In part, this was an inevitable product of the process of investment and diffusion to ensure that the best practice is adopted, especially when the rate of change is high. Furthermore, the nature of the sources has to be borne in mind as military leaders are not prone to say that they have adequate resources. Nevertheless, in some states, expenditure was low. The USA had the world's largest economy, but its military was not prepared for a major conflict. In 1938, the army could only put six divisions in the field. Due to the treaty restrictions on capital ships, the American navy was smaller in 1938 than in 1925, with the important exceptions of cruisers and aircraft carriers, but it was one of the world's leading navies.[4] Moreover, there were improvements in the American military, both in equipment, notably aeroplanes, and also planning with development in what would subsequently be called operational art and preparations for joint operations.[5]

At the same time, particular problems arose from the range of commitments of the major powers. This was especially the case for the imperial ones, Britain, France, Italy, and Japan, but Germany and the Soviet Union each also had to consider challenges on two fronts. Furthermore, the large size of the militaries made the cost of improving them especially high; indeed, the burden of sustaining forces that were so numerous, in particular feeding, clothing, housing and arming such numbers, was a serious problem.

This issue accentuated the tendency to focus on key sectors, which helped encourage debate about their identity. The emphasis on the leading sectors of mass militaries was an attempt to reconcile the apparent needs for both quality and mass in modern warfare. This was seen, for example, in the French army, where the development of mechanized and motorized divisions was intended to provide a mobility capable of countering any German advance in Belgium, as a prelude to an engagement by the mass army with its infantry and artillery. Similarly, the Germans emphasized élite units as a force multiplier ahead of the mass army.

In discussing these years, it is easy to adopt an approach that centres on new weaponry and related operational doctrines. Inter-war mechanization of armies led to a focus on the combination of firepower and mobility. Subsequently, those who adopted this approach were to be heavily praised, for example the writings of Charles de Gaulle in the early 1930s, especially *Le Fil de l'épee* (1932) and *Vers l' armée de métier* (1934), translated as *The Army of the Future* (1940). These were much touted later, notably by himself, as prescient for his recognition of the need for a professional army of movement, relying on a large and mobile armoured corps, and de Gaulle was presented as a prophet in the wilderness, his stance prefiguring his later rejection of the Vichy government of Marshal Pétain, a more conventional military figure. However, de Gaulle altogether failed to see the significance of air power, either in a military support role or as an independent arm. Mostly, de Gaulle just wanted a much bigger professional army and foresaw a rerun, on more mobile lines, of the Great War. His support for a professional army was not appropriate for a political order committed to conscription.[6]

More generally, it is necessary to note the lack of clarity about what constituted military progress, the variety of responses and the role of political suppositions. To take the lack of clarity about what constituted military progress, the processes of lesson-learning and doctrinal innovation sound far more clear-cut and easier than are, in fact, the case. The same is also true of the contemporary and subsequent evaluation of these processes. For example, Tukhachevsky's interest in 'deep battle' and mechanization are usually praised, but can be criticized for exaggerating the economic potential of the Soviet Union, for failing to pay due attention to the actual state and capability of the Red Army in the late 1930s, and for under-estimating the importance of the defensive. One particular problem concerns the assessment of 'anti-'strategies and tactics. If, for example, the doctrine and technology of a period favours the offensive, then investing in the defensive can be seen as anachronistic or, more favourably, as a way to try to lessen the impact of the offensive. In the latter view, it can be regarded as prescient, or even forward-looking.

Turning to individual states, an emphasis on tanks[7] could make static defences seem limited, but, by the 1930s, both Fuller and Liddell Hart had come to appreciate that tank offensives could be blunted by an effective defence, as was actually to be the case in the Second World War, notably with the German invasion of the Soviet Union in 1941. At the same time, alongside tactical constraints, there was an appreciation in Britain of the operational possibilities created by the tank. This appreciation was seen within the army by practical modernizers, but they had to be more aware of financial restrictions than the publicists criticizing from outside.[8] Liddell Hart remained a contentious figure. In 1939, Sir John Dill, Commander of the 1st British Corps in France, complained about the 'incalculable' harm done by Liddell Hart, adding:

thanks largely to Liddell Hart's advice, battalions were cut down. The argument was that it is fire power, not man power that is wanted on the battlefield. That may be true up to a point but at night, in fog, and when the enemy uses smoke, one must have men on the ground.[9]

Promoted Chief of the Imperial General Staff in May 1940, Dill was an undistinguished holder of the post and was removed by Churchill in December 1941.

France was to be rapidly defeated in 1940, and, in that light, it is all-too-easy to neglect the policies of the state in Western Europe with the largest army for most of the inter-war period. Spending heavily on the military, despite taking a long time in the 1930s to recover from economic crisis, the French devoted considerable effort to preparing for another war with Germany. Maxime Weygand, as Chief of the General Staff, Vice-President of the Supreme War Council and Army Inspector-General from 1930 to 1935, was convinced that Germany was France's key enemy, and he focused French planning on this threat. This effort included the construction, from 1930, of the Maginot Line of in-depth fortifications to cover the eastern frontier with Germany[10], named after André Maginot, the French Minister of Defence from 1928 to 1930.

Like the British defences at Singapore, the Maginot Line, which was to be bypassed by the German advance in 1940, is often treated as both failure and anachronism. However, French strategy was more nuanced and flexible than most accounts would admit. Leaving aside the important point that the fortifications constrained attacking options, the French had not abandoned the concept of the offensive. Instead, drawing on the experience of the Great War, French military doctrine emphasized the role of artillery, which was both a defensive and an offensive arm. Fortifications were regarded not as a definition of a defensive stance, but as an aspect of a force structure that could support an offensive and/or a defensive strategy. French war planning in the early 1920s, notably Plan of 1924, envisaged a speedy invasion of Germany, while, from 1933, the emphasis shifted to advancing to fight the invading Germans in Belgium.[11] The Maginot Line was intended to be by-passed, in order to channel the Germans into Belgium

Montgomery-Massingberd, who visited France in 1935, commented on the strength of the fortifications facing Italy – 'tunnelled as they are under 40 or

50 feet of rock, with embrasures for guns and machine guns covering every approach' – but he was also very impressed by French developments with mechanization. The Maginot Line was seen by Montgomery-Massingberd as offering protection and a support for operational mobility:

> My recollections of our attacks against strong lines during the war, even with masses of heavy guns and tanks, is that this frontier, in three or four years will be practically impregnable, always provided of course that the French keep up their present garrison and maintain everything at the standard they are doing at present. Here again the underlying idea of economy in men so as to set free as many troops as possible for the mobile army.[12]

French tank strength was built up and the best French tanks, the Char B, had far thicker armour than its German counterpart. Nevertheless, the French failed to develop an effective doctrine for their armour. Tanks were seen, like artillery, as best integrated with infantry that they were to support as if mobile artillery, and not as a separate arm capable of shock action.[13] However, it is unclear that tanks designed for shock action would have been a good use of French resources. If the Germans had not advanced through the Ardennes and if the French army had been better trained, then French defensive doctrine might have done the job. The French also had major colonial commitments and, in order to be able to exert power in the Mediterranean, put strenuous effort into developing their navy.

To the east, its lengthy frontiers vulnerable to German attack from the north, west and south-west, Poland put its emphasis on avoiding the Czech fate in 1938, both by defending the full extent of its borders, and by being part of an alliance system. The Polish victory over Russia in 1920, not least at Komarów, the last cavalry battle in Europe, led to a mistaken confidence in the continued value of the methods used then. The Poles did not match the mechanization of the German and Soviet armies in the 1930s, in part because of a lack of financial resources. Sikorski pressed the value of mechanized warfare and the tank, but he was out of favour with Pilsudski, who was dictator from 1926, when he staged a coup, until his death in 1935. Although, in the late 1930s, the Polish military came to understand the value of tanks, they were too far behind their rivals.[14] By 1939, the Polish cavalry, about a tenth of the men under arms, was armed with anti-tank weapons and heavy machine-guns, and was trained to fight dismounted, the horses being employed to change position after an action-in short, for mobility, not shock action.[15] Nevertheless, the Polish army was weak in tanks and in anti-tank guns and training.

German rearmament

From the low base of 100,000 men permitted under the Versailles settlement, Hitler built up the German military, although rearmament took time, not least in creating the necessary industrial capability. Secret British reports in early 1934 indicated a significant increase in German land and air strength.[16] On 1 October 1934, Hitler ordered a trebling of army size to 300,000 men, as well as the creation of an (illegal) air force. The *Luftwaffe* became independent from the army in March 1935, and its existence was publicly acknowledged that summer.

Rather than respond to the fiscal strains of 1934 by restraining rearmament, Hitler pressed ahead, ordering the military in October 1935 to rearm as fast as possible. The Four-Year Plan, initiated in 1936, was designed to ensure self-sufficiency and readiness to go to war in four years. Hitler set out to strengthen the German position by negotiating agreements with Italy and Japan in late 1936, and by constructing the West Wall fortifications to protect the Western frontier with France. The aim of these enhancements was not to secure stability, but to provide strategic flexibility for German aggression.

Responding to Hitler

In a key step, Hitler unilaterally remilitarized the Rhineland on 7 March 1936: it provided military protection for the Ruhr and was also a springboard for action against France. Backed by air action, 22,000 German troops, joined by 14,000 paramilitaries, entered the demilitarized zone although, initially, only 3,000 troops were sent across the Rhine. The German fleet was also prepared for action.

The French, however, had no capability for a significant rapid response in 1936. Their army was largely intended for defensive roles, and its equipment and training for mobile action was limited. Expenditure heavily focused on fortifications, notably the Maginot Line, and 1935 was the nadir of inter-war French military expenditure. There were no detailed plans for a response to the German action, the size of which was greatly exaggerated, and Gamelin did not wish to risk war.[17]

Moreover, far from responding forcefully against this breach of the Versailles peace settlement, the British sought to discourage the French from acting. Belgium also did not provide support. Indeed, that spring, Belgium rejected the 1920 secret military convention with France and, instead, opted for neutrality. This was not expected to protect her from German attack if war broke out, but it did not make French planning easier.

In hindsight, Western passivity in 1936 marked a major step in Nazi expansionism, but, at the time, it was not seen in such a stark light. Furthermore, differences between Britain and France in their views of European development, the very limited nature of Anglo-French military cooperation over the previous decade, and their lack of preparedness, were understood by contemporaries as a poor basis for joint action. In 1933, the British were unwilling to make common cause with France towards Germany[18], and this remained their policy. More robust policies focused on alliance with France were rejected.[19] Moreover, the Anglo-German naval agreement of 1935 was regarded by the French as a betrayal.

In response, France, which had already passed a two-year conscription law in March 1935 and begun to increase arms spending, sought allies against Hitler elsewhere. There was no shortage of forces to accumulate in an anti-German alliance and in pursuit of the idea of one also including Poland, Czechoslovakia and the Soviet Union, Gamelin visited Warsaw in August 1936. However, his visit helped convince the French government of the incompatibility of the Eastern European powers and thus of the impossibility of such an alliance. Such an assessment was supported by the fate of the Rambouillet deal with Poland agreed the following month which provided armaments credits and help to the Polish defence industry. In the event, this agreement was unable to stop Poland from adopting a neutralist alignment, one also characterized by hostility to Czechoslovakia. This belief led the French to move away from Eastern European diplomacy, minimizing their commitments to Poland and Czechoslovakia, and, instead, to plan for a long war with Germany and to try to improve relations with Britain[20], which they allowed to take the lead in the Munich Crisis of 1938.

Appeasement, the Anglo-French failure to confront Germany, Japan and Italy, was a matter of goals and means. The attempt to contain the Axis powers short of war failed, but, however mishandled, the *Realpolitik* involved was not inherently dishonourable. Moreover, a wish to seek a negotiated alternative to war was widespread across the political spectrum. In Britain, far from being a characteristic of reprehensible Conservatives, not to say fellow-travelling neo-Fascists, the desire to avoid war and the related opposition to rearmament were also notably strong among liberal opinion and on the Left, and particularly so prior to the Munich Crisis of 1938.

On the part of Britain, an effort to sway Germany towards better behaviour and a sense that compromise with Germany was possible, combined with a lack of interest in the areas threatened by German expansionism, encouraged a conciliatory search for a settlement, as did the extent that few were in other than denial about what Nazism was really like, both in domestic and international policy. Neville Chamberlain, Prime Minister from 1937 to 1940, feared that war would lead to the collapse of the British Empire and would also wreck the domestic policies of the Conservative-dominated National Government for which he had previously served from 1931 as Chancellor of the Exchequer. He was correct on both counts. Chamberlain wanted a small defence budget to help in economic recovery.[21] Ministers also assumed that, if conflict broke out with Germany, then Japan might be encouraged to attack Britain's Asian empire, which was correctly seen as militarily and politically vulnerable.

Appeasement was designed to avoid unwelcome alliances as well as war. Unhappy with Britain's allies and potential allies, and unwilling to explore the path of confronting Hitler by making him uncertain about the prospects of collective action against Germany, the British government preferred to negotiate directly with Hitler. This political response was matched by Chamberlain's focus on deterrence by a stronger navy and, in particular, air force, each of which was to be based in Britain, rather than through an army that was to be sent to the Continent.

The occupation of the Rhineland, like rearmament, could be seen as an attempt to regain Germany's former position. But when Hitler occupied Austria on 12 March 1938, uniting it with Germany in the *Anschluss* (union) of 13 March, this was more than a revision of the Versailles settlement. The map of Europe had been fundamentally redrawn. This step was possible because of the rapprochement between Mussolini and Hitler in 1936. That year, the Austrian government was pressed by Mussolini to settle its differences with Hitler, and the latter's promise, in April 1937, to leave Italy with its post-war gains from Austria ensured that Mussolini would accept *Anschluss* as he promised to do on the eve of the German occupation.

Under great pressure from Hitler, the Austrian government, nevertheless, called a national referendum on independence for 13 March 1938, but, on 10 March, large-scale Nazi demonstrations across Austria helped cow opposition. On 11 March, Hitler ordered the occupation to go ahead while the Austrian government crumbled before Nazi pressure and a Nazi-dominated cabinet was appointed. A formal request for German troops was sent, but Hitler had already ordered them to cross the border the next morning. The occupation began on 12 March and there was scant opposition. Some opponents and Jews were murdered during the takeover. Austria and Germany became *Grossdeutschland* (Greater Germany).

The Austrian economy and currency reserves could now contribute to the build-up of the German war economy, which was also strengthened by the addition of Austrian manpower. The small Austrian army was broken up and absorbed into the German army. Czechoslovakia's southern frontier was now exposed to German attack, and Germany gained frontiers with Hungary, Yugoslavia and Italy. Like the German re-occupation of the Rhineland, the *Anschluss* led to a programme for French rearmament, although the weak state of the French armaments industry ensured that production did not rapidly respond, and indeed not really until 1939.[22]

The Munich Crisis

The Versailles settlement had left to Czechoslovakia those parts of Bohemia and Moravia where there was an ethnic majority of Germans: the Sudeten Germans. This was unacceptable to Hitler, who sought the union of all Germans in one state and was determined to destroy Czechoslovakia, a democratic state that looked to the great powers for support. However, Czechoslovakia was very different to Austria as the bulk of the population was totally opposed to German takeover, although there was a serious weakness in the failure to create a state in which the Slovaks and the Sudeten Germans felt represented. Czechoslovakia was wealthier than Austria and had a larger and more determined army. In addition, France was an ally of Czechoslovakia. Hitler's pressure on Czechoslovakia therefore caused grave anxiety for part of the German army leadership.

Nevertheless, a crisis built up over the summer of 1938 as Germany prepared for war while virulent anti-Czech propaganda was incessantly produced in Germany. On 12 September 1938, Hitler told the Nazi Party rally at Nuremberg that there would be war if the Sudeten Germans did not receive self-determination. While Britain attempted to negotiate a settlement, Hitler renewed his threats of war with Czechoslovakia, in the event only to accept a settlement negotiated with Britain, France and Italy, the Munich agreement of 29 September 1938.

Hitler himself felt thwarted as he had wanted a short and successful war with Czechoslovakia. However, concern over the prospect of a more general war leading to conflict with Britain and France had led Mussolini to become more cautious, and, without the support of his ally, Hitler cancelled the mobilization order and decided to rely on negotiations. Mussolini's position had indeed been regarded as significant by the British Chiefs of Staff, notably because of the threat to Egypt.[23]

Prior to the Munich agreement, Britain and France had threatened action if Hitler tried to pre-empt a negotiated settlement of the Sudeten question. In fact, by the agreement, the Czech frontier was to be revised to satisfy the Sudeten Germans. On 1 October, the Sudetenland was occupied by the German army.

Pacifism in British and French society and opinion[24] affected their governments' policies. So did anti-Communism, but suspicion of the Soviet Union as a potential ally against Germany also owed much to the purge of the military leadership. Soviet opportunism, which extended to considering closer relations with Germany, was also a serious handicap. The Soviets mobilized 330,000 troops in 21–24 September 1938, deploying most of them close to the Polish frontier, while there was also the potential of a Soviet airlift to support the Czechs. However, Stalin was very cautious, not least as he feared being drawn in to fight Germany on behalf of British interests.

Britain was also affected by the reluctance of the Dominions, especially Canada and South Africa, to fight Germany. With Roosevelt guaranteeing Canada's security in his Kingston, Ontario speech in September 1938, there appeared less reason to risk war. With isolationism strong, the USA played no real role in the crisis, which itself ensured that it took an important part.

Czechoslovakia also received no support from Yugoslavia and Romania, its allies in the Little Entente. Hungary and Poland, with which Czechoslovakia had poor relations, used the crisis to make gains at Czechoslovakia's expense. On 2 October, Polish troops moved into the Teschen area, while, on 2 November, the Hungarians occupied an area of southern Czechoslovakia with a population of over a million in an agreement brokered by Mussolini. Poland also moved troops to the frontier of Lithuania in order to intimidate the latter into settling its frontier dispute on Polish terms, which it did in January 1939.

Anglo-French fears in 1938 may have been excessive, given the weaknesses of the Nazi regime, not least a lack of enthusiasm among the German generals, as well as the deficiencies of the German military[25], the weaknesses of the German frontier defences, and the lack of German strength for any attritional conflict. British intelligence, and notably the Air Staff, exaggerated German military capabilities with regard to Britain and Czechoslovakia.[26] The *Luftwaffe* lacked the training and range to launch a bomber offensive against Britain, while the number estimated for German reserve and armoured divisions was too high. Moreover, poor leadership by French politicians was matched by the French high command, and French military intelligence overestimated the rate of German rearmament.[27]

It is too easy in hindsight, however, to criticize the leaders of the period and to underrate their genuine and understandable fear of causing a second 'Great War'. In many respects, the Munich agreement was part of the legacy of the Great War. Germany may have been weaker than was thought, but was determined to gain its objectives. There were also serious weaknesses in the British and French militaries. Gamelin talked of invading Italy and marching thence on Vienna, but the French army was not ready for attack, the planned mechanized forces were woefully unprepared, and there was a serious shortage of new aircraft, anti-aircraft guns and anti-tank guns. Moreover, suspicion between Britain and France harmed cooperation against Hitler.[28] In May 1939, General Sir Ronald Adam, the Deputy Chief of the Imperial General Staff, noted:

> The crisis in September 1938 emphasised the danger in the assumption that a Continental commitment was to be given a low order of priority. It also focused sharply the fact that, even when the programme was complete, our forces would be inadequate for a major Continental war.[29]

Indeed, the British Expeditionary Force that was to be sent to France in September 1939 after war had broken out were small, short of rifles, and poorly trained for conflict with the Germans, although, contrary to frequent remarks, it was well-equipped in many respects, notably in tanks.[30] A sense of only slow institutional improvement is suggested by the British army committee that in 1938 recommended the merger of the Royal Tank Corps and the newly mechanized cavalry regiments. The committee noted that, in the past, troops had been trained within their own regiments, but that 'this system is impracticable for a corps equipped with armoured fighting vehicles, and it is clear that in future training will be necessary at a depot equipped with suitable vehicles and staffed by technically qualified instructors'.[31] At the time of Munich, the RAF had only a few modern fighters, while its bombers were weak. The radar network was incomplete. Moreover, British command and control systems were inadequate. Due to the financial situation, there had been no large-scale army manoeuvres for several years.

As a part of an alliance including Britain and America, the Red Army was to play the key role in destroying the German army in 1944–5, but, in 1938–9, this alliance and role did not seem really feasible, either militarily or diplomatically. The loss of talented officers in the purges and the promotion of men whom Stalin could trust, many of whom were mediocre and unwilling to challenge his views, affected the calibre of command. Moreover, poor training systems compromised fighting quality, there were serious organizational weaknesses, and the expansion in size of the late 1930s was not matched by a comparable increase in effectiveness. It is difficult to separate out factors, but the expansion in size may have been more significant than the purges in explaining the weaknesses of the Red Army in 1939–41.[32] The value of the Soviet Union as an ally was doubted by the British Chiefs of Staff.[33]

The Red Army proved ill-equipped, ill-trained and badly led when it was sent against Finland in November 1939. However, the Red Army persisted in that Winter War and eventually won.[34] Moreover, in August 1939, the Soviets had decided to build two new powerful tanks, the T-34 and the KV-1.

Alongside the deficiencies of the forces that could have been arrayed against Germany, it was not as easy to create a German war army as Hitler had envisaged or as Göring announced on 14 October 1938. There was a shortage of the necessary trained troops and reservists, as well as of military stores and the relevant industrial capacity. Shortages in raw materials hit German armaments' production. The last, in fact, was to be greatly helped by the German seizure of Czech armaments, industry and raw materials in March 1939. This seizure doubled the quantity of artillery the Germans controlled, while the strength of German armour when Poland was attacked in September 1939 owed much to the seizure of Czech tanks and military-industrial capacity.

German rearmament had a 'shop window' character and failed in many ways. There was little appropriate long-term planning, and aside from the serious shortage of iron and steel that hit German weapons production, there was a lack of skilled workers, while Germany's fiscal situation greatly exacerbated the problems created by the shift to oil-based weapon systems. There was simply not the oil to meet Göring's bold plan to take the *Luftwaffe's* strength to 21,000 aeroplanes by the end of 1942. The shortage of oil also made the plans for a much larger navy and tank force implausible, while there was neither the shipbuilding nor dockyard capacity for the naval construction programme that was endorsed in December 1938 to January 1939, in part a response to Hitler's anger with the British role at Munich. At the same time, the scale of rearmament was deliberately exaggerated in order to intimidate likely opponents.

1939

Eventually, on 15 March 1939, Hitler destroyed his victim, Czechoslovakia, and was able to do so without encountering armed resistance, because the country had been much weakened by internal dissent between Czechs and Slovaks, and by a loss of frontier fortifications and easily defended positions as a result of the Munich agreement. The Munich agreement had been followed by Slovakia becoming autonomous, but relations between Czechs and Slovaks deteriorated sharply.

Fears that Slovakia would become independent led the Czech government to occupy the Slovak capital, Bratislava, on 10 March 1939. Hitler then bullied the Slovak leaders into declaring independence and seeking protection against the Czechs. Under the threat of attack, including the bombing of Prague, the Czech President yielded to pressure and agreed to Bohemia and Moravia becoming a German protectorate. The President ordered the Czech army not to resist. On 16 March 1939, moreover, with Hitler's encouragement, Hungarian forces occupied Ruthenia, the easternmost part of Czechoslovakia. Hungary, where the Revisionist League had been established as a semi-official body in 1927, had earlier been ready to accept the *Anschluss*. Also, on 23 March 1939, the threat of invasion and bombing led Lithuania to agree to German demands for the cession of Memel (Klapeida).

The Munich Crisis and its aftermath led British policymakers to appreciate more clearly the danger posed by Hitler who was increasingly pushing his aim of a new world order in which Germany was a superpower. The seizure of Bohemia and Moravia on 15 March 1939 and Hitler's renunciation of the guarantees he had made at Munich showed that his ambitions were not restricted to bringing all Germans under one state, while he was increasingly willing to pursue opportunities without considering the risks involved. In a further sign of developing instability, an envious Mussolini invaded Albania on 7 April, Good Friday, in a badly managed affair that was successful in part because there was no real opposition: 22,000 Italian troops landed and King Zog promptly fled.

Neville Chamberlain, the British Prime Minister, and Édouard Daladier, his French counterpart, responded to Hitler by pressing ahead with rearmament.

In Britain, the Territorial Army was doubled in size, conscription was introduced, and Leslie Hore-Belisha, the Secretary of State for War, moved ahead with the modernization of the army. Chamberlain also sought to create an alliance system capable of deterring and intimidating Hitler, a policy supported by a French government that was less frightened of Germany than at the time of Munich.[35]

Despite the resulting guarantees of British and French support to Poland, made on 31 March, and Romania, Hitler persisted with his plan for an attack on Poland, for which he had given instructions on 25 March. On 28 April, Hitler renounced the 1934 German-Polish Non-Aggression Pact and the 1935 Anglo-German Naval Agreement. To give substance to the British and French guarantees, it seemed necessary to bring in the Soviet Union. However, negotiations for a triple alliance of Britain, France and the Soviets collapsed largely because Britain and France could not satisfy the Soviets on the issue of Polish and Romanian consent to the passage of Soviet forces in the event of war with Germany. Romania, where King Carol II had rejected the idea of a reconciliation with the Soviet Union in 1936, was suspicious about Soviet intentions about Bessarabia and fearful of the German reaction if it agreed to the British approach.[36] Earlier, the idea of a four-power declaration by Britain, France, Poland and the Soviet Union had fallen foul of Polish opposition. In light of the Soviet invasion of Poland in 1920, as well as what was to happen in 1939–41, the Soviets brutally conquering part of Poland, Polish concerns are understandable. However, the Poles were also naïve in imagining that Germany could be restrained without active Soviet assistance. Stalin was totally untrustworthy, but the Poles had no viable alternative.

Hitler believed that Britain and France would not fight, especially after he secured a non-aggression pact with Stalin, concluded on 23–24 August, and named after their manipulative Foreign Ministers, Ribbentrop and Molotov. The pact stipulated no war between the two powers for ten years, while secret clauses determined spheres of influence in eastern Europe.[37] Hitler was therefore freed from the prospect of a two-front war against major powers. As such, it appeared possible to avoid the stalemate of the Great War.

However, Hitler wanted only a limited war against Poland and, when the pact failed to lead Britain and France to abandon their guarantees to Poland, postponed the attack on Poland. This provided Britain and France with the apparent opportunity to negotiate a settlement between Germany and Poland, but Hitler was only interested in weakening Anglo-French support for Poland. His threats did not work because Poland stood firm while Britain and France felt war necessary in order to preserve honour and the international system, and to stop Hitler.[38] In the event, the German attack on 1 September 1939 led Britain and France to declare war two days later.

13

Conclusions

Taking the long view, it is unquestionable that what the British Empire has most reason to fear in the future is a Russo-German combination.

GENERAL STAFF REPORT, 'THE MILITARY SITUATION IN RUSSIA', JULY 1919[1]

The view from 1940

The rapid fall of France to German forces in June 1940 was both a total contrast with the Great War and marked the final end of the inter-war period militarily and politically. The defeat of the imperial systems of France and Britain in their European heartland ensured that Germany would only be stopped as a superpower if the Soviet Union and America came into the war, and also meant that a major American role would be necessary to defeat Japan once it entered the war in December 1941. The fall of France also marked the end of limited war because the new British government under Winston Churchill was not interested in a compromise peace dictated by a victorious Germany, which was, indeed, on offer. This decision meant that the conflict would continue until the actions of these other powers played a decisive role.

'Machine has triumphed over man', observed the war correspondent John Langdon-Davies of the Spanish Nationalists' capture of Toledo in 1936.[2] In his juxtaposition, he repeated a frequent theme. The 1940 German campaign might appear to demonstrate the wisdom of those who had seen the future of war in tanks, mobility and the offensive. Indeed, Liddell Hart was later to claim part of the credit for German success. The theme of a prophet ignored in his own country but heeded elsewhere proved attractive to commentators and appeared to add a military counterpart to the idea that Britain had been betrayed politically by Appeasement.

However, just as options are rarely simple, so military change is far from straightforward. Most notably, the Germans were not really preparing for *blitzkrieg* and, instead, learned from their successful war of manoeuvre in Poland in September 1939 what could be achieved, although a lack of training was also apparent in 1939. The Germans were also helped by the Polish deployment, notably defending the full extent of their borders and lacking defence in depth, as well as by complete German air superiority and Soviet intervention on the German side.[3]

The ad hoc nature of *blitzkrieg* helps put supposed German operational brilliance in its proper context. Moreover, much of the German army in 1939 was heavily reliant on railways and draught animals. Moving toward *blitzkrieg* was linked to retraining actively after the Poland campaign as the Germans made more profitable use than their opponents of the 'Phoney War' or lull on the Western Front in the harsh winter of 1939–40, and to the politics of command preference within the German army, as Hitler felt emboldened to advance particular generals. The Anglo-French forces failed to respond to German success in Poland with an appropriate training regime.[4]

The rapid defeat of France in 1940 reflected German military strengths at the tactical and operational levels that helped overcome the superior numbers of well-equipped opponents.[5] The Germans launched their offensive on 10 May, pushed across the Meuse River on 13 May, reached the English Channel on 21 May, took the surrender of the Dutch on 14 May and of the Belgians on 27 May, entered Paris on 14 June, and dictated terms to the French on 22 June. For less than 30,000 of their own troops killed, Germany had transformed the situation in western Europe.

However, it is also fairly well established that the effectiveness of the *blitzkrieg* was exaggerated by commentators under the spell cast by the sheer shock and drama of the German offensives. As a result, commentators have overrated the impact on war of military methods which, in practice, represented more of an improvisation than the fruition of a coherent doctrine. The potential of weaponry and logistics based on the internal combustion engine was less fully grasped than talk of *blitzkrieg* might suggest, not least because much of the German army was unmechanized and walked into battle. Alongside the effective tactical and operational use of the armoured tip of the army, the contribution and quality of the German infantry and artillery were significant.

As another qualification of the standard *blitzkrieg* approach, the Germans encountered serious problems in fighting their way across the Meuse River against French resistance.[6] Subsequently, the French artillery-infantry defence at Gembloux proved effective[7], while the British counter-attack on 21 May had an impact on German policy, as exaggerated flank fright, especially on the part of Hitler, led to the slowing down of the tempo of German advance.[8]

More generally, the success of the risky German strategy owed much to the serious deficiencies of French strategy and planning, particularly the deployment of mechanized reserves on the advancing left-flank so that, in fact, they were not available in a reserve capacity[9], and, linked to this, the absence of defence in depth. The experience of the Polish campaign was also significant for the Germans who would probably have been less successful had they attacked the French in 1938. In 1940, as with the Allies (but not, earlier in the year, Germans) in 1918, the attacking side won. The ability to take the initiative was a key point, as was the opponents' response. In 1918, the Allies had responded more effectively than they were to do in 1940 to German attack. Greater German mobility was an important factor in 1940, not least the triumph of an operational war of movement over position warfare, but it was not the only factor. Indeed, French strategic and operational inadequacies, rather than deficiencies in weaponry, ensured that inter-war German efforts at innovation, which had aimed at incremental improvement, produced, instead, a 'striking and temporarily asymmetrical operational revolution'.[10] The French were outmanoeuvred in part because their attempt to take the initiative contributed to a disastrous position. The German army's key advantage was not superior equipment but greater intellectual flexibility.

Arguing back in order to make judgements on decisions, risks neglecting the extent to which the unexpected came to the fore. For example, in 1940–1, the *Luftwaffe*, which was designed essentially for tactical purposes, was called upon to play a strategic role against Britain and was unable to fulfil this role.

The suppression of aerial defence proved more difficult than had been anticipated, and the same was true of bold talk about using air power to prevent
warships from operating. Moreover, despite the heavy casualties and terrible
damage that did result in Britain, the German air offensive proved less deadly
and disruptive than had been anticipated prior to the war.

A key element, again, was that of politics. In 1939, by allying with Hitler,
Stalin proved more than willing to subordinate the cause of international
Communism, about which he was anyway dubious, to that of state-expansion
in concert with Germany. This process was facilitated by a shared hostility to
Britain and its liberalism. This hostility stemmed from a rejection of liberal
capitalism as a domestic agenda for liberty and freedom, but also hostility to it
as an international agenda focused on opposition to dictatorial expansionism.
Just as Britain had fought to protect Belgium in 1914, so it went to war in 1939
in response to the invasion of another weak power, Poland.

The resulting German-Soviet system proved short-lived, as Hitler attacked
the Soviet Union in June 1941, while, in the meantime, Britain and the
Soviet Union did not fight each other, despite the Soviet invasion of Poland.
Nevertheless, the combination of Germany and the Soviet Union underlined
the extent to which military considerations, such as the force structure
of the British military, were secondary to the parameters and tasking set
by political alignments. In 1939, it proved necessary for Britain to fight
Germany, but its ally Italy did not come into the war until June 1940 while,
conversely, there was consideration in Britain and France of hostilities with
the Soviet Union.

In the event, the initial campaign of the Second World War, that in Poland,
scarcely involved the British or French. Their emphasis on resting on the
defensive and using the indirect means of an attritional economic warfare
based on the strength of the Western economies and naval blockade to weaken
Germany[11] could not save Poland, and, indeed, was not intended to do so. The
Royal Navy found itself focusing on German submarines and surface raiders,
rather than on fleet actions with the Italian or Japanese navies. Yet, combined
with political will, popular support, potent air defence and the backing of
the empire, the navy's strength was to ensure that German strategy failed in
1940. Britain fought on and Germany was deprived of the quick victory it had

prepared for.[12] As with Japan in 1938–9, the weakness of a flawed strategic insight became apparent.

Longer-term perspectives

The themes in this book are those of variety and unpredictability, the importance of the Far East, and the significance of civil wars. These themes were to be overshadowed from 1939, but have come to the fore again in recent years. That should return our attention to the importance of the earlier inter-war period. So also should the significance of China as a rising power and the extent to which the conflicts of the 1920s and 1930s, both with Japan and domestically, play a central role in the Chinese popular account of history and in the political legitimation of the Communist party. As such, this period is more important than the earlier development of the 'Eastern Question' from the 1850s. Chinese weakness, Japanese revival, and American, Russian and British activity and expansionism, provided a link from the 1850s to the mid-twentieth century. However, it is the 1920s and 1930s that are more important to the development and identity of modern China, as China's international crisis then rose to a height while the foundation and growth of the Communist Party can be presented as a counter to this crisis.

Given the demographic weight of China, it is striking that more attention is not paid to it in general military histories. There are problems with language, sources and the partisanship of some of the literature[13], but, after the end of the Russian Civil War, conflicts in China involved the largest numbers of troops and caused the most casualties in both the 1920s and the 1930s. Moreover, far from being 'primitive' militarily, whatever that means, these conflicts were able to deliver verdicts, notably in terms of (partial) Chinese unification in the 1920s and of preventing Japan from winning victory in the 1930s. Both of these, especially the second, were of considerable importance for world history. What happened in the Far East in the 1920s and 1930s was more important for the history of that period than is generally recognized, while the rise of China today also makes what happened there in the 1920s and 1930s of great importance.

To turn to Europe, the use of Appeasement as a potent political and military *leitmotif* in the West also reflects the continuing relevance of the period, while inviting discussion of the rationale of past decisions. Indeed, 'Munich' has repeatedly served as a key point in public strategic debate, notably being used to justify intervention in the Suez Crisis of 1956 and against Iraq in 2003.[14]

The issues of policy, tasking, strategy, doctrine and force structure facing Britain in the 1920s and 1930s are also of considerable relevance for America today. Imperial strategic commitments for Britain included interests in the Middle East, the extensive presence in South and South-East Asia, and the route to Australasia. The combination of these commitments posed a problem in responding to particular crises. Judging between commitments was central whether expenditure rose or not. In Britain, it proved possible to take a peace dividend after the Great War, and the cuts recommended by the Geddes Committee in 1922 – the Geddes Axe – hit military expenditure most heavily. In the 1930s, however, as expenditure rose, debates over priorities became even more bitter not least because competing threats interacted with rivalry between the services.

Parallels with the modern USA are noticeable, not least the limitations of alliance politics, with the Dominions, especially Canada, posing 1930s' Britain problems comparable to most of America's allies today. Moreover, British 'small war' on India's North-West Frontier and American constabulary duties in the Philippines are pointers to the West's recent development of counter-insurgency or COIN policies.[15] So also with the use of air power.[16]

Lastly, although much of the period was scarcely a preparation for the Second World War, this was far less true of the Soviet Union, Nazi Germany, Japan and China, while by 1938, at the latest, a major conflict increasingly appeared likely to other powers. Thus, any history of the war requires a discussion of developments and planning prior to it, not least the extent to which there were action-reaction cycles. These cycles were the case not only between the powers as they anxiously sought to follow each others' moves, but also between preparations and what the conflicts of the period suggested about military capability and possibilities. Without a study of the years 1918–39, the Second World War is difficult to follow, and impossible to do so in East Asia where it really began in 1937.

Notes

Preface

1 J. Black, *The Age of Total War, 1860–1945* (Westport, Connecticut, 2006), *War Since 1945* (London, 2004) and *War Since 1990* (London, 2009).

2 J. Eloranta, 'Twentieth Century Military Spending Patterns', in G. Kassimeris and J. Buckley (eds), *The Ashgate Research Companion to Modern Warfare* (Farnham, 2010), pp. 152–5.

3 C. Kinvig, *Churchill's Crusade: The British Invasion of Russia, 1918–1920* (London, 2006); A. Zamoyski, *Warsaw 1920: Lenin's Failed Conquest of Europe* (Basingstoke, 2008).

Introduction

1 J. Black, *Rethinking Military History* (London, 2004).

2 General Staff, 'The Situation in Turkey, 15th March, 1920', NA. CAB. 24/101 fol. 315.

3 Wilson to Churchill, 9 June, Air Staff Memorandum, Churchill to Cabinet, 15 June 1920, NA. CAB. 24/107 fols 253, 262–3, 250.

4 S. T. Ross, *American War Plans 1890–1939* (London, 2002), pp. 121–6.

5 J. Latimer, *1812. War with America* (Cambridge, Massachusetts, 2007), pp. 407–8.

6 The Stimson Doctrine named after President Hoover's Secretary of State, Henry Stimson, denounced Japanese aggression in Manchuria.

7 D. Edgerton, *Britain's War Machine. Weapons, Resources and Experts in the Second World War* (London, 2011), pp. 11–65.

8 LH. MM. 10/6; NA. CAB. 24/259.

9 J. P. Harris, 'Obstacles to innovation and readiness: the British Army's experience 1918–1939', in W. Murray and R. H. Sinnreich (eds), *The Past as Prologue. The Importance of History to the Military Profession* (Cambridge, 2006), p. 216.

Chapter 1

1 NA. WO. 106/6238, p. 19.

2 M. Pawley, *The Watch on the Rhine. The Military Occupation of the Rhineland* (London, 2007).

3 NA. CAB. 24/84 fol. 282.

4 J. D. Smele, *Civil War in Siberia: The Anti-Bolshevik Government of Admiral Kolchak, 1918–1920* (Cambridge, 1998).

5 LH. Kennedy 2/2.

6 General Staff report, NA. CAB. 24/84 fol. 284.

7 G. Swain, *Russia's Civil War* (Stroud, 2000).

8 LH. Kennedy 2/2.

9 G. Leggett, *The Cheka: Lenin's Political Police* (2nd edn, Oxford, 1986), p. 17.

10 V. N. Brovkin, *Behind the Front Lines of the Civil War. Political Parties and Social Movements in Russia, 1918–1922* (Princeton, New Jersey, 1994).

11 O. Figes, *A People's Tragedy. The Russian Revolution 1891–1924* (London, 1996), p. 768.

12 B. W. Blouet, *Halford Mackinder* (College Station, Texas, 1987), p. 174.

13 B. Isitt, *From Victoria to Vladivostok: Canada's Siberian Expedition, 1917–19* (Vancouver, 2010).

14 War Office report on military situation, revised up to 19 January 1921, NA. CAB. 24/120 fol. 56.

15 V. G. Liulevicius, *WarLand on the Eastern Front: Culture, National Identity and German Occupation in World War I* (Cambridge, 2000), pp. 228–32.

16 Hankey, Report to Cabinet, July 1920, NA. CAB. 24/110.

17 NA. WO. 106/6238, pp. 19–23; A. Zamoyski, *Warsaw 1920: Lenin's Failed Conquest of Europe* (London, 2008).

18 P. Latawski ed., *The Reconstruction of Poland, 1914–23* (London, 1992).

19 E. Mawdsley, *The Russian Civil War* (London, 1987).

20 D. Bloxham and R. Gerwarth (eds), *Political Violence in Twentieth-Century Europe* (Cambridge, 2011).

21 K. Hitchins, *I.I.C. Brătianu* (London, 2011), pp. 96, 102; A. V. Prusin, *The Lands Between. Conflict in the East European Borderlands, 1870–1992* (Oxford, 2010).

22 T. H. Tooley, *National Identity and Weimar Germany: Upper Silesia and the Eastern Border, 1918–1922* (Lincoln, Nebraska, 1992); T. K. Wilson, *Frontiers of Violence: Conflict and Identity in Ulster and Upper Silesia, 1918–1922* (Oxford, 2010).

23 M. Adam, *The Little Entente and Europe, 1920–1929* (Budapest, 1993).

24 B. Destani and J. Tomes (eds), *Albania's Greatest Friend. Aubrey Herbert and the Making of Modern Albania. Diaries and Papers 1904–1923* (London, 2011), p. 315.

25 P. Kenez, 'Pogroms and White Ideology in the Russian Civil War', in J. Klier and S. Lawbroza (eds), *Pogroms: Anti-Jewish Violence in Modern Russian History* (New York, 1992), pp. 293–313.

26 M. R. Ebner, *Ordinary Violence in Mussolini's Italy* (Cambridge, 2011).

27 General Staff, 'The Situation in Turkey, 15th March, 1920', NA. CAB. 24/101 fol. 315.

28 D. M. Leeson, *The Black and Tans. British Police and Auxiliaries in the Irish War of Independence, 1920–1921* (Oxford, 2011).

29 Chetwode to Montgomery-Massingberd, 1 July 1921, LH MM 8/22.

30 W. Sheehan, *A Hard Local War. The British Army and the Guerrilla War in Cork 1919–21* (Barnsley, 2011), esp. pp. 169–76.

31 A. F. Parkinson, *Belfast's Unholy War: The Troubles of the 1920s* (Dublin, 2004).

32 Z. Steiner, *The Lights that Failed: European International History, 1919–1933* (Oxford, 2005).

33 E. Kuhlman, 'American Doughboys and German *Fräuleins*: Sexuality, Patriarchy, and Privilege in the American-Occupied Rhineland, 1918–23', *Journal of Military History*, 71 (2007), p. 1104.

34 W. A. McDougall, *France's Rhineland Diplomacy, 1914–1924* (Princeton, New Jersey, 1978).

35 War Office report on military situation, revised up to 19 January 1921, NA. CAB. 24/120 fol. 54; K. Neilson, *Britain, Soviet Russia and the Collapse of the Versailles Order, 1919–1939* (Cambridge, 2006).

36 P. Holquist, *Making War, Forging Revolution: Russia's Continuum of Crisis, 1914–1921* (Cambridge, Massachusetts, 2002).

37 Zamoyski, *Warsaw 1920*, p. 133.

38 J. Borzecki, *The Soviet-Polish Peace of 1921 and the Creation of Interwar Europe* (New Haven, Connecticut, 2008).

39 Foreign Countries Report, 14 June 1922, NA. CAB. 24/155 fol. 138.

40 D. R. Stone, 'The Prospect of War? Lev Trotskii, the Soviet Army, and the German Revolution in 1923', *International History Review*, 25 (2003), pp. 799–817, esp. pp. 801–2.

41 W. D. Jacob, *Frunze: The Soviet Clausewitz* (The Hague, 1969); J. J. Schneider, *The Structure of Strategic Revolution: Total War and the Roots of the Soviet Warfare State* (Novato, California, 1994); M. von Hagen, *Soldiers in the Proletarian Dictatorship: The Red Army and the Soviet Socialist State, 1917–1930* (Ithaca, New York, 1990); J. Jacobson, *When the Soviet Union Entered World Politics* (Berkeley, California, 1994).

42 Steiner, *Lights that Failed*; P. Jackson, 'French Security and a British "Continental Commitment" after the First World War: a Reassessment; *English Historical Review*, 126 (2011), pp. 384–5.

43 P. O. Cohrs, *The Unfinished Peace after World War I: America, Britain, and the Stabilisation of Europe, 1919–1932* (Cambridge, 2006).

44 A. Adamthwaite, *Grandeur and Misery. France's Bid for Power in Europe, 1914–1940* (London, 1995).

45 General Staff, 'The Situation in Turkey, 15th March 1920', NA. CAB. 24/101 fol. 315; Chetwode to Montgomery-Massingberd, 1 July 1921, LH. MM. 8/22.

46 B. J. Fischer, *King Zog and the Struggle for Stability in Albania* (Boulder, Colorado, 1984).

47 S. Ben-Ami, *Fascism from Above: the Dictatorship of Primo de Rivera in Spain, 1923–1930* (Oxford, 1983).

48 A. Polonsky, *Politics in Independent Poland 1921–1939: The Crisis of Constitutional Government* (Oxford, 1972).

49 R. S. Grayson, *Austen Chamberlain and the Commitment to Europe: British Foreign Policy 1924–29* (London, 1997).

50 Vansittart, 'An Aspect of International Relations in 1931', May 1931, NA. CAB. 24/225, fol. 182. On Vansittart, see K. Neilson and T. G. Otte, *The Permanent Under-Secretary for Foreign Affairs, 1854–1946* (London, 2009).

51 Military Appreciation of the Situation in Europe, March 1931, NA. CAB. 24/220.

Chapter 2

1 Churchill, Secretary of State for War, Memorandum for Cabinet, 15 June 1920, NA. CAB. 24/107 fol. 250.

2 M. Thomas, 'Bedouin Tribes and the Imperial Intelligence Services in Syria, Iraq and Transjordan in the 1920s', *Journal of Contemporary History*, 38 (2003), pp. 543, 560.

3 Enclosure in General Staff, 'The Situation in Turkey, 15th March, 1920', NA. CAB. 24/101 fol. 317.

4 Enclosure in General Staff, 'The Situation in Turkey, 15th March, 1920', NA. CAB. 24/101 fol. 317.

5 Y. Güçlü, 'The Struggle for Mastery in Cilicia. Turkey, France, and the Ankara Agreement of 1921', *International History Review*, 23 (2001), pp. 593–7.

6 Rawlinson to Montgomery-Massingberd, 21 September 1922, LH MM 8/27; General Staff, 'The Situation in Turkey, 15th March, 1920', NA. CAB. 24/101 fols 311, 315.

7 R. S. Simon, *Spies and Holy Wars. The Middle East in twentieth-century crime fiction* (Austin, Texas, 2011). For example, Sax Rohmer, *The Mask of Fu Manchu* (London, 1932).

8 R. Blake, *The Unknown Prime Minister: The Life and Times of Andrew Bonar Law,*

1858–1923 (London, 1955), p. 448; K. O. Morgan, *Consensus and Disunity: The Lloyd George Coalition Government, 1918–1922* (Oxford, 1979), pp. 323–42.

9 *New York Tribune*, 24 July 1921.

10 *New York Tribune*, 6 August 1921.

11 J. E. Alvarez, 'Tank Warfare during the Rif Rebellion', *Armor*, 106 (1997), pp. 26–8.

12 *The Times*, 20 January 1925.

13 D. S. Woolman, *Rebels in the Rif: Abd el Krim and the Rif Rebellion* (Stanford, California, 1968); J. Chandler, 'Spain and her Moroccan Protectorate, 1898–1927', *Journal of Contemporary History* (1975), pp. 301–22 and 'The Responsibilities for Annual', *Iberian Studies* (1977), pp. 68–75; C. R. Pennell, *A Country with a Government and a Flag: The Rif War in Morocco, 1921–1926* (Wisbech, 1986); S. E. Fleming, *Primo de Rivera and Abd-el-Krim: The Struggle in Spanish Morocco, 1923–1927* (New York, 1991).

14 J. E. Alvarez, 'Between Gallipoli and D-Day: Alhucemas, 1925', *Journal of Modern History*, 63 (1999), pp. 75–98.

15 P. S. Khoury, *Syria and the French Mandate: the Politics of the Arab Nationalism, 1920–1945* (Princeton, New Jersey, 1987).

16 M. Evans, *Conflict in Afghanistan: Studies in Asymmetric Warfare* (London, 2005), pp. 89–95.

17 LH. Ismay 3/1/1–83, quotes pp. 55, 58.

18 A. Gordon, 'Time after Time in the Horn of Africa', *Journal of Military History*, 74 (2010), pp. 140–3; M. Page, *A History of The King's African Rifles* (Barnsley, 2011), pp. 22–4.

19 J. Lewis, *Racing Ace. The Fights and Flights of Samuel 'Kink' Kinkead* (Barnsley, 2011), pp. 104–8.

20 P. M. Holt and M. W. Daly, *A History of the Sudan* (5th edn, Harlow, 2000), p. 103.

21 NA. WO. 33/2764, p. 257.

22 Rawlinson to Montgomery-Massingberd, 8 November 1922, LH. MM. 8/27.

23 *The Times*, 6 June 1923.

24 Note by the General Staff on British Military Liabilities, 9 June 1920, NA. CAB. 24/107 fols 255, 259; Military Report on Mesopotamia (Iraq), Area 1 (Northern Jazirah), 1922, NA. WO. 33/2758, p. 39.

25 D. Omissi, *Air Power and Colonial Control: The Royal Air Force 1919–1939* (Manchester, 1990); C. Townshend, 'Civilisation and "Frightfulness": Air Control in the Middle East Between the Wars', in C. Wrigley ed., *Warfare, Diplomacy and Politics* (London, 1986), pp. 142–62; P. Satia, 'The Defense of Inhumanity: Air Control in Iraq and the British Idea of Arabia', *American Historical Review*, 111 (2006), pp. 16–51.

26 R. K. Mazumder, 'When Strong Men Meet: Recruited Punjabis and Constrained

Colonialism', in H. Islamoğlu and P. C. Perdue (eds), *Shared Histories of Modernity. China, India and the Ottoman Empire* (New Delhi, 2009), pp. 147–204, esp. 187–9.

27 D. G. Boyce, 'From Assaye to the *Assaye*: Reflections on British Government, Force and Moral Authority in India', *Journal of Military History*, 63 (1993), pp. 643–68; N. Collett, *The Butcher of Amritsar. General Reginald Dyer* (London, 2005), pp. 251–67.

28 P. S. Gupta, 'The Debate on Indianisation', in Gupta and A. Deshpande (eds), *The British Raj and Its Indian Armed Forces 1857–1939* (New Delhi, 2002), pp. 228–69.

29 Rawlinson to Montgomery-Massingberd, 21 September 1922, LH. MM. 8/27.

30 C. G. Segrè, *Fourth Shore: the Italian Colonisation of Libya* (Chicago, Illinois, 1974).

31 P. Holquist, 'Violent Russia, Deadly Marxism? Russia in the epoch of violence, 1905–21', in A. Kocho-Williams ed., *The Twentieth-Century Russia Reader* (Abingdon, 2011) pp. 114–15.

32 M. Broxup, 'The Last *Chazawat*: The 1920–1921 Uprising', and A. Avtorkhanov, 'The Chechens and Ingush during the Soviet Period', in M. Broxup ed., *The North Caucasus Barrier* (London, 1992), pp. 112–45, 157–61, 183.

33 A. Khalid, 'The Soviet Union as an Imperial Formation. A View from Central Asia', in A. L. Stoler et al (eds), *Imperial Formations* (Santa Fe, New Mexico, 2007), pp. 121–2.

34 J. Fisher, 'Major Norman Bray and Eastern Unrest in the British Empire in the aftermath of World War I', *Archives*, 27 (2002), p. 51.

35 S. Roskill, *Admiral of the Fleet Earl Beatty* (London, 1980), p. 299.

36 H. Schmidt, *The United States Occupation of Haiti, 1915–1934* (New Brunswick, New Jersey, 1971); B. J. Calder, *The Impact of Intervention: the Dominican Republic during the US occupation of 1916–1924* (Austin, Texas, 1984).

37 *The Times*, 9 December 1929.

38 *The Times*, 3 January 1928.

39 *The Times*, 28 July 1927, 21 March 1928.

40 L. D. Langley, *The Banana Wars: An Inner History of American Empire, 1900–1934* (Lexington, Kentucky, 1983).

41 C. D. Laurie and R. H. Cole, *The Role of Federal Military Forces in Domestic Disorders, 1877–1945* (Washington, 1997), pp. 277–301.

42 S. K. Fung, *The Diplomacy of Imperial Retreat: Britain's South China Policy, 1924–1931* (Oxford, 1991).

43 R. Ileto, 'Religion and Anti-colonial Movements', in N. Tracy ed., *The Cambridge History of South-East Asia* vol. 2 (Cambridge, 1992), p. 238.

44 K. C. Ulrichsen, *The Logistics and Politics of the British Campaigns in the Middle East, 1914–22* (Basingstoke, 2010).

45 T. Moreman, '"Small Wars" and "Imperial Policing": The British Army and the Theory and Practice of Colonial Warfare in the British Empire, 1919–1939', *Journal of Strategic*

Studies, 19 (1966), pp. 105–31; G. Kudaisya, '"In Aid of Civil Power": The Colonial Army in Northern India, c. 1919–42', *Journal of Imperial and Commonwealth History*, 32 (2004), pp. 41–68.

46 B. C. Denning, 'Modern Problems of Guerrilla Warfare', *Army Quarterly*, 13 (1927), pp. 347–54.

47 D. Killingray, 'A Swift Agent of Government: Air Power in British Colonial Africa, 1916–39', *Journal of African History*, 25 (1984), pp. 429–44; J. L Cox, 'A Splendid Training Ground: the Importance to the RAF of Iraq, 1913–32', *Journal of Imperial and Commonwealth History*, 13 (1985), pp. 157–84.

48 W. Ryan, 'The Influence of the Imperial Frontier on British Doctrines of Mechanised Warfare', *Albion*, 15 (1983), pp. 123–42; E. Spiers, 'Gas and the North-West Frontier', *Journal of Strategic Studies*, 6 (1983), pp. 94–112.

49 *The Times*, 5 July 1924.

50 R. Adelson, *London and the Invention of the Middle East. Money, Power, and War 1902–1922* (New Haven, Connecticut, 1995).

51 H. B. Elliston, 'China in the World Family', *Foreign Affairs*, 7 (1929), p. 622.

52 B. Prasad, *Defence of India: Policy and Plans* (New Delhi, 1963), p. 138.

Chapter 3

1 P. Young, *The Presidency of Yuan Shih-k'ai: Liberalism and Dictatorship in Early Republican China* (Ann Arbor, Michigan, 1977).

2 B. Elleman, *Modern Chinese Warfare, 1795–1989* (London, 2001); J. Sheridan, *Chinese Warlord: the career of Feng Yu'hsiang* (Stanford, California, 1966); D. Gillin, *Yen His-shan in Shansi Province, 1911–1949* (Princeton, New Jersey, 1967); S. R. MacKinnon, 'The Peiyang Army, Yuan Shih-k'ai, and the Origins of Modern Chinese Warlordism', *Journal of Asian Studies*, 23 (1973); H-s Ch'i, *Warlord Politics in China, 1916–1928* (Stanford, California, 1976); O. Wou, *Militarism in Modern China: The Career of Wu P'ei-fu, 1916–39* (Canberra, 1978); E. A. McCord, *The Power of the Gun: The Emergence of Chinese Warlordism* (Berkeley, California, 1993).

3 X. Guoqi, *China and the Great War: China's Pursuit of a New National Identity and Internationalization* (Cambridge, 2005).

4 On Zhang Zuolin, G. McCormack, *Chang Tso-lin in northeast China: 1911–1928* (Stanford, California, 1977).

5 J. Black, *War. The Cultural Turn* (Cambridge, 2012).

6 S. T. Ross ed., *American War Plans, 1919–1941. I. Peacetime War Plans, 1919–1935* (New York, 1992), p. 194.

7 *The Times*, 9 March 1926.

8 *The Times*, 28 May, 6 September 1927.

9 *The Times*, 9 March 1926.

10 *The Times*, 28 May 1927.

11 *The Times*, 3 September 1927.

12 H. van de Ven, *Warfare and Nationalism in China, 1925–1945* (London, 2003).

13 H. van de Ven, 'Introduction', in van de Ven ed., *Warfare in Chinese History* (Leiden, 2000), p. 24.

14 A. Waldron, *From War to Nationalism: China's Turning Point, 1924–5* (Cambridge, 1995).

15 Report, 11 January 1927, NA. CAB. 24/184 fols 40–3.

16 Y. Zhang, 'The Shandong Battlefield during the Northern Expedition', in L. Yu-ning ed., *Chiang Kai-shek and China*, vol. 2 (Armonk, New York, 1988), pp. 3–65.

17 D. A. Jordan, *The Northern Expedition: China's National Revolution of 1926–1928* (Honolulu, Hawai'i, 1976); J. Taylor, *The Generalissimo: Chiang Kai-shek and the Struggle for Modern China* (Cambridge, Massachusetts, 2009), pp. 84–5.

18 J. Fitzgerald, *Awakening China: Politics, Culture and Class in the Nationalist Revolution* (Stanford, California, 1996).

19 *The Times*, 23 December 1927.

20 S. Cronin, 'Conscription and Popular Resistance in Iran, 1925–1941', *International Review of Social History*, 43 (1998), pp. 451–71.

21 L. B. Poullada, *Reform and Rebellion in Afghanistan, 1919–1929* (Ithaca, New York, 1973).

22 L. McLoughlin, *Ibn Saud. Founder of a Kingdom* (Basingstoke, 1993), pp. 61–131; M. Darlow and B. Bray, *Ibn Saud. The Desert Warrior and his Legacy* (London, 2010), pp. 261–377.

23 J. Meyer, *The Cristero Rebellion: The Mexican People Between Church and State, 1926–1929* (Cambridge, 1976); M. Butler, *Popular Piety and Political Identity in Mexico's Cristero Rebellion: Michoacán, 1927–1929* (Oxford, 2004).

24 A. Grünberg, *The Chayanta Rebellion of 1927, Potosí, Bolivia* (DPhil. Oxford, 1996), p. 137.

25 F. Katz, *The Life and Times of Pancho Villa* (Stanford, California, 1998), p. 782.

26 J. Buchenau, *The Last Caudillo. Alvaro Obregón and the Mexican Revolution* (Chichester, 2011), pp. 132–5.

Chapter 4

1 E. A. Huelfer, *The 'Casualty Issue' in American Military Practice: The Impact of World War I* (Westport, Connecticut, 2003).

2 A. Green, *Writing the Great War: Sir James Edmonds and the Official Histories, 1915–1948* (London, 2003).

3 E. C. Kiesling, *Arming Against Hitler: France and the Limits of Military Planning* (Lawrence, Kansas, 1996).

4 D. Juniper, 'Gothas Over London', *RUSI Journal*, 148 no. 4 (August 2003), p. 79.

5 G. C. Peden, *Arms, Economics and British Strategy. From Dreadnoughts to Hydrogen Bombs* (Cambridge, 2007), p. 162.

6 A. R. Millett and W. Murray (eds), *Military Effectiveness II. The Interwar Period* (Cambridge, 1988); H. R. Winton and D. R. Mets (eds), *The Challenge of Change: Military Institutions and New Realities, 1918–1941* (Lincoln, Nebraska, 2000).

7 Rawlinson to Montgomery-Massingberd, 16 July 1923, LH. MM. 8/28.

8 J. Sweet, *Iron Arm: The Mechanisation of Mussolini's Army, 1920–1940* (Westport, Connecticut, 1980).

9 J. B. Crowley, 'Japanese Army Factionalism in the early 1930s', *Journal of Asia Studies*, 21 (1962), pp. 309–26; L. A. Humphreys, *The Way of the Heavenly Sword: The Japanese Army in the 1920s* (Stanford, California, 1995).

10 J. Kipp, 'Military Reform and the Red Army, 1918–1941: Bolsheviks, Voyensopetsy, and Young Commanders', in H. Winton ed., *The Challenge of Change: Military Institutions and New Realities, 1918–1941* (Lincoln, Nebraska, 2000); R. W. Harrison, *The Russian Way of War: Operational Art, 1904–1940* (Lawrence, Kansas, 2001).

11 P. Fox, '"A New and Commanding Breed": German Warriors, Tanks and the Will to Battle', *War and Society*, 30 (2011), p. 22.

12 J. Maiolo, *Cry Havoc. How the Arms Race Drove the World to War, 1931–1941* (London, 2010), p. 66.

13 D. Massam, *British Maritime Strategy and Amphibious Capability, 1900–40* (DPhil. Oxford, 1995).

14 W. O. Odom, *After the Trenches: The Transformation of US Army Doctrine, 1918–1939* (College Station, Texas, 1999).

15 Montgomery-Massingberd to Chetwode, 3 December 1928, LH. MM. 10/1.

16 Montgomery-Massingberd to Chetwode, 3 December 1928, LH. MM. 10/1.

17 D. E. Johnson, *Fast Tanks and Heavy Bombers: Innovation in the US Army, 1917–1945* (Ithaca, New York, 1998).

18 G. F. Hofman, *Through Mobility We Conquer: The Mechanisation of U.S. Cavalry* (Lexington, Kentucky, 2006).

19 W. Murray, 'Does Military Culture Matter?', *Orbis*, 43 (1999), pp. 34–5.

20 Chetwode to Montgomery-Massingberd, 21 July 1921, LH. MM. 8/22. For the value of cavalry, S. Badsey, *Doctrine and Reform in the British Cavalry, 1880–1918* (Aldershot, 2008).

21 LH. Foulkes papers, 2/18, 6/102–8, 112.

22 Sixth Annual Report of the Department, NA. WO. 33/1128, p. 19.

23 J. F. C. Fuller, *Tanks and the Great War 1914–1918* (London, 1920).

24 Report on India, 1926, Rutgers, Fuller, Box 4, pp. 4, 48.

25 LH. MM. 9/5/7, memorandum by Colonel Lindsay, p. 2.

26 B. H. Reid, "'Young Turks, or Not So Young?" The Frustrated Quest of Major-General J. F. C. Fuller and Captain B. H. Liddell Hart', *Journal of Military History*, 73 (2009), pp. 147–75.

27 A. Danchev, *Alchemist of War: The Life of Basil Liddell Hart* (London, 1998); B. H. Reid, *Studies in British Military Thought: Debates with Fuller and Liddell Hart* (Lincoln, Nebraska, 1998).

28 Montgomery-Massingberd to Lincolnshire branches of the British Legion, 15 June 1940, LH. MM. 10/10.

29 H. Strachan, *The Politics of the British Army* (Oxford, 1997), p. 153.

30 A. Gat, *British Armour Theory and the Rise of the Panzer Arm: Revisiting the Revisionists* (London, 2000).

31 J. S. Corum, *The Roots of Blitzkrieg: Hans von Seeckt and German Military Reform* (Lawrence, Kansas, 1992); R.M. Citino, *The Path to Blitzkrieg: Doctrine and Training in the German Army, 1920–1939* (Boulder, Colorado, 1999).

32 M. Strohn, *The German Army and the Defence of the Reich. Military Doctrine and the Conduct of the Defensive Battle, 1918–1939* (Cambridge, 2010).

33 G-l Vardi, 'The Change from Within', in H. Strachan and S. Scheipers (eds), *The Changing Character of War* (Oxford, 2011), pp. 80–4.

34 T. Travers, *How The War Was Won. Command and Technology in the British Army on the Western Front, 1917–1918* (London, 1992), pp. 179–82.

35 D. Stevenson, *With Our Backs to the Wall. Victory and Defeat in 1918* (London, 2011), pp. 212–22.

36 J. Stone, 'The British Army and the Tank', in T. Farrell and T. Terriff (eds), *The Sources of Military Change. Culture, Politics, Technology* (Boulder, Colorado, 2002), p. 193.

37 Minute by the General Staff, September 1919, NA. CAB. 24/89 fol. 11.

38 Chetwode to Montgomery-Massingberd, 6 September 1921, LH. MM. 8/22.

39 Montgomery-Massingberd to Chetwode, 18 January 1929, LH. MM. 10/2.

40 General Staff, 'The situation in Turkey, 15 March 1920', NA. CAB. 24/101 fol. 315.

41 Chetwode to Montgomery-Massingberd, 23 October 1922, LH. MM. 8/22.

42 Rawlinson to Montgomery-Massingberd, 23 October 1922, LH. MM. 8/27.

43 LH. MM. 9/5/7, quotes pp. 9–10, 21.

44 LH. Milne papers, Box 3, quote p. 3.

Chapter 5

1 S. Roskill, *Naval Policy between the Wars. I, The Period of Anglo-American Antagonism, 1919–1929* (London, 1968); E. O. Goldman, *Sunken Treaties: Naval Arms Control Between the Wars* (University Park, Pennsylvania, 1994); P. P. O'Brien, *British and American Naval Power: Politics and Policy, 1900–1936* (Westport, Connecticut, 1998); E. Goldstein and J. H. Maurer, *The Washington Naval Conference: Naval Rivalry, East Asian Stability, and the Road to Pearl Harbor* (Ilford, 1994).

2 J. T. Kuehn, 'The U.S. Navy General Board and Naval Arms Limitation: 1922–1937', *Journal of Military History*, 74 (2010), p. 1159.

3 R. D. Burns, 'Regulating Submarine Warfare, 1921–41: A Case Study in Arms Control and Limited War', *Military Affairs*, 35 (1971), pp. 56–63.

4 NA. CAB. 29/117 fol. 78; R. W. Fanning, *Peace and Disarmament: Naval Rivalry and Arms Control, 1922–1933* (Lexington, Kentucky, 1995); D. C. Evans and M. R. Peattie, *Kaigun: Strategy, Tactics and Technology in the Imperial Japanese Navy, 1887–1941* (Annapolis, Maryland, 1997).

5 J. Sumida, '"The Best Laid Plans": the Development of British Battle-Fleet Tactics, 1919–1942', *International History Review*, 14 (1992), pp. 682–700.

6 H. T. Bussemaker, 'Confronting Japan: The Dutch Dilemma, 1904–1941', *National Institute for Defense Studies [Japan] International Forum on War History: Proceedings* (August 2009) p. 69

7 BL. Add. 49045 fols 1–2.

8 *The Times*, 6 September 1927.

9 I. M. Philpott, *The Royal Air Force . . . the Inter-war Years. I. The Trenchard Years, 1918 to 1929* (Barnsley, 2005), pp. 194–208.

10 C. G. Reynolds, *The Fast Carriers: The Forging of an Air Navy* (New York, 1968); G. Till, 'Adopting the Aircraft Carrier. The British, American, and Japanese Case Studies', in W. Murray and A. R. Millett (eds.), *Military Innovation in the Interwar Period* (Cambridge, 1996), pp. 191–226.

11 G. Till, *Air Power and the Royal Navy, 1914–1945* (London, 1989).

12 T. C. Hone, N. Friedman, and M. D. Mandeles, *American and British Aircraft Carrier Development, 1919–1941* (Annapolis, Maryland, 1999); T. Wildenberg, *Destined for Glory: Dive Bombing, Midway, and the Evolution of Carrier Airpower* (Annapolis, Maryland, 1998).

13 BL. Add. 49699 fol. 84.

14 Re 1921, B. Bestani and J. Tomes (eds), *Albania's Greatest Friend*, p. 339.

15 BL. Add. 49045 fols. 1–2.

16 J. Ferris, '"It is our business in the Navy to Command the Seas": The Last Decade of British Maritime Supremacy, 1919–1929', in K. Neilson and G. Kennedy (eds), *Far*

– *Flung Lines: Studies in Imperial Defence in Honour of Donald Mackenzie Shurman* (London, 1997), pp. 124–70.

17 E. S. Miller, *War Plan Orange: The U.S. Strategy to Defeat Japan, 1897–1945* (Annapolis, Maryland, 1991).

18 A. A. Nofi, *To Train the Fleet for War: The U.S. Navy Fleet Problems, 1923–1940* (Newport, Rhode Island, 2010); I. Hata, 'Admiral Yamamoto and the Japanese Navy', in S. Dockrill ed., *From Pearl Harbor to Hiroshima: The Second World War in Asia and the Pacific, 1941–45* (New York, 1994), p. 58.

19 Report by the Chiefs of Staff, 11 January 1927, NA. CAB. 24/184 fols 42–3.

20 S. T. Ross ed., *Peacetime War Plans, 1919–1935* (New York, 1992), pp. 13–14.

21 C. M. Bell, *The Royal Navy, Seapower and Strategy Between the Wars* (Stanford, California, 2000).

22 W. R. Braisted, *Diplomats in Blue: U.S. Naval Officers in China, 1922–1933* (Gainesville, Florida, 2009).

23 K. Neilson, 'The Defence Requirements Sub-Committee, British Strategic Foreign Policy, Neville Chamberlain and the Path to Appeasement', *English Historical Review*, 118 (2003), p. 675.

24 I. Cowman, *Dominion or Decline. Anglo-American Naval Relations in the Pacific, 1937–1941* (Oxford, 1996).

25 O. C. Chung, *Operation Matador: Britain's War Plans against the Japanese 1918–1941* (Singapore, 1997).

26 S. E. Pelz, *Race to Pearl Harbor: The Failure of the Second London Naval Conference and the Onset of World War II* (Cambridge, Massachusetts, 1974); R. G. Kaufman, *Arms Control During the Pre-Nuclear Era: The United States and Naval Limitation Between the Two World Wars* (New York, 1990).

27 For these claims, P. Padfield, *Maritime Dominion and the Triumph of the Free World* (London, 2009).

28 S. Asada, *From Mahan to Pearl Harbor: The Imperial Japanese Navy and the United States* (Annapolis, Maryland, 2006).

29 D. C. Evans and M. R. Peattie, *Kaigun: Strategy, Tactics, and Technology in the Imperial Japanese Navy, 1887–1941* (Annapolis, Maryland, 1997), pp. 271–82.

30 J. Reardon, 'Breaking the U.S. Navy's "Gun Club" Mentality in the South Pacific', *Journal of Military History*, 75 (2011), pp. 533–64.

31 R. G. Kaufman, *Arms Control During the Pre-Nuclear Era: The United States and Naval Limitation Between the Two World Wars* (New York, 1990).

32 B. Rieger, *Technology and the Culture of Modernity in Britain and Germany, 1890–1945* (Cambridge, 2005).

33 T. R. Philbin, *The Lure of Neptune. German-Soviet Naval Collaboration and Ambitions, 1919–1941* (Columbia, South Carolina, 1994), p. xiv.

34 H. H. Herwig, 'Innovation Ignored: The Submarine Problem – Germany, Britain, and the United States, 1919–1939', in Murray and Millett (eds), *Military Innovation*, pp. 227–64.

35 R. Mallett, *The Italian Navy and Fascist Expansionism, 1935–1940* (London, 1998).

36 Sub-Committee Annual Review, 12 Oct. 1933, NA. CAB. 24/244 fol. 136.

37 A. Marder, 'The Royal Navy and the Ethiopian Crisis of 1935–36', *American Historical Review*, 75 (1970), pp. 1327–56.

38 T. R. Maddux, 'United States-Soviet Naval Relations in the 1930s. The Soviet Union's Efforts to Purchase Naval Vessels', in D. J. Stoker and J. A. Grant (eds), *Girding for Battle. The Arms Trade in a Global Perspective, 1815–1940* (Westport, Connecticut, 2003), p. 207.

39 J. Rohwer and M. S. Monakov, *Stalin's Ocean-Going Fleet Soviet: Naval Strategy and Shipbuilding Programmes 1935–1953* (London, 2001); S. McLaughlin, 'USSR', in V. P. O'Hara, W. D. Dickson and R. Worth (eds), *On Seas Contested. The Seven Great Navies of the Second World War* (Annapolis, Maryland, 2010), p. 260.

40 J. Wise, *The Anglo-Chilean naval association as a case study to illustrate the Royal Navy's contribution to British peacetime foreign policy, 1925–1970* (PhD., Exeter, 2011), Chapter Four.

41 P. Kennedy, 'HMS *Dreadnought* and the Tides of History', in R. J. Blyth, A. Lambert and J. Rüger (eds), *The 'Dreadnought' and the Edwardian Age* (Farnham, 2011), p. 227.

42 P. P. O'Brien, *British and American Naval Power: Politics and Policy, 1900–1936* (Westport, Connecticut, 1998); H. P. Willmott, *The Last Century of Sea Power, II: From Washington to Tokyo, 1922–1945* (Bloomington, Indiana, 2010).

43 A. Marder, *From the Dardanelles to Oran. Studies of the Royal Navy in War and Peace 1915–1940* (Oxford, 1974), p. 61; C. M. Bell, 'Winston Churchill and the Ten Year Rule', *Journal of Military History*, 74 (2010), p. 1125.

44 J. Ferris, 'The last decade of British maritime supremacy, 1919–1929', in K. Neilson and G. Kennedy (eds), *Far Flung Lines* (London, 1997), pp. 155–62.

45 NA. CAB. 16/109, fol. 9.

46 J. Maiolo, *The Royal Navy and Nazi Germany, 1933–9* (London, 1998).

47 *The Times*, 9 March 1926.

48 Report by the Chiefs of Staff Sub-Committee, 4 Ap. 1927, NA. CAB. 24/186 fols 108–9.

49 Report by the Chiefs of Staff Sub-Committee, 12 November 1937, NA. CAB. 24/273 fol. 147.

50 K. Neilson, 'The Royal Navy, Japan, and British Strategic Foreign Policy, 1932–1934', *Journal of Military History*, 75 (2011), pp. 505–31.

51 J. Moretz, *The Royal Navy and the Capital Ship in the Interwar Period: An Operational Perspective* (London, 2002), p. 253.

52 Chiefs of Staff Sub-Committee, report, 9 February 1937, NA. CAB. 24/268, fol. 104.

272   *Notes*

Chapter 6

1 Simon, 'The Crisis in Europe', 28 February 1933, NA. CAB. 24/239.

2 J. J. Born, *Winged Gospel: America's Romance with Aviation, 1900-1950* (New York, 1983); M. Paris, *Winged Warfare: The Literature and Theory of Aerial Warfare in Britain, 1859-1917* (Manchester, 1992) and 'The Rise of the Airmen: The Origins of Air Force Elitism, c. 1890-1918', *Journal of Contemporary History*, 28 (1993), pp. 123-41; R. Wohl, *A Passion for Wings: Aviation and the Western Imagination* (New Haven, Connecticut, 1994); P. Fritzsche, 'Machine Dreams: Airmindedness and the Reinvention of Germany', *American Historical Review*, 98 (1993), pp. 685-709; S. W. Palmer, *Dictatorship of the Air: Aviation Culture and the Fate of Modern Russia* (Cambridge, 2006). For futurology, R. Panchasi, *Future Tense: The Culture of Anticipation in France Between the Wars* (Ithaca, New York, 2009).

3 A. Barros, 'Razing Babel and the Problems of Constructing Peace: France, Great Britain, and Air Power, 1916-28', *English Historical Review*, 126 (2011), pp. 75-115, esp. 75-7, 114.

4 T. C. Imlay and M. D. Toft (eds), *The Fog of Peace and War Planning: Military and Strategic Planning under Uncertainty* (Abingdon, 2006).

5 Chetwode, Deputy Chief of the Imperial General Staff, to Montgomery-Massingberd, 20 July 1921, LH. MM. 8/22.

6 Admiralty memorandum on functions of the Air Ministry, 7 January 1919, NA. CAB. 24/73.

7 A Gallop, *The Martians Are Coming! The True Story of Orson Welles' 1938 Panic Broadcast* (Stroud, 2011), pp. 66-9.

8 C. Segrè, 'Giulio Douhet: Strategist, Theorist, Prophet?', *Journal of Strategic Studies*, 15 (1992), pp. 69-80.

9 N. Parton, *The Evolution and Impact of Royal Air Force Doctrine, 1919-1939* (London, 2011).

10 N. Parton, 'The Development of Early RAF Doctrine', *Journal of Military History*, 72 (2008), pp. 1155-77.

11 M. Smith, *British Air Strategy Between the Wars* (Oxford, 1984), pp. 83-4.

12 M. Smith, '"A Matter of Faith": British Strategic Air Doctrine Between the Wars', *Journal of Contemporary History*, 15 (1980), pp. 423-42.

13 Chamberlain, 'The Role of the British Army', 11 December 1936, NA. CAB. 24/265 fol. 265.

14 S. Roskill, *Admiral of the Fleet Earl Beatty* (London, 1980), p. 317.

15 A. F. Hurley, *Billy Mitchell: Crusader for Air Power* (New York, 1964).

16 W. F. Trimble, *Admiral William A. Moffett: Architect of Naval Aviation* (Washington, 1994).

17 B. D. Watts, *The Foundations of US Air Doctrine: The Problem of Friction in War* (Maxwell Air Force Base, Alabama, 1984); S. L. McFarland, *America's Pursuit of Precision Bombing 1910–1945* (Washington, 1995).

18 J. Ferris, 'The theory of a "French air menace": Anglo-French relations and the British Home Defence Air Force programmes of 1921–25', *Journal of Strategic Studies*, 10 (1987), pp. 62–83 and 'Fighter Defence Before Fighter Command: The Rise of Strategic Air Defence in Great Britain, 1917–1934', *Journal of Military History*, 63 (1999), pp. 845–84; N. Gibbs, *Grand Strategy. I: Rearmament Policy* (Oxford, 1976), p. 543; N. Gibbs, *Grand Strategy I: Rearmament Policy* (Oxford, 1976), p. 543

19 U. Bialer, *The Shadow of the Bomber: The Fear of Air Attack and British Politics, 1932–1939* (London, 1980); G. G. Lewis, '"I see Dead People": Air-Raid Phobia and Britain's Behavior in the Munich Crisis', *Security Studies*, 13 (2003-4), pp. 230–72.

20 Report by ministerial committee as amended and approved by Cabinet on 31 July 1934, NA. CAB. 24/250 fol. 113 and attached information from Chiefs of Staff Sub-Committee, fols 126–8.

21 R. J. Overy, *The Air War 1939–1945* (London, 1980), p. 25.

22 F. H. Winter, *Prelude to the Space Age: The Rocket Societies, 1924–1940* (Washington DC., 1983); A. Kosmodemyansky, *Konstantin Tsiolkovskiy* (Moscow, 1985).

23 M. J. Bollinger, *Warriors and Wizards: the Development and Defeat of Radio-Controlled Glide Bombs of the Third Reich* (Annapolis, Maryland, 2010).

24 Ministerial Committee, 16 July 1934, NA. CAB. 24/250 fol. 119.

25 S. Ritchie, *Industry and Air Power: The Expansion of British Aircraft Production, 1935–1941* (London, 1997); J. Buckley, *Air Power in the Age of Total War* (London, 1999), pp. 109–10.

26 R. E. Bilstein, 'Airplanes', in C. Pursell ed., *A Companion to American Technology* (Oxford, 2005), p. 263.

27 D. Edgerton, *Britain's War Machine. Weapons, Resources and Experts in the Second World War* (London, 2011), pp. 37–9.

28 D. Omissi, *Air Power and Colonial Control: The Royal Air Force 1919–1939* (Manchester, 1990).

29 *Times*, 9 Mar. 1926.

30 M. Mauer and C. F. Senning, 'Billy Mitchell, the Air Service, and the Mingo County War', *West Virginia Historian*, 30 (Oct. 1968), pp. 339–50.

31 *The Times*, 10 January 1927.

32 L. McLoughlin, *Ibn Saud* (Basingstoke, 1993), pp. 81, 221.

33 Lieutenant-General Congreve, Commander Egyptian Expeditionary Force. Appreciation of the Situation. Egypt and Palestine, 4 May 1920, NA. CAB. 24/107 fol. 258.

34 Chiefs of Staff, 'The Situation in China', 4 April 1927, NA. CAB. 24/186 fol. 108.

35 Thompson, memorandum on Spain, 13 October 1937, NA. CAB. 24/271 fol. 303.

36 R. J. Overy, 'From "Uralbomber" to "Amerikabomber": the *Luftwaffe* and strategic bombing', *Journal of Strategic Studies*, 1 (1978), pp. 154–78.

37 E. L. Homze, *Arming the Luftwaffe: the Reich Air Ministry and the German Aircraft Industry 1919–39* (Lincoln, Nebraska, 1976); K. A. Maier, 'Total War and Operational Air Warfare', in Maier et al., *Germany and the Second World War II* (Oxford, 1991), pp. 31–59; J. S. Corum, *The Luftwaffe: Creating the Operational Air War, 1918–1940* (Lawrence, Kansas, 1997); Corum and R. R. Muller, *The Luftwaffe's Way of War: German Air Force Doctrine, 1911–1945* (Baltimore, Maryland, 1998).

38 J. S. Corum, *Wolfram von Richthofen: Master of the German Air War* (Lawrence, Kansas, 2008).

39 J. Hayward, 'The Luftwaffe's Agility: An Assessment of Relevant Concepts and Practices', in N. Parton ed., *Air Power: The Agile Air Force* (Shrivenham, 2007), pp. 40–9.

40 S. Robertson, *The Development of RAF Bombing Doctrine, 1919–1929* (Westport, Connecticut, 1995); P. S. Meilinger, 'Trenchard and "Morale Bombing": The Evolution of Royal Air Force Doctrine Before World War II', *Journal of Military History*, 60 (1996), pp. 243–70.

41 LH. MM. 10/6.

42 J. S. Corum, 'The Spanish Civil War: Lessons Learned and Not Learned by the Great Powers', *Journal of Military History*, 62 (1998), pp. 313–34.

43 L. Robineau, 'French Air Policy in the Interwar Period and the Conduct of the Air War Against Germany from September 1939 to June 1940', in H. Boog ed., *The Conduct of the Air War in the Second World War* (Oxford, 1992), pp. 85–107.

44 S. W. Palmer, *Dictatorship of the Air: Aviation Culture and the Fate of Modern Russia* (Cambridge, 2006).

45 U. Bialer, *Shadow of the Bomber*, p. 132; G. G. Lee, '"I See Dead People": Air-Raid Phobia and Britain's Behavior in the Munich Crisis', *Security Studies*, 13 (2003–4), pp. 230–72.

46 B. R. Farnham, *Roosevelt and the Munich Crisis: A Study of Political Decision-Making* (Princeton, New Jersey, 1997).

47 Milne, 'The Role of the Air Force in Relation to the Army', LH. Milne, Box 3.

Chapter 7

1 H. James, *The End of Globalization: Lessons from the Great Depression* (Cambridge, Mass., 2001).

2 J. Jackson, *The Politics of Depression in France 1932–1936* (Cambridge, 1985).

3 P. Edgar, *Sir William Glasgow* (Newport, New South Wales, 2011), pp. 292–4.

4 Lindley, paper for Cabinet 'The Policy of Japan', 20 May 1933, NA. AB. 24/241 fol. 203.

5 L. Collingham, *The Taste of War. World War Two and the Battle for Food* (London, 2011), pp. 58–60, 31.

6 D. Stone, 'The First Five-Year Plan and the Geography of Soviet Defence Industry', *Europe-Asia Studies*, 57 (2005), pp. 1047–63.

7 N. S. Simonov, '"Strengthen the Defence of the Land of Soviets": The 1927 "War Alarm" and Its Consequences', *Europe-Asia Studies* (1996).

8 W. Murray, 'British grand strategy, 1933–1942', in Murray, R. H. Sinnreich and J. Lacey (eds), *The Shaping of Grand Strategy. Policy, Diplomacy, and War* (Cambridge, 2011), p. 151.

9 D. Edgerton, *Britain's War Machine. Weapons, Resources and Experts in the Second World War* (London, 2011).

Chapter 8

1 H. Rosinski, 'The Strategy of the Sino-Japanese Conflict', *Pacific Affairs*, 11 (1938), p. 43. See also, W. H. Mallory, 'Japan Attacks: China Resists', *Foreign Affairs*, 16 (October 1937), pp. 141–2.

2 A. Waldron, *From War to Nationalism: China's Turning Point, 1924–1925* (Cambridge, 1996).

3 A. Dirlik, *The Origins of Chinese Communism* (Oxford, 1989).

4 E. J. Perry, *Shanghai on Strike: The Politics of Chinese Labor* (Cambridge, 1995).

5 B. G. Martin, *The Shanghai Green Gang: Politics and Organised Crime, 1919–1937* (Berkeley, California, 1996).

6 D. S. Sutton, 'German Advice and Residual War Lordism in the Nanking Decade: Influences on Nationalist Military Training and Strategy', *China Quarterly*, 9, no. 91 (1982).

7 B. Yang, *From Revolution to Politics: Chinese Communists on the Long March* (Boulder, Colorado, 1990).

8 Mao Zedong, *On Guerrilla Warfare*, translated by S.B. Griffith (Urbana, Illinois, 2000), pp. 41–2, 80.

9 *Ibid.*, p. 46.

10 *Ibid.*, p. 47.

11 R. Zhang, 'The National Army from Whampoa to 1949', in D. A. Graff and R. Higham (eds), *A Military History of China* (Boulder, Colorado, 2002), pp. 193–209.

12 Memorandum by Sir V. Wellesley on Anglo-Japanese Relations, 1 February 1932, NA. CAB. 24/228 fol. 66.

13 I. Nish, *Japan's Struggle with Internationalism. Japan, China and the League of Nations, 1931-3* (London, 1993). More generally, see his *Japanese Foreign Policy in the Interwar Period* (Westport, Connecticut, 2002).

14 B. A. Shillony, *Revolt in Japan: The Young Officers and the February 26, 1936 Incident* (Princeton, New Jersey, 1973); S. Wilson, *The Manchurian Crisis and Japanese Society, 1931-1933* (London, 2002).

15 L. Young, *Japan's Total Empire: Manchuria and the Culture of Wartime Imperialism* (Berkeley, California, 1997); Y. T. Matsusaka, *The Making of Japanese Manchuria, 1904-1932* (Cambridge, Massachusetts, 2001).

16 R. J. Smethurst, *A Social Basis for Prewar Japanese Militarism. The Army and the Rural Community* (Berkeley, California, 1974).

17 W. A. Skya, *Japan's Holy War: The Ideology of Radical Shintō Ultranationalism* (Durham North Carolina, 2009).

18 B. Victoria, *Zen at War* (New York, 1997).

19 H. Bix, *Hirohito and the Making of Modern Japan* (New York, 2000). For a more positive view, S. Large, *Emperor Hirohito and Shōwa Japan: A Political Biography* (London, 1992).

20 S. Jun' Ichiro, 'The Quest for International Justice and Asianism in a "New Order in East Asia"; Fuminaro Konoe and His Vision of the World', in W. Murray and T. Ishizu (eds) *Conflicting Currents. Japan and the United States in the Pacific* (Santa Barbara, 2010) pp. 58-60.

21 E. Drea, *Japan's Imperial Army: Its Rise and Fall, 1853-1945* (Lawrence, Kansas, 2009).

22 A. Cox, 'The Effects of Attrition on National War Effort: the Japanese Army Experience in China, 1937-38', *Military Affairs*, 32 no. 2 (October 1968), pp. 57-62.

23 O. Yoshitake, *Konoe Fumimaro: A Political Biography* (Tokyo, 1983).

24 E. Kinmonth, 'The Mouse that Roared: Saitō Takao, Conservative Critic of Japan's "Holy War" in China', *Journal of Japanese Studies*, 25 (1999), pp. 331-60.

25 'The Present Sino-Japanese Military Situation', report by Chiefs of Staff, 9 December 1939, NA. CAB. 66/4/2 p. 16.

26 M. R. Peattie, E. Drea and H. van de Ven (eds), *The Battle for China: Essays on the Military History of the Sino-Japanese War of 1937-1945* (Stanford, California, 2010).

27 L. Lincoln, *The Japanese Army in North China, 1937-1941: Problems of Political and Economic Control* (Oxford, 1975); P. Coble, *Facing Japan: Chinese Domestic Politics and Japanese Imperialism, 1931-1937* (Cambridge, Massachusetts, 1991).

28 D. P. Barrett and L. N. Shyu (eds), *Chinese Collaboration with Japan: The Limits of Accommodation* (Stanford, California, 2001); T. Brook, *Collaboration: Japanese Agents and Local Elites in Wartime China* (Cambridge, Massachusetts, 2005).

29 M. R. Peattie, *Ishiwara Kanji and Japan's Confrontation with the West* (Princeton, New Jersey, 1975), pp. 304-5.

30 G. Kasza, *The State and the Mass Media in Japan, 1918-1945* (Berkeley, California, 1988).

31 L. Pincus, *Authenticating Culture in Imperial Japan: Kūki Shūzō and the Rise of National Aesthetics* (Berkeley California, 1996).

32 G. Bunker, *The Peace Conspiracy: Wang Ching-wei and the China War 1937-1941* (Cambridge, Massachusetts, 1972).

33 J. Fogel ed., *The Nanjing Massacre in History and Historiography* (Berkeley, California, 2000); P. Li ed., *Japanese War Crimes: The Search for Justice* (New Brunswick, New Jersey, 2003); S. Richter and W. Höpken, *Vergangenheit im Gesellschaftskonflikt: ein Historikerstreit in Japan* (Cologne, 2003); R. B. Jeans, 'Victims or Victimizers? Museums, Textbooks, and the War Debate in contemporary Japan', *Journal of Military History*, 69 (2005), pp. 149–95; B. T. Wakabayashi ed., *The Nanking Atrocity, 1937–38: Complicating the Picture* (New York, 2007).

34 P. Duara, *Sovereignty and Authenticity: Manchukuo and the East Asian Modern* (Lanham, Maryland, 2003).

35 W. Dunn, *The Soviet Economy and the Red Army, 1930–1945* (Westport, Connecticut, 1995); L. Samuelsson, *Plans for Stalin's War Machine: Tukhachevskii and Military-Economic Planning, 1925–1941* (Basingstoke, 1999).

36 D. Stone, *Hammer and Rifle: The Militarisation of the Soviet Union, 1926–1933* (Lawrence, Kansas, 2000).

37 J. Haslam, *The Soviet Union and the Threat from the East 1933–1941: Moscow, Tokyo and the Prelude to the Pacific War* (Basingstoke, 1992).

38 J. P. Fox, *Germany and the Far Eastern Crisis, 1931–1938: A Study in Diplomacy and Ideology* (Oxford, 1982).

39 J. Erickson, *The Soviet High Command. A Military-Political History 1918–1941* (3rd edn, London, 2001), p. 499.

40 A. Sella, 'Khalkhin-Gol: The Forgotten War', *Journal of Contemporary History*, 18 (1983), pp. 658–67; A. Coox, *Nomonhan: Japan Against Russia 1939* (Stanford, California, 1985); E. Drea, *Nomonhan: Japanese-Soviet Tactical Combat, 1939* (Fort Leavenworth, Kansas, 1981); D. Nedialkov, *In the Skies of Nomonhan. Japan versus Russia May–September 1939* (Manchester 2011).

41 A. Best, *British Intelligence and the Japanese Challenge in Asia, 1914–1941* (Basingstoke, 2002); D. Ford, *Britain's Secret War Against Japan, 1937–1945* (Abingdon, 2006); K. Kotani, *Japanese Intelligence in World War II* (Oxford, 2009), pp. 111–14. For a more positive account, G. Kennedy, 'Anglo-American Strategic Relations and Intelligence Assessments of Japanese Air Power 1934–1941', *Journal of Military History*, 74 (2010), pp. 737–73.

42 J. E. Dreifort, *Myopic Grandeur: The Ambivalence of French Foreign Policy towards the Far East, 1919–1945* (Kent, Ohio, 1991).

43 M. Thomas, 'Economic Conditions and the limits to mobilisation in the French Empire, 1936–1939', *Historical Journal*, 48 (2005), pp. 494–6.

44 M. A. Barnhart, *Japan Prepares for Total War: the Search for Economic Security, 1919–1941* (Ithaca, New York, 1987).

Chapter 9

1 *The Times*, 24 April 1936.

2 LH. MM. 10/6.

3 *The Times*, 7 April 1936.

4 Secretary of State for War to Cabinet colleagues, 17 January 1936, NA. CAB. 24/259.

5 G. B. Künzi, 'Total Colonial Warfare. Ethiopia', in R. Chickering and S. Förster (eds), *The Shadows of Total War. Europe, East Asia, and the United States, 1919–1939* (Cambridge, 2003), p. 315 fn. 10.

6 S. Morewood, 'The Chiefs of Staff, the "Men on the Spot" and the Italo-Abyssinian Emergency, 1935–36', in G. Grün, D. Richardson and G. Stone (eds), *Decisions and Diplomacy* (London, 1995), pp. 88–99 and *The British Defence of Egypt 1935–1940. Conflict and the Crisis in the Eastern Mediterranean* (Abingdon, 2005), pp. 76–81; D. B. Strang, '"The Worst of All Worlds": Oil Sanctions and Italy's Invasion of Abyssinia, 1935–1936', *Diplomacy and Statecraft* (2008), pp. 210–35.

7 NA. CAB. 23/83.

8 L. McLoughlin, *Ibn Saud*, pp. 145–6.

9 M. Bernal, 'The Nghe-tinh Soviet Movement, 1930–1931', *Past and Present*, 92 (1981), pp. 148–68; T. Rettig, 'French Military Policies in the Aftermath of the Yên Bay Mutiny, 1930: Old Security Dilemmas Return to the Surface', *South East Asia Research*, 10 (2002), pp. 309–31; M. Thomas, 'Fighting "Communist banditry" in French Vietnam: The Rhetoric of Repression after the Yen Bay Uprising, 1930–1932', *French Historical Studies*, 33 (2010).

10 M. Thomas, *Empires of Intelligence. Security Services and Colonial Disorder after 1914* (Berkeley, California, 2008), pp. 281, 269, 272.

11 M. Thomas, 'At the Heart of Things? French Imperial Defence Planning in the Late 1930s', *French Historical Studies*, 21 (1998), pp. 325–61.

12 M. E. Ochonu, *Colonial Meltdown: Northern Nigeria in the Great Depression* (Athens, Ohio, 2009).

13 N. Arielli, *Fascist Italy and the Middle East, 1933–40* (Basingstoke, 2010).

14 T. Moreman, '"The Greatest Training Ground in the World": the Army in India and the North-West Frontier, 1901–1947', in D. P. Marston and C. S. Sundaram (eds), *A Military History of India and South Asia: From the East India Company to the Nuclear Era* (Bloomington, Indiana, 2008), pp. 123–30.

15 Report by Ministerial Committee as amended and approved by Cabinet on 31 July 1934, NA. CAB. 24/250 fol. 111.

16 A. Warren, *Burma 1942* (London, 2011), pp. 9, 19.

17 Chiefs of Staff Sub-Committee, 'The Situation in the Far East', 31 March 1933, NA.

CAB. 24/239 fol. 284, 'Imperial Defence Policy', 12 October 1933, NA. CAB. 24/244 fol. 138; Committee of Imperial Defence, 6 April 1933, NA. CAB. 24/239 fol. 287.

18 A. Muldoon, *Empire, Politics and the Creation of 1935 India Act: Last Act of the Raj* (Farnham, 2009).

19 A Military Appreciation of the Present World Situation, NA. CAB. 24/234 fol. 165.

20 NA. CAB. 16/109 fol. 15.

21 War Office to Cabinet, 4 December 1936, NA. CAB. 24/265 fol. 220.

22 Chiefs of Staff Sub-Committee, 'Appreciation of the Situation in the Event of War Against Germany', 14 September 1938, NA. CAB. 24/278 pp. 345–59.

23 LH. Adam 2/3, pp. 2–3.

24 D. E. Showalter, 'Plans, Weapons, Doctrines: The Strategic Cultures of Interwar Europe', in R. Chickering and S. Förster (eds), *The Shadows of Total War: Europe, East Asia, and the United States, 1919–1939* (Cambridge, 2003), pp. 55–81.

25 G. Kennedy, '1935: A Snapshot of British Imperial Defence in the Far East', in Kennedy and K. Neilson (eds), *Far-Flung Lines: Studies in Imperial Defence* (London, 1997), pp. 190–216.

26 J. Ferris, *Intelligence and Strategy: Selected Essays* (London, 2005), pp. 120–7; G. Kennedy, 'Anglo-American Strategic Relations and Intelligence Assessments of Japanese Air Power 1934–1941', *Journal of Modern History*, 74 (2010), pp. 772–3.

Chapter 10

1 R. Chickering and S. Förster (eds), *The Shadows of Total War. Europe, East Asia, and the United States, 1919–1939* (Cambridge, 2003).

2 P. M. Ynsfran ed., *The Epic of the Chaco: Marshal Estigarribia's Memoir of the Chaco War, 1932–38* (Austin, Texas, 1950).

3 *The Times*, 14 May 1934.

4 D. H. Zook, *The Conduct of the Chaco War* (New York, 1960).

5 *The Times*, 28 October 1933.

6 J. W. Lindsay, 'The War over the Chaco: A Personal Account', *International Affairs*, 14 (1935), p. 237.

7 *The Times*, 21 May 1934.

8 B. Farcau, *The Chaco War: Bolivia and Paraguay, 1932–1935* (Westport, Connecticut, 1996); M. Hughes, 'Logistics and the Chaco War: Bolivia versus Paraguay, 1932–1935', *Journal of Military History*, 69 (2005), pp. 411–37.

9 Lindsay, 'Chaco', p. 239.

10 Memoranda by the Foreign Secretary, 18 July 1934, 28 January 1935, NA. CAB. 24/250, 253; *League of Nations. Fifteenth Assembly. Report of the Delegates of the United Kingdom, 30 November 1934* (London, 1934), pp. 7–9.

11 For an example from 1877–8, M. P. O'Connor, 'The vision of soldiers: Britain, France, Germany and the United States observe the Russo-Turkish War', *War in History*, 4 (1997), pp. 257–75.

12 J. M. Young, *The Brazilian Revolution of 1930 and the Aftermath* (New Brunswick, New Jersey, 1967); R. M. Levine, *The Vargas Regime: The Critical Years, 1934–1938* (New York, 1970); J. P. Woodward, *A Place in Politics: São Paulo, Brazil, from Seigneurial Republicanism to Regionalist Revolt* (Durham, North Carolina, 2009).

13 L. Bethell ed., *The Cambridge History of Latin America*, vol. 8 (Cambridge, 1991).

14 H. S. Klein, 'David Toro and the Establishment of "Military Socialism" in Bolivia', *Hispanic American Historical Review*, 45 (1965), pp. 25–52; M. Falcoff and F. B. Pike (eds), *The Spanish Civil War, 1936–1939: American Hemispheric Perspectives* (Lincoln, Nebraska, 1982).

15 I. Al-Marashi and S. Salama, *Iraq's Armed Forces: An Analytical History* (Abingdon, 2008).

16 H. G. Marcus, *Haile Selassie. I: The Formative Years, 1892–1936* (Berkeley, California, 1987).

17 D. Omissi, *Air Power and Colonial Control*, p. 131.

18 S. Cronin, 'Building and Rebuilding Afghanistan's Army: An Historical Perspective', *Journal of Military History*, 75 (2011), pp. 60–1.

Chapter 11

1 L. Viola, *Peasant Rebels under Stalin. Collectivization and the Culture of Peasant Resistance* (Oxford, 1996); R. R. Reese, 'Red Army Opposition to Forced Collectivization, 1929–30: the Army Wavers', *Slavic Review*, 55 (1996), pp. 24–45.

2 J. E. Álvarez, 'The Spanish Foreign Legion during the Asturian Uprising of October 1934', *War in History*, 18 (2011), pp. 200–24.

3 Report of the Committee on the Mechanised Cavalry and Royal Tank Corps, NA. WO. 33/1512, pp. 7–8.

4 C. D. Laurie and R. H. Cole, *The Role of Federal Military Forces in Domestic Disorders, 1877–1945* (Washington, 1997), pp. 367–89.

5 M. S. Alexander, *The Republic in Danger: General Maurice Gamelin and the Politics of French Defence, 1933–1940* (Cambridge, 1992).

6 J. Casanova, *The Spanish Republic and Civil War* (Cambridge, 2010).

7 Thompson, memorandum on Spain, 13 October 1937, NA. CAB. 24/271 fol. 303.

8 R. H. Whealey, *Hitler and Spain: The Nazi Role in the Spanish Civil War, 1936–1939* (Lexington, Kentucky, 1989).

9 Reichenau lecture, NA. CAB. 24/277 fol. 281.

10 J. Corum, 'The Spanish Civil War: Lessons Learned and Not Learned by the Great Powers', *Journal of Military History*, 62 (1998), pp. 313–34; M. Alpert, 'The Clash of the Spanish Armies: Contrasting Ways of War in Spain, 1936–39', *War in History*, 6 (1999), pp. 331–51; M. Hughes and E. Garrido, 'The "European Aldershot" for the Second World War? The Battle of the Ebro, 1938', *RUSI Journal*, 147 no. 6 (December 2002), pp. 76–81.

11 NA. WO. 106/1576, pp. 1–7. For a commentary, originally published in 1938, by a conservative French air power specialist: General Maurice Duval, *Lessons of the War in Spain*, edited by M. E. Chapman (Reading, Massachusetts, 2006).

12 NA. WO. 105/1580, pp. 2–7.

13 A. Beevor, *The Battle for Spain. The Spanish Civil War 1936–1939* (London, 2007 edn), pp. 384–5.

14 P. Preston, *The Politics of Revenge. Fascism and the military in twentieth-century Spain* (London, 1990), pp. 41–2.

15 C. Jerez-Farrán and S. Amago (eds), *Unearthing Franco's Legacy: Mass Graves and the Recovery of Historical Memory in Spain* (Notre Dame, Indiana, 2010).

16 A reference to a Gilbert and Sullivan comic operetta that featured a plodding police force and an unbattleworthy general.

17 Rutgers, Fuller, Box 4, Italy-Abyssinian War Diary, pp. 16–17.

18 J. Gooch, *Mussolini and His Generals: The Armed Forces and Fascist Foreign Policy, 1922–1940* (Cambridge, 2008).

19 A. Gat, *Fascist and Liberal Visions of War: Fuller, Liddell Hart, Douhet, and Other Modernists* (Oxford, 1998).

20 R. Mallett, *Mussolini and the Origins of the Second World War, 1933–1940* (Basingstoke, 2003); G. B. Strang, *On the Fiery March: Mussolini Prepares for War* (Westport, Connecticut, 2003).

21 R. M. Salerno, *Vital Crossroads. Mediterranean Origins of the Second World War, 1935–1940* (Ithaca, New York, 2002).

22 C. Ipsen, *Dictating Demography. The Problem of Population in Fascist Italy* (Cambridge, 1996).

23 J. Noakes, 'The Nazi Revolution', in M. Donald and T. Rees (eds), *Reinterpreting Revolution in Twentieth-Century Europe* (London, 2001), pp. 109–10.

24 Secret information, NA. CAB. 24/250 fol. 123.

25 L. E. Jones, 'Franz von Papen, Catholic Conservatives, and the Establishment of the Third Reich, 1933–1934', *Journal of Modern History*, 83 (2011), pp. 309–12.

26 R. J. Evans, *The Third Reich in Power 1933–1939* (London, 2005), pp. 642–5.

27 I. Lukes, 'The Tukhachevsky Affair and President Edvard Benes: Solutions and Open Questions', *Diplomacy and Statecraft*, 7 (1996), pp. 505–29.

28 J. A. Getty and O. V. Naumov, *The Road to Terror: Stalin and the Self-Destruction of the Bolsheviks, 1932–1939* (New Haven, Connecticut, 1999), p. 446.

29 Comparison of the strength of Great Britain with that of certain other Nations. Report by Chiefs of Staff, 12 November 1937, circulated to Cabinet, 3 Dec. 1937, NA. CAB. 24/273, fol. 152.

Chapter 12

1 Report, NA. CAB. 24/273 fol. 145.

2 B. J. C. McKercher, 'Deterrence and the European Balance of Power: The Field Force and British Grand Strategy, 1934–1938', *English Historical Review*, 123 (2008), p. 129.

3 J. Haslam, 'Comintern and Soviet Foreign Policy, 1919–1941', in R. G. Suny ed., *The Cambridge History of Russia, III: The Twentieth Century* (Cambridge, 2006), pp. 648–9.

4 S. T. Ross ed., *Plans for Global War: Rainbow-5 and the Victory Program, 1941* (New York, 1992), p. x.

5 M. R. Matheny, *Carrying the War to the Enemy: American Operational Art to 1945* (Norman, Oklahoma, 2011).

6 B. Bond and M. Alexander, 'Liddell Hart and de Gaulle: The Doctrines of Limited Liability and Mobile Defence', in P. Paret ed., *Makers of Modern Strategy* (Princeton, New Jersey, 1986), pp. 598–623.

7 M. R. Habeck, *Storm of Steel: The Development of Armor Doctrine in Germany and the Soviet Union, 1919–1939* (Ithaca, New York, 2003).

8 H. Winton, *To Change an Army. General Sir John Burnett-Stuart and British Armoured Doctrine, 1927–1938* (London, 1988).

9 Dill to Montgomery-Massingberd, 25 September, 18 November 1939, LM. MM. 10/14.

10 A. Kemp, *The Maginot Line: Myth and Reality* (London, 1981).

11 E. Kiesling, 'Resting Uncomfortably on Its Laurels: The Army of Interwar France', in H. Winton ed., *The Challenge of Change: Military Institutions and New Realities, 1918–1941* (Lincoln, Nebraska, 2000), pp. 1–24; D. E. Showalter, 'Le que l'armée française avait compris de la guerre moderne', in M. Vaisse ed., *Mai–Juin 1940: Défaite française, victoire allemand, sous l'oeil des historiens étrangers* (Paris, 2000), pp. 29–58.

12 Montgomery-Massingberd to Viscount Halifax, Secretary of State for War, 17 August 1935, LH. MM. 10/4/1. On the forts in this area, J. E. Kaufmann et al, *The Maginot Line* (Barnsley, 2011), pp. 74–83.

13 R. A. Doughty, *The Seeds of Disaster: The Development of French Army Doctrine, 1919–1939* (Hamden, Connecticut, 1985); E. Kiesling, *Arming against Hitler: France and the Limits of Military Planning* (Lawrence, Kansas, 1996).

14 P. D. Stachura, 'The Battle of Warsaw, August 1920, and the Development of the Second Polish Republic', in Stachura ed., *Poland Between the Wars, 1918–1939* (Basingstoke, 1998), pp. 54–5.

15 A. Suchcitz, 'Poland's Defence Preparations in 1939', in Stachura ed., *Poland*, pp. 54–5.

16 Summary of Evidence in regard to the Progress of German Rearmament, NA. CAB. 24/250 fols 123–5.

17 S. A. Schuker, 'France and the Remilitarization of the Rhineland, 1936', *French Historical Studies*, 14 (1986), pp. 299–338.

18 P. Jackson, 'French Intelligence and Hitler's Rise to Power', *Historical Journal*, 41 (1998), p. 821.

19 M. L. Roi, *Alternative to Appeasement. Sir Robert Vansittart and Alliance Diplomacy, 1934–1937* (Westport, Connecticut, 1997).

20 N. Jordan, *The Popular Front and Central Europe. The Dilemmas of French Impotence, 1918–1940* (Cambridge, 1992).

21 R. Self, *Neville Chamberlain: A Biography* (Aldershot, 2006).

22 J. Jackson, *The Fall of France. The Nazi Invasion of 1940* (Oxford, 2003), p. 13.

23 Chiefs of Staff Sub-Committee, 'Appreciation of the Situation in the event of war against Germany', 14 September 1938, NA. CAB. 24/278, pp. 350, 354–5.

24 B. Morris, *The Roots of Appeasement. The British Weekly Press and Nazi Germany during the 1930s* (London, 1991).

25 W. Murray, 'The War of 1938', in R. Cowley ed., *More What If?* (London, 2003), p. 261.

26 W. K. Ward, *The Ultimate Enemy: British Intelligence and Nazi Germany, 1933–1939* (Ithaca, New York, 1985).

27 P. Jackson, *France and the Nazi Menace: Intelligence and Policy Making, 1933–1939* (Oxford, 2000).

28 M. Dockrill, *British Establishment Perspectives on France, 1936–40* (London, 1999).

29 LH. Adam 2/3, pp. 2–3.

30 D. Edgerton, *Britain's War Machine. Weapons, Resources and Experts in the Second World War* (London, 2011), pp. 62–4.

31 NA. WO. 33/1512, p. 3.

32 D. M. Glantz, *Stumbling Colossus: The Red Army on the Eve of World War* (Lawrence, Kansas, 1998); B. M. Gerard, 'Mistakes in Force Structure and Strategy on the Eve of the Great Patriotic War', *Journal of Slavic Military Studies*, 4 (1991), pp. 471–86.

33 Report by the Chiefs of Staff Sub-Committee, 12 November 1937, NA. CAB. 24/273 fols 146–7.

34 R. R. Reese, 'Lessons of the Winter War: A Study in the Military Effectiveness of the Red Army', *Journal of Military History*, 72 (2008), pp. 825–52, esp. 826, 852.

35 T. Imlay, *Facing the Second World War: Strategy, Politics, and Economics in Britain and France, 1938–1940* (Oxford, 2003).

36 D. B. Lungu, *Romania and the Great Powers, 1933–1940* (Durham, North Carolina, 1989).

37 G. K. Roberts, *The Unholy Alliance: Stalin's Pact with Hitler* (London, 1991).

38 R. Overy, *1939: Countdown to War* (London, 2009).

Chapter 13

1 NA. CAB. 24/84 fol. 285.

2 J. Langdon-Davies, *Behind the Spanish Barricades* (London, 1936; London, 2007 edn), p. 202.

3 S. J. Zaloga and V. Madej, *The Polish Campaign, 1939* (New York, 1985); A. B. Rossino, *Hitler Strikes Poland: Blitzkrieg, Ideology, and Atrocity* (Lawrence, Kansas, 2003).

4 N. Smart, *British Strategy and Politics During the Phony War* (Westport, Connecticut, 2003).

5 R. H. S. Stolfi, 'Equipment for Victory in France', *History*, 55 (1970), pp. 1–20.

6 R. A. Doughty, 'Myth of the *Blitzkrieg*', in L. J. Matthews ed., *Challenging the United States Symmetrically and Asymmetrically: Can America be Defeated?* (Cambridge, Pennsylvania, 1998), pp. 57–79; J. S. Corum, 'Myths of *Blitzkrieg*: The Enduring Mythology of the 1940 Campaign', *Historically Speaking*, 6 (2005), pp. 11–13, citing P. Raborg, *Mechanized Might: The Story of Mechanized Warfare* (New York, 1942), p. 255; See, more generally, J. Jackson, *The Fall of France. The Nazi Invasion of 1940* (Oxford, 2003).

7 J. A. Gunsburg, 'The Battle of Gembloux, 14–15 May: The "Blitzkrieg" Checked', *Journal of Military History*, 64 (2000), pp. 97–140.

8 K. H. Frieser, *The Blitzkrieg Legend. The 1940 Campaign in the West* (Annapolis, Maryland, 2005), pp. 286–7.

9 M. S. Alexander, 'The Fall of France, 1940', *Journal of Strategic Studies*, 13 (1990), pp. 10–44; N. Jordan, 'Strategy and Scapegoatism: Reflections on the French National Catastrophe, 1940', in J. Blatt ed., *The French Defeat of 1940: Reassessments* (Providence, Rhode Island, 1998), pp. 13–38.

10 W. Murray, 'May 1940: Contingency and Fragility of the German RMA', in M. Knox and W. Murray (eds), *The Dynamics of Military Revolution 1300–2050* (Cambridge, 2001), pp. 173; E.O. Goldman and L. C. Eliason (eds), *The Diffusion of Military Technology and Ideas* (Stanford, California, 2003), p. 349.

11 T. C. Imlay, *Facing the Second World War: Strategy, Politics, and Economics in Britain and France, 1938–40* (Oxford, 2003); N. Smart, *British Strategy and Politics During the Phony War* (Westport, Connecticut, 2003).

12 D. E. Showalter, 'German Grand Strategy: A Contradiction in Terms?', *Militärgeschichtliche Mitteilungen*, 48 (1990), pp. 65–102.

13 R. Mitter, *The Manchurian Myth: Nationalism, Resistance and Collaboration in Modern China* (Berkeley, California, 2000).

14 *Munich 1938: Mythes et réalités* (Paris, 1979); Y. F. Khong, *Analogies at War: Korea, Munich, Dien Bien Phu, and the Vietnam Decisions of 1965* (Princeton, New Jersey, 1992); D. Chuter, 'Munich, or the Bloods of Others', in C. Buffet and B. Heuser (eds), *Haunted by History: Myths in International Relations* (Oxford, 1998), pp. 65–79; J. Record, *Making War, Thinking History. Munich, Vietnam and Presidential Uses of Force from Korea to Kosovo* (Annapolis, Maryland, 2002), and 'The Use and Abuse of History. Munich, Vietnam and Iraq', *Survival*, 49 (2007), pp. 163–80.

15 M. M. Matthews, *An Ever Present Danger: A Concise History of British Military Operations on the North-West Frontier, 1849–1947* (Fort Leavenworth, Kansas, 2010).

16 J. Hayward ed., *Air Power, Insurgency and the 'War on Terror'* (Cranwell, 2009).

Selected further reading

The emphasis here is on recent works. Earlier scholarship can be approached through these valuable studies. It is always useful to consult the *Journal of Military History*, *War in History* and the *International History Review*.

Alexander, M. S. (1992), *The Republic in Danger: General Maurice Gamelin and the Politics of French Defence, 1933–1940*.

Asada, S. (2006), *From Mahan to Pearl Harbor: The Imperial Japanese Navy and the United States*.

Bialer, U. (1980), *The Shadow of the Bomber: The Fear of Air Attack and British Politics, 1932–1939*.

Buckley, J. (1999), *Air Power in the Age of Total War*.

Chickering, R., and Förster, S. (eds) (2003), *The Shadows of Total War. Europe, East Asia, and the United States, 1919–1939*.

Citino, R. M. (1999), *The Path to Blitzkrieg: Doctrine and Training in the German Army, 1920–1939*.

Corum, J. S. (1992), *The Roots of Blitzkrieg: Hans von Seeckt and German Military Reform*.

Doughty, R. A. (1985), *The Seeds of Disaster: The Development of French Army Doctrine, 1919–1939*.

Drea, E. J. (2009), *Japan's Imperial Army: Its Rise and Fall, 1853–1945* (2009).

Gat, A. (1998), *Fascist and Liberal Visions of War: Fuller, Liddell Hart, Douhet and Other Modernists*.

Glantz, D. M. (1998), *Stumbling Colossus: The Red Army on the Eve of World War II*.

Harris, J. P. (1995), *Men, Idea and Tanks: British Military Thought and Armoured Forces, 1903–1939*.

Harrison, R. W. (2001), *The Russian Way of War: Operational Art, 1904–1940*.

Kier, E. (1997), *Imagining War: French and British Military Doctrine Between the Wars*.

Kiesling, E. (1996), *Arming Against Hitler: France and the Limits of Military Planning*.

Knox, M. (2000), *Common Destiny: Dictatorship, Foreign Policy, and War in Fascist Italy and Nazi Germany*.

Langley, L. D. (2002), *The Banana Wars. US Intervention in the Caribbean 1898–1934*.

McCann, F. (2003), *Soldiers of the Pátria: A History of the Brazilian Army, 1889–1937*.

McCord, E. A. (1993), *The Power of the Gun: The Emergence of Chinese Warlordism*.

Mallett, R. (1998), *The Italian Navy and Fascist Expansionism, 1935–1940*.

Mawdsley, E. (1987), *The Russian Civil War.*

Mockler, A. (1985), *Haile Selassie's War: the Italian-Ethiopian Campaign, 1935–1941.*

Murray, W., and Millett, A. R. (eds) (1996), *Military Innovation in the Interwar Period.*

Omissi, D. (1990), *Air Power and Colonial Control: The Royal Air Force 1919–1939.*

Peden, G. C. (2007), *Arms, Economics, and British Strategy: From Dreadnoughts to Hydrogen Bombs.*

Reese, R. R. (2000), *The Soviet Military Experience.*

Swain, G. (2000), *Russia's Civil War.*

Waldron, A. (1996), *From War to Nationalism. China's Turning Point 1924–1925.*

Willmott, H. P. (2010), *The Last Century of Sea Power, II: From Washington to Tokyo, 1922–1945.*

Index